Coaching Soccer:
Match Strategy and Tactics

Luca Prestigiacomo

**Library of Congress
Cataloging - in - Publication Data**

Coaching Soccer:
Match Strategy and Tactics
Luca Prestigiacomo

ISBN No. 1-59164-055-5
Lib. of Congress Catalog No. 2003094651
© 2003

Editing
Bryan R. Beaver

Cover Photography
EMPICS Ltd.

Printed by
DATA REPRODUCTIONS
Auburn, Michigan

Reedswain Publishing
612 Pughtown Road
Spring City, PA 19475
800.331.5191
www.reedswain.com
info@reedswain.com

CON.tents

This is a good book, written with passion and competence about the tactical management of a soccer match.
It will help the public see things from the point of view of the coach, and understand how, as far as he is concerned, a match lasts for much longer than those all-important 90 minutes. It gives excellent insight into the preparation hidden behind the plays that are put on show during the competition itself.

Luciano Spalletti
Coach of Udinese
(Serie A - Italy)

Acknowledgments to the author.

Up to now there has been no specific text in the whole literary panorama in Italy that could be considered a means of discussion for coaches going in to face the problems relative to a match, and showing how to play good soccer and how to create the right mentality in the team.

If our idea for the book has now been given form in a work of finished quality, that is thanks to Luca, who has handled things in a serious, meticulous and detailed way. He has succeeded in the difficult task of putting forward the psychological qualities that a coach must combine with his tactical know-how so that he can intervene before, during and after a match.

I would like to thank the author and congratulate him on the way he has created this book. He has thought deeply and everything he writes will help clarify the tactical and psychological difficulties that the coach is facing and will have to overpower so that his team arrives at higher and higher levels.

Massimo Lucchesi

INTRODUCTION

No doubt about it, the match is the peak - the topmost summit of soccer, its living moment.

The match is what really interests and attracts most of the people that follow this sport: from the mad fans to the journalists; from the relaxed, thoughtless families who prefer to watch the event from the tranquillity of their homes to the workers and the school kids that have spent the whole week looking forward to Sunday afternoon when they can go and watch the team that they support; from the children whose imagination takes fire when they see their heroes at work to the so called experts, always ready to praise or criticize the work of any given coach or player; from the club directors and managers who want to know that their investments have been confirmed on the field to the older supporters telling stories about when they were present in the stadium to see the most famous players of all time on the field and the glorious teams in which they performed.

What with the multiplication of the matches and the mushrooming of the competitions in which they are involved (Championship, Champions League, Uefa Cup, Italian Cup, etc.), it would be no exaggeration to say that football matches measure out the lives of millions of fans the world over.

This does not only happen at high levels. All down the categories, players, relatives and anyone who is interested just can't wait for Sundays and the moment when they can all 'let off steam', each in his own way and depending on his role.

The man whose special job it is to make all these different dreams come true is, of course, the coach. It is clear as well that his approach to the match will be totally different from anyone else's, for this is the final countdown as far as he is concerned, the moment of truth when all his work is to be judged and when he himself will witness whether it has been positive or not. And, keeping in mind that the responsibility for the success or failure of the team is usually to be laid at his own doorstep, this is a good chance for him to reflect on what has gone wrong if he has been defeated. Then, rolling up his sleeves, he must present himself at the next training session with even greater application and desire to succeed.

As we will see, however, the coach's job has many facets and not all are so closely connected to the match itself. All we wish to say for the moment is that the week's preparation for a single match, his ability to 'read' what is in store so as to 'straighten out' the critical situations it might present - as well as the analysis he will be making after it is over - are all qualities that the modern, qualified and competent coach will be in need of so that he can attain first class results with his team, by performing in a way that will be judged both positive and convincing by the spectators and the journalists. No truly good coach can neglect this phase of his work whatever his personal convictions may be. All those little tasks regarding the preparation of the single match are but signs of how he is taking care of details - and it is this that frequently divides a careless coach from one who is meticulous in treating every aspect of commanding a soccer team.

The match is the point of reference for all things - even as far as the coach is concerned. From the moment the team starts its preparation in the summer, every training session and each single exercise is directed towards the various competitions to be faced. It goes without saying, therefore, that the specific preparation for each single upcoming match is even more pertinent to the way in which the coach is shouldering his responsibility to his fans and to himself. This constitutes success for him: putting a team on the field that can satisfy the spectators, and, at the same time - give him those vital three points.

CHAPTER 1

THE COACH'S ROLE

THE FIGURE OF THE COACH AND ITS EVOLUTION IN TIME

The role of the coach has taken on different patterns down the years and experts have often been of widely diverse opinion about his importance.

Historically speaking, tactical evolution and the growing interest of the masses in the game of soccer in general have led to the coach assuming a role that puts him more and more on the front line. Initially, of course, he was a very marginal figure: his task was limited mainly to improving the technical ability of the players, to keeping them fit and to giving them general advice about their attitude on the field. From a tactical point of view, he would conform himself to solutions which, even though they were in continual transformation (in the first half of the last century there were tumultuous and incessant changes in fashions concerning playing systems), never really tended to glorify his particular role. Neither the coaches themselves nor the press gave much thought to the figure of the trainer.

Since the 50s the figure of the coach has grown in importance as a result of the development of new and sophisticated tactics, and today he is the protagonist in the shadow (but not in the shade) behind any soccer team.

There can be no doubt today that the coach plays an all important role in a soccer team, and that the achievement of the group depends to a great extent on his work. Yet, it is the team's style of play that he really instigates, its mentality, what we call its philosophy. It is no accident that we often connect and even identify a team with the name of the coach who has brought it to success, though there are critics who, even today, would tend to reduce and depreciate his importance.

True, the coach does not enter the field, and, no doubt about it, what happens on the pitch depends to a great extent on the players themselves: their technical ability and their attitudes, their 'soccer' intelligence (to coin a phrase), their drive and their willingness to respect and carry out the tactical guidelines the coach has given them, their physical form, their personal relationships with teammates and the weight of their own experience in the game.

And still, as we have already said, apart from being in a position to improve on all these individual aspects of his players, the coach can also become the real protagonist of the team, labeling them with his own authentic 'trade mark' - a well-defined mentality and perfect playing organization.

LEADING THE TEAM: TWO MODELS IN CONTRAST

In the attempt to clarify what we are getting at we must first of all distinguish between two general categories of coaches present on the scene today in relation to the extent to which they become the protagonist or headliner of the team.

On one side there are coaches who do not have any well-defined tactical preferences, and who, therefore, adapt their team's playing style to their own players' characteristics, to the opponents they happen to be facing on the day and to whether they are playing at home or away. If the coach is a capable one, he will make the best of his players and the team will have a highly pragmatic approach. This type of coach does not usually give the team any particular philosophy of play in terms of their general attitude. Depending on the circumstances, the team will play in attack or in defense, adapting itself to the team it is playing against. The team put on the field by coaches of this type will usually vary its tactical set-up, its own playing system and the specific movements it makes in both phases. Many of these coaches will often put their trust in the inventions and the improvisations of the players themselves, relying on the most technically skilled individual to build up play, and confiding in his physical form from one match to another. There is a tendency here to create ranks of importance among the players, because there will be a distinction in the team between 'stars' and mere 'supporting players'. We can say, in the end, that the reputation of such coaches is not so conspicuous, and that , when their teams are successful, their contribution is not so marked and is not taken into such high account by the critics.

The second category of coach is given a good deal of personal credit for the success of his team - and becomes the front man. In the first place, these coaches convey a distinct mentality to their teams in terms of general attitude (their sides very often have a positive attacking temperament); but it is above all their tactical organization which is seen to be coordinated in every detail. The coach has freed the team of individual improvisation and aims for collective play that is well-defined, easily recognizable and based on innovative tactical themes. The style and the level of play expressed by the team all bear the marked appearance of the coach's own ideas, and he does not only manage to make the best of the potential of his players, but can go beyond, managing to obtain extraordinary results from a high level of play even if - from the point of view of each single individual - the group that he has on hand would probably have performed much more modestly had they been managed in the 'traditional' way. Furthermore, coaches like these show little inclination to adapt themselves pragmatically to rival teams and to the circumstances, and do not even like to distinguish between home and away matches.

With such coaches we do not usually get ranks and grades of importance among the players. No one player is to be considered indispensable, and, at the same time, each single player feels that he is as important as any other. There are not players who must be waited on, or others who are burdened down with all the difficult work - and everyone knows that he is at the service of the group. This outlook leads to the point where, in cases where the individual's abilities are not sufficient, the group as a whole steps in with the winning mentality imparted by the coach. As well as this, there is a degree of tactical organization that leaves nothing to chance and refuses to base itself on single episodes. In the end, of course, even the individual gains from this situation, because he is able to express himself better, intensifying his own performance in the collective play of the team.

We can say that this type of coach is like the conductor of an orchestra. He has to 'synchronize' his musicians, who, though they may be excellent at playing their own instrument, would only give rise to an annoying din without the presence of someone who can organize them. Or, again, he is like a film director, who defines the story line and the single scenes of his film (its aesthetics if you like, the qualities that make it pleasing) and even each separate line put across by the actors; or he is like an engineer who must create a work of architecture that is exact and functional in all its details and which will be both stable and a pleasure for all to see.

To tell the truth, in real life the sharp difference between these two kinds of coach is not always so clear, and there are many distinctions and demarcations to be made.
There are coaches who leave large margins to the invention and improvisation of their players, but do not like to adapt themselves to the opponents on the day. They prefer to give their team a well-defined configuration and outlook (as far as their degree of offensiveness is concerned).
In the same way, there are coaches who give their teams a rigid tactical organization so as to reduce any kind of improvisation on the field, but who usually vary their attitude and set up, making it sometimes more or sometimes less accommodating.

This classification only wishes to point out in as general a way as possible that there are two main manners of interpreting the role of the coach in reference to how much he will be influencing the players on the team in their performances

Yet, I would like to add that it is this second type of coach that I consider more modern, more suitable and positive, even if I fully respect the undoubted abilities and competence of those belonging to the first class. When they are successful, the 'pragmatic' coaches undoubtedly demonstrate just how well they can manage the human material at their disposition in relation to the various situations, but the 'ideological' coaches (we will call them this because they give their teams a continuous playing philosophy) display even more skill because (whatever the players they are using) they have enforced a precise identity on the team, enabling them to impose their play against any opponent.

THE COACH'S TASKS

Having had a look at the important role played by a modern coach, we can now try to delineate the tasks and responsibilities he is to carry through in order to make the most of his team's potential. No matter what ideas he has about the part he is to play, it goes without saying that he must try to do his job with as much dedication and attention to detail as possible so as to oversee his duties as a 'guide' to his players.

THE PLANNING PHASE

The work of a coach is divided into three main phases.
The first of these, which we could call the 'planning' phase, is concerned with defining the general strategy of the team: the guidelines and the attitude that the players will have to keep to during the match in order to arrive at their double aim - to win and to put on an enjoyable show for the public, who, having paid the ticket, have a right to expect as much.
As we have already said in the first part of this introduction, the best way to fulfill this double aim is to apply offensive soccer based on detailed tactical organization.
This first phase also includes that 'mental' preparation of the group, which the coach will have to be particularly careful about, so as to get his group ready for those things that go beyond mere tactics. The first things he must get over to his players are the principles of total soccer: offensiveness, a feeling for the group, collaboration and reciprocal assistance. The team must be looked upon as a compact block moving on the whole field - to the point where everyone is at the same time both a defender and a forward. The various roles must be interchangeable so that there are no specialized individual tasks - and this in order to create a more global, universal concept of the part played by each single member. Great stress must be given to the importance and the task of the player without the ball in both phases so that he can be active and at the center of the action at all times (becoming the real focus of the play) and enabling him to give special meaning to the concepts 'space' and 'time'. Defensive play should begin in our opponent's half, in the first place to force the rival team to play as far away as possible from our goal, but

also to crush them into their own area so that we will have as many chances to shoot as possible. As we will see, tactically speaking all this will result in our adopting a zonal defense system and in our using innovative methods like pressing and off-side.

The coach must then see to it that the players are all thinking in the same way: that their heads are all tuned in on the same wavelength.

The mental preparation of the group must also include the more 'noble' concepts like fair play, the respect for your opponent and the written and unwritten rules of the sport. It is important that the coach gives his players a sense of accepting the result, of not being bad losers, because after all soccer is a game and not a war in which the end justifies the means. The tactics of renunciation used by some coaches are a negative thing, but the exaggerated pursuit of victory at all costs leads to behavior that can be serious from the sporting point of view: simulated fouls, violent fouls, incorrect conduct, sneaky 'tactical fouls', not to mention doping and out-and-out violence.

The mental preparation of the group must also be finalized to give them the idea that their application, their will, their work and all they put into it are indispensable to attaining results. The players must understand that every move they make, every exercise carried out in a training session is a contribution towards getting on top of their opponents. In other words, during training sessions the players must get used to having to concentrate.

The coach will also have to impart the 'winning' mentality, which can be summed up in this way: having a sense of belonging to a collective group, taking to the field with the intention of winning and convincing without ever looking for a more deliberately contrived result, never going over the moon when you are successful or getting depressed when you have been defeated. The coach must cultivate things like self-respect in his players, unity of intents, determination and a conviction of their own worth; and at the same time he must eliminate any sign of presumption in their attitude.

Of course the mental preparation of the group will be a long and complicated process and will call for qualities in the coach that go beyond his skill in getting technical and tactical themes across to his players.

His difficulty in this phase will also be connected to the cultural maturity of the individual players, which is often not very well-developed in fact, and tends instead to force them into a way of acting that is the very opposite to what we have been listing here. The coach must be good at divulging all these principles, using his ability as a communicator to catch the attention of his players and fill them with enthusiasm. In some cases, like the question of self-respect for example, he will even need to turn himself into something of a psychologist.

THE PROGRAMMING PHASE

The second phase, or programming phase, concerns the definition of the tactics the team will be using in order to put their strategy and mentality into practice on the field. The coach will now begin his work of instruction so that the players can assimilate the tactical measures that have been established.
Let us have a look at the best tactical attitudes to adopt so that the team will be offensive, collective and spectacular.
In the possession phase our maneuvers must be fast, fluid, based on incessant movements without the ball which are synchronized among all the players. Everyone must participate in the play, which will have to be varied, unpredictable and intense. The circulation of the ball needs to be rapid (one or two touch play) and build up must make the best of both the width and the depth of the field with the players correctly set out in ranks. There must be continuous use of change of play, and we need at all times to be looking for and making the most of numerical superiority around the ball. We must exploit the entire range of finishing touch techniques (cuts, dump and rebound passes, overlapping, crosses, combinations). The players must be close together and never too far from the ball, and the members of the team must widen themselves out and shorten up so as to make the best use of the flanks and at the same time to be compact and ready to help each other. Short passes are preferable to medium or long range ones, the ball should be kept as much as possible to the ground and a collective solution (a pass) is always better than an individual one (dribbling), which will be allowed, at most, in the last fifteen yards, and even then only if the player in possession has no other better solutions open to him. We must clearly stress the importance of the concepts of playing time and space.

In the non-possession phase, we should adopt a zonal defense system, the better to make use of the collaboration between the players. We can get the best coverage of space by using the zone, and we will be marking our opponents in a collective way because our defenders will be moving in relation to the ball and their teammates and only in the last place with the opponents. Against a zone defense, an attacker has the feeling that he is playing 1 against 11, on account of the great pressure automatically brought to bear on him. By shifting towards the ball, the defenders - who will also be using the principles of anticipatory marking on opponents who are present in their zone of general competence - reduce the space on the strong side of the field, creating numerical superiority. They will also cover each other using the defense diagonal, so guaranteeing closure on an opponent who has dribbled past a teammate or has eluded an attempt at anticipation. The constant doubling up of marking on the opposing player in possession is closely connected with zonal defense, as are pressing - which can be carried out on the whole field, keeping the team tight and short - and the use of offside tactics. The defense must not only play in depth and in line, keeping to the correct distance from the mid field (there should not be more than fifteen yards from one section to the other, while never more than eight / nine yards should separate one player from another in the same section), but they must be ready at all times to carry out a good defensive shift, moving up or back depending on the tactical situation so as to take depth from their opponent's play while at the same time making the best use of the advantages of the offside rule.

Also, the goalkeeper has important tasks in both phases, interpreting his role in the modern fashion - a role which has been revolutionized by the innovations of total soccer. In the attacking phase he must be able to set up play using his feet and give support to the defenders in possession. In the phase of non-possession he must be ready to change himself into an 'extra sweeper' should there be a mistaken application of offside tactics on the defenders' part, when he will come out to intervene on the opponent making for the goal.

As far as teaching methods go, the coach will follow an itinerary that goes from the general to the particular, from what is easy, building up to what is more difficult.

The first thing the coach must do is make sure his team has grasped the general principles of collective and individual tactics. From a collective point of view the principles for the attacking phase are: zigzag placement, making the best use of width, mobility and unpredictability. From the point of view of the individual, we have: getting free of marking, moving with the ball, passing the ball, receiving the ball and protecting the ball. The collective principles of the defense phase are the following: zigzag placement, reducing space, aggressiveness, balancing and playing for time; these are the principles from the point of view of the individual: defending the goal, contrasting, anticipating, marking and taking up position. One thing that must be introduced at once is the concept of pressing, making sure everyone is clear about pressure, pressing (defensive, offensive and ultra-offensive), stand-by phase, aggressive pressing phase, strong and weak side of the field, and invited pressing.

All this must come about by using technical and tactical theme exercises finalized to the development of these particular skills.

Instruction will then proceed with the preparation of a specific tactical system. At this stage of the coach's job, the tactical principles earlier put across in a general way will now be applied specifically to the set up the team will be assuming on the playing field. Here, we begin to set out in detail the particular plays we will be using in both phases.

In the attacking phase, the coach will see to the creation of the triangles and rhombi of play that are so important in the zigzag placement that will lead to good maneuvers during the build up. It is also important to take care of specific subgroups of players (pairs, three-man groups, chains and sections).

These subgroups must blend with each other so as to offer a wide range of plays involving the entire team. At the start, the coach will suggest the movements to be made, but he should then allow the team to decide which offensive solutions are best in each case, and these will have to be diversified all the time so that the maneuvers are fluid, fast, dynamic and unpredictable. The coach must make sure that the movements without the ball are correctly timed and coordinated and that they are taking place in the right place and at the right moment. The team must repeat all these things again and again until they have become almost automatic.

In the defense phase, the coach will begin by working with each single section, paying particular attention to how to carry out defense diagonals and pyramids, shifting movements, doubling up within the section and the right balance between covering spaces, marking the zone and how to deal with numerical inferiority.

It is especially important with the defense section to teach them how to make vertical backward and forward movements (defensive shifts) and how to 'pass on' the marking of opposing attacking players on the basis of their movements. At the same time, the strikers will have to learn how to carry out pressing on the defenders playing against them and how to cover the passing lines.

At a certain point, the movements of the single sections will need to be integrated: first uniting the defense line with the mid field, and then adding the attacking front.

Working on the defense/midfield block, we can look at doubling up of marking between players of two sections, and, in similar circumstances, covering space as you move up or back or shifting movements on the flanks.

At last, we get to the complete team: practicing ultra-offensive pressing and the help that the strikers must give the midfield line, above all by moving backwards to double up the marking.

The goalkeeper must participate in the exercises concerning both phases if he is to interpret his role in the way already mentioned. The coach must balance the time he has on hand with the team in order to give the same care and attention to both phases.

Keeping in mind that as well as all this, the team needs to get the right athletic preparation (often the job of a specialized trainer), you will see how important it is to combine the technical and tactical work, making sure that exercises of instruction play a role even in the physical preparation of the players.

You must not neglect the transition phase, i.e., when play switches from one phase to the other: counterattacking and getting back into position need to be given detailed attention.

In this second part of his work the coach will be trying to improve the technical ability of the single player, and he will also be keeping an eye on how well the players are getting into things mentally. The players' mind needs to be trained as much or even more than his feet, because the second depend on the first. Each individual must be able to resolve every situation in which he finds himself on the field - and he must do so as quickly as possible. Training sessions should be thought of in this way: improving the players' ability to re-elaborate on problems in ever shorter intervals of time. The coach must come up with psycho-tactical and psycho-technical training exercises in order improve the speed of the players' thinking, their vision of play, the capacity of their perceptions and the readiness to make decisions.

Another important thing in this phase of the work is to give practice on finding solutions for inactive balls.

THE MICRO-PROGRAMMING PHASE

At this point we finally get to the third phase of the coach's work - which is the subject that we will be studying in this book.

We could call this 'the micro-programming' phase because we are here talking about specific work over a short period - usually a week.

As we have already seen, the first two phases aim to give the team that universal organization and mentality to be used against any opponent, also making sure the team understands the tactics and schemes of play that can be used in situational contexts, so making it both independent and aware.

The third phase is all about the week's preparation for the next match on the calendar, how to 'read' and analyze it in real time and make any possible tactical modifications that might become necessary as a result of whatever critical situations may come out.

In this phase, the coach must be able to make all changes required by the team's tactical organization so that nothing is left to chance and his players can enter the field in the best possible conditions.

The players must be left with no doubts about how to face the match, in particular about those tactical solutions that are to be preferred against the opponents of the day. In the attacking phase, for example, the wide range of solutions that have previously been presented to the team must now be classified so as to indicate which of them will be of greater use in getting past this particular defense line; and in the non-possession phase we will fix on which shifting moves will be the most effective in obstructing the rival team's offensive ability.

Coaches who want to prepare their teams' organization in every detail must dedicate the greatest possible care to the coming match, which represents, as we have already pointed out, the pivot around which everything else rotates in soccer - from the simple fans to those more closely involved in the work itself.

In any case, the team's general preparation may be of the highest possible standards, but we would be forced to say it was incomplete if this was not accompanied by attention to each single match.

No doubt about it, every coach will prepare the match in a different way depending on his culture, his ideas, his way of interpreting his own role - just as his approach to the competition itself will depend on his personality and his particular inclinations.

Some coaches will prepare the match by adapting themselves completely to the opponent of the day, to the point of even modifying the team's mentality and playing system. Others will operate a series of tactical solutions that are as irritating as they are pragmatic; and still others only make some little changes to the tactical set up, holding on to the team's original philosophy, its general layout and its playing system.

Without repeating the explanations that have already been given, we believe this last reaction to be the best and most intelligent way of confronting a match.

We could compare a soccer team to a Formula One racing car: it has its own shape and well-defined characteristics, and yet at the same time from race to race it undergoes small but decisive alterations to its set up (different types of tires, different height of the wings, different amount of fuel in the tank, etc.). We could say the same thing about a soccer team: by our careful study of the opposing team, and by keeping other variables in mind, we will 'instruct' our players in how to behave on the field and will be able to make little changes to our original general arrangement, still remaining faithful to the outlines of our play.

The coach should try to avoid exaggerated tactical moves that risk turning a soccer match into a game of chess, blocking the potential ability of the players.

It should be made clear from the very start that the preparation and handling of a match must not be looked upon only from a tactical point of view, but also in a psychological way. We must pay close attention to the team's mental approach to the match, and even during play the coach must be able to monitor the players' psychological situation moment by moment, making whatever interventions he thinks necessary in real time.

Two contrasting psychological conditions can play a negative role: anxiety, when we think the opponents are better than us; and overconfidence, when we imagine they are not nearly as good. We will be dealing more broadly with the mental preparation for a match in Chapter 8.

MATCH PREPARATION

The preparation for each single match is an important part of the coach's work.

Preparing the match means making an analysis of all those factors regarding the next game which will be a basis for deciding how to behave against the opposing team on a tactical or psychological level.

We can say that each match is a different story in that the team will always be operating in different circumstances. First of all, each week we will be playing against a different team, with a different tactical organization, a different playing system - or, a different interpretation, at least, of the same system - a different mentality with different physical and psychological characteristics of the players.

Another thing you have to keep in mind is that with each passing week our own team will be in a different psycho-physical condition and, depending on the period of the year, at a different level of preparation from a tactical and athletic point of view.

And that is not all; other elements and other variables guarantee that each match we play will be unique and unrepeatable: first of all the match itself (depending on the championship we are playing in), whether it is at home or away, the preceding performances of both the teams, the weather conditions and as a consequence the conditions of the field of play - all these things that identify a single match will become the object of the coach's careful study and analysis so that he can take care of every detail of his team's preparation.

FIXED AND VARIABLE ELEMENTS

The first thing to do so to make the best of your chances when preparing your team's match strategy is to distinguish between 'fixed' and variable elements. Fixed elements are those aspects of the team's attitude and tactical organization which we can never change no matter whom we are playing against and in what circumstances; varied elements on the other hand are the things that are open to modification depending on the team we are to face and on other factors.

The team's mentality and philosophy and its attacking attitude are things which, in my opinion, should not be modified match after match. The team should always go on the field in order to win and convince, playing offensive spectacular soccer.

Another thing: by changing the playing system in a systematic way we will spoil all the work that has been done before. As we have seen in the introduction, the coach has been following a precise itinerary step by step in order to create the movements connected with the playing system that he has chosen; switching that from match to match would mean putting players on the field without firm points of reference. The mechanisms of play would begin to creak and the players would inevitably begin to improvise in a more or less marked way depending on how well they have grasped those general tactical principles we were looking at earlier. I do not wish to put any stress on playing systems as such: theoretically no one system is better than any others, just as the attacking nature of a team does not depend on the system in itself, but on other factors, first of all the general attitude and the number of players actively taking part in the build up phase. The system is only a graphic representation of the team's general set up on the field, which is something destined to vary all the time if we wish to play soccer in a dynamic way. And yet, as we have already said, in order to be able to play as well as possible every player must have exact points of reference on the ground so that he can always find his teammates with his eyes closed in whatever phase, and so that he will always know how they will be moving as play develops. The player who knows where his team-mates are positioned will gain time in the mental elaboration of play. This is even more important in modern soccer with its emphasis on pressing and the short team because players no longer has the time to receive, observe, decide and carry out, but must rather observe and decide first of all, and then receive and carry out that which he has already decided.

Other fixed elements of a team are its way of building up play and the main movements in the attacking phase. In order to make the best possible use of both the width and the depth of the field we will always need rapid maneuvers of one or two touch plays and the collective participation of the whole team as well as those specific moves and plays that the coach considers of fundamental importance.

Even in the non-possession phase, what must not vary is the philosophy with which a team faces its opponents.

If necessary, what we can change are our finishing touch techniques first of all; we may also prefer to bring certain playing schemes into greater focus, and downgrade others.

Depending on the particular characteristics of the team we are facing, we will decide what kind of finishing touch techniques to use: cuts, dump and rebound passes and breaking in through the center; or setting up the shot at goal by using crosses and overlapping on the flanks; or again we might go for tight combinations.

We must try to list our offensive movements in order of importance so as to show the team which are the best for getting past their opponent's defense system, above all to create and make the best of situations of numerical superiority. Apart from that, the coach will also need to tell the team what defensive moves they are to use most frequently and how to develop play in the build up phase.

Other 'variable' elements in a soccer team are the definition of doubling up on marking and the way pressing and shifting movements are to be applied.

Doubling up on marking first of all: based principally on the opponent's system, the coach must decide which of his players will be doubling up, in what parts of the field and in what way (doubling up in the same section, doubling up between different sections, by moving backwards or moving forwards).

Pressing and shifting movements depend on the opponent as well, and the coach will give indications about how to contrast their set up. For example, the strikers will have to behave in different ways with a three or four man defense in order to reduce their playing space and time. The shifting moves on the sidelines are the principle ones to undergo change in reference to how the adversaries are lined up on the field.

In some cases the coach will supply the team with real tactical modifications; in others he will limit himself to giving them advice - depending on the importance of the factors to be taken into consideration. The coach's aim is to make sure the team becomes as independent and as aware as possible so as not to have to teach the players over and over again how to deal with a three man defense, with cuts, with overlapping, etc.
To sum up, the coach must try to give the team a sense of universal organization that is so ingrained that he need only give advice and suggestions on how to face each match, at the same time carrying out tactical 'revision' with some theme exercises. This will not take away too much time from the main work - perfecting the general organization of the team.

SPECIFICATIONS TO ANALYZE AND THEIR IMPLICATIONS CONCERNING OUR TEAM'S STRATEGIC CHOICES.

Before getting to grips with the next seven closely interconnected chapters, we need to have a look at the itinerary that we will be following. First of all we will be having a look at the parameters to keep in mind when preparing the match, starting from our study of the opposing team. This study will concern tactical, technical, psychological and athletic elements. We will be explaining how each of these complementary factors can influence the tactical set up of our team, modifying some of its details.
Our treatment will go on to consider the state of our own team: the level of tactical organization that we have reached, our physical and psychological condition. Once again in this sphere, we will indicate how the coach will have to adjust the tactical set up to the state of his team, keeping in mind the information he has gathered and the idea he has built up about the rival team.
In Chapter 7 we will be having a closer look at the other factors mentioned above.
At this point we can speak about how to prepare a match from a strictly practical point of view. By capitalizing on what has

emerged from his analysis of all the factors we have indicated, the coach must now work out how to make sure that his team enters the field in the best possible way so as to play a match that leaves nothing to chance.

In this connection, we will be looking at how the coach should manage the weekly training sessions. He will have to decide which sessions will be dedicated to perfecting the detailed tactical organization so necessary for the play and the clearly defined style of his team; and he will also have to find all the time necessary for the operative preparation of the next match.

As far as this second type of training session is concerned, we will be giving a series of technical / tactical exercises so that the players will be able to grasp the particular themes that will be developed during the coming game. Furthermore, we will be explaining how to prepare training matches that simulate the tactical situations the team will have to face.

It is also important to stress the psychological preparation for the match. Psychology is vital to soccer and the team's mental state has a primary role to play in its preparation. Without suitable training for their 'heads', the players' strategy, tactics and playing schemes would be of no use at all, just as it is of no use giving your legs athletic training if they are not 'guided' by your mind. The coach must follow this aspect if he wants the team to perform as well as possible. He must also impart a winning mentality to the players, which is something that derives directly from psychology.

We will be outlining how the coach is to behave with the team during the week, getting rid of any presumptuous attitudes leading the players to underestimate their opponents, or, resolving any cases of anxiety that might exist.

In Chapter 9, finally, we will be showing what criteria the coach should use in order to select the best team to put on the field on the day of the match.

CHAPTER 2

STUDYING THE OPPOSING TEAM

As we have already said, studying the opposing team means having a good look at them from a tactical, technical, psychological and athletic point of view.

We carry out this study by carefully watching the last few matches they have played. It is not enough to have a look at their very last match because one of the things that we want to find out more about is their 'fixed' and 'variable' elements. Only by making a comparison of their last three matches (at the very least), will we be able to define the team's permanent characteristics and how they usually modify their normal set up to contrast the opposition. In this way we can deduce how the rival coach will probably behave in relation to our own characteristics, thus enabling us to make the right countermoves in anticipation.

THE AIMS OF OUR STUDY

Having made an analysis of our opponents, we will be able to formulate the necessary modifications and tactical countermoves so that our team enters the field fully prepared for the match. Apart from these countermoves, our analysis of the rival team will also enable the coach to give more general advice and suggestions about how to get into the game.

In the second place, our study of the opponent will make us aware of what kind of opponent we will be facing.

It is always important to have some idea who we are facing, without even considering the tactical countermoves that we might make and anything else that is closely connected to our preparation for a particular match. A soccer team just cannot come out on the field without knowing anything about its adversaries.

His pure and simple curiosity should encourage the good coach to find out as much as he can about his opponent's characteristics, if only to compare the playing level reached by his own team with that of his next opponent.

Let us now have a look at how to watch your opponents' matches.

HOW TO OBSERVE THE OPPOSING TEAM

Finding as much information as you can about the opposing team is not always so easy or convenient. Here, everything will depend on the category in which you are playing and the resources and predisposition of your club.

The best thing is to be in a position to use a network of collaborators who can help the coach by giving him the necessary material regarding the opponents.

We should also say that the ideal conditions are that the person who is to observe the opposing team should be able to do so 'live' and in the stadium, because it is not possible to see the whole field on video.

With the help of a small number of trusted observers who can follow the matches of the teams we are interested in, we should be able to gather a sufficient amount of information without creating too much organizational difficulty. Clearly, we need to give detailed instructions to the observers about what we wish to find out, making sure they draw up an accurate report of each match. If the club's resources permit it, we will certainly find out more about the teams we are interested in if we can also have a look at videocassettes of their previous matches.

Unfortunately, if you are playing in the 'lower' categories, you can not 'let loose' your observers to go and watch the opposing teams. In these categories you generally have to make do with a small number of collaborators, sometimes limited to the assistant coach, the instructor of the goalkeepers, and the athletic trainer - if not fewer. Keeping in mind that in most cases the opponent you wish to observe will be playing its preceding match at the same time you are, you cannot allow such close collaborators to miss out on your match and go off to follow the upcoming opponent.

Getting people you do not trust to follow your next opponents is not a good move either - particularly if you are not sure of their soccer competence, above all from a tactical point of view.

In any case, when you do get the chance to have a look at an opponents' match, it is a good idea to follow precise guidelines so that you will be observing things in the best way possible. When a coach is following a match 'live' he should - before the starting whistle is blown - make a detailed list of all the things that interest him. In fact, in order to facilitate his observations, he should first draw up a sort of prospectus laid out subject by subject, under which he can jot down all those elements of the opposing team that he is interested in. Then, as the match is being played he can take note of everything he sees on the field and whatever he considers important to his inquiry. If he wishes he could also simply take note of these things as they come to him during the match, and then later organize his notes into summary form.

We must say, however, that watching a live match does not always allow you to collect a great quantity of information. There is no replay button to be pressed and you cannot have a second look at any single play in order to bring out all its hidden meanings and tactical implications. The apparent simplicity of any single play can, when it has undergone careful vivisection, lead to important and unsuspected occasions for deeper examination. The coach must try to draw out all he can from each single play - right down to any details that looked insignificant at first glance.

It follows that the classic notes taken down on a piece of paper are not enough. We could even say that having to take notes might create still more problems for the observer because as he looks down at his piece of paper to write, he will be missing some important play in the match itself.

One way of getting over this is by arming yourself with a little cassette recorder so that you can catch what you want or what you think is useful on tape in real time, without having ever to bend your head. At a later time the coach or the observer can transfer the contents of the tape onto the prospectus he has already prepared.

One of the advantages a coach has when he is watching a match played by an upcoming opponent is that he can concentrate entirely on this team, without giving too much consideration to their rivals on the day.

Nevertheless, it is important to understand how the team under scrutiny is behaving in relation to their opponents in order to deduce as much as possible about their adaptability. To do that we must make a note of how the other team is lined up, but this will be only a brief and essential analysis, allowing us to focus entirely on our future opponent.

It goes without saying that if the coach has the chance to watch the opponent on cassette he must watch and re-watch the single plays that most deserve attention.

This is undoubtedly the best situation for the coach, who can take all the time he needs to analyze the things about his opponents that are of particular interest to him, pausing the tape whenever he wishes to write down his considerations.

Remember that you must try to look at as many matches as possible. Following a single match without being able to get a second look at the most interesting plays can often leave you with mere 'impressions' or 'sensations'. A coach who wants to come to grips with all the details without leaving anything at all to chance must carry out a 'scientific' job.

Let us now have a look at the specifications that must be kept in mind and then analyzed when watching an opponent's match. We will start with tactics.

CHAPTER 3

ANALYSIS OF THE TACTICAL PARAMETERS

THE PLAYING SYSTEM AND ITS INTERPRETATION

Our study of the playing system regards:

☐ The team's placement on the field during the attacking phase.
☐ The team's placement on the field during the defense phase.
☐ Interpretation of the system in terms of general attitude.

The first two points are important because, as soccer is a dynamic game, the team will be placing itself in different ways depending on the phase to be interpreted. Just to give a couple of examples, there are teams that use a three-man defense, but only during the possession phase. In the defense phase, the back line inevitably becomes a four or even a five man defense. It is not accurate, therefore, to say that this team is using the 3-4-3 or the 3-5-2 or the 3-4-1-2. As the team has a three man defense only during the offense phase, it would be more correct to say: in the attacking phase the team adopts the 3-4-3 system (or the 3-5-2 or the 3-4-1-2), while in the defense phase we have a 5-4-1 system (or the 5-3-2).

The three man defense is an extreme case, but this is a concept we can apply to many other situations. We often say that a team with the 4-4-2 set up is defensive; but this is a mistake if you do not keep in mind that this system is a 4-4-2 only in the defense phase, while the two side mid fielders often move up during the attacking phase and position themselves as wings beside the two strikers, with the side backs shifting into the mid field so that the system is now a sort of 2-4-4.

The list of how the various systems change in reaction to the phase being interpreted would be a long one: the 4-3-3 becomes a 4-5-1 in the defense phase, the 4-3-1-2 and the 4-2-3-1 both become a 4-4-2 in defense etc.

This is the reason behind the third point in our analysis of our opponent's system: everything depends on how they are interpreting it. In itself, the system is just a set of numbers which tell us little or nothing about how the opposing team will actually be playing. What counts in soccer is the movements that are made; dynamism, not immobility. The system is neither defensive nor offensive in itself. A 5-4-1 could be an offensive system if it is interpreted in a certain way during the attacking phase, with the mid fielders and the defenders breaking in continuously, changing the system into a 3-4-3. Furthermore, teams using a single striker are actually more inclined to base their play on ball possession and elaborate build up. The striker cannot move too far into depth but must come to meet the mid fielders or the defenders in possession so as to give them a sure point of reference in a vertical direction.

On the contrary, the 4-3-3 can be a defensive system if the team defends with 9 players (transforming the system into a 4-5-1), and above all if in the possession phase we keep sending the ball vertically to the strikers, who will be the only players to participate actively in that phase. Teams with a three man attack often tend to use only their three strikers beyond the ball line. Occupying the whole of the attacking front, they give a great number of points of reference to the team in a vertical direction, and so the sub phase of build up will be based on immediate build up or maneuvered counterattack.

What we are trying to demonstrate is that the coach needs to evaluate the way in which the rivals are interpreting their system. To do so he must keep in mind a number of other factors concerning the opposing team, in particular the following: the general mentality of the team, the number of players that participate in the two phases, the level at which they go into pressing, the type of defensivee system (man marking or zonal defense), the degree to which the team is capable of adapting itself, how they build up play (and as a consequence whether they exploit the width of the field more than the depth), the movements carried out most frequently by the various players and how much freedom is given to the individual.

Another thing to remember is that a system can often be heavily personalized. You can sometimes see a 4-4-2 where one of the two side mid fielders is constantly positioned as a wing during the attacking phase; or a 3-5-2 with one of its two side mid fielders integrating himself invariably with the backs during the defense phase no matter where the ball happens to be, while the other always remains in the mid field.

What matters to us for the moment is that the coach must understand the opposing team's placement on the field in both phases of play. More particularly, he must consider the set up not only section by section, but also on the flanks and at the center (the center of the defense, the center of the mid field, the center of the attack). He must also keep in mind the possible presence of 'hybrid' placements: cases where you find a player half way between one section and another, or between the flanks and the center of the field. Two such examples are the side mid fielders of the 3-5-2 - positioned in the mid field or even in attack during the attacking phase, and, during the defense phase, at the sides of the defense - and the two inside / side mid fielders of the 4-3-3, who are placed half way between the center of the field and the flanks. In the first example, the 'hybrid' position is connected to the transition from one phase to another, so transforming the system from a 3-5-2 to a 5-3-2. In the second case the position is 'hybrid' in both phases and does not bring about any change of system (though it must be pointed out that the half wings of the 4-3-3 play wider in the attacking phase and tighter in the defense phase).

It is not difficult, however, to evaluate all these things. It is enough to see how the team sets itself up during a stop in play, standing by before going into the attacking or the defense phase. When waiting for a ball to be kicked back into play or for the kick off, the placement of the team is clear for all to see, and so also the system to which it makes reference. When making out his report about the opponent's system the coach must carefully identify any change that is made from one phase to another and possible 'hybrid' positions and personalized situations - as we have seen. It is not enough to say that the team is positioned according to this or that system, but the situation must be broken down into all its details.

COMPARING PLAYING SYSTEMS

Once you have established the system used by your opponent you have to compare it with your own so as to take all the necessary counter measures. Comparing two systems means working out all the possible numerical situations: section by section, on each flank, at the center of the defense, at the center of the field and at the center of the attack. We have to make the best of our numerical superiority, eliminate the situations of numerical inferiority and turn the numerical equality to our own advantage.

By making the most of our numerical superiority we free men to receive passes and create empty spaces that can be attacked. As a result, it will be easier for us to get near our opponent's goal, keeping in mind that our opponents will be finding it difficult to get to grips with our advantage because they will be forced to shift without the ball being in movement.

Generally speaking, the countermoves we make to contrast our opponent's system should tend to magnify the defects of their set up (both those inherent to the system itself, and those created by the excellence of our own), while at the same time eliminating - or in any case reducing - the good points of their play (inherent to it or in relation to the defects of our own).

We will have to decide if it is better to exploit the width or the depth of the field during the attacking phase, and we must choose which finishing touch techniques to use in order to get past their defense system and which plays will be most useful in creating and making the best of situations of numerical superiority.

In the defense phase, we must establish how to shift so as to contrast the opposing set up as well as we can, and in what zone and with which players to double up the marking, trying at the same time to force the opposition into playing where they find it most difficult. We must also give our players instructions on how best to confront the typical movements of the opponent's system.

ANALYSIS OF MENTAL ATTITUDE

We must try to sum up the opponent's general attitude to the match, which will reflect their mentality and philosophy of play. Above all we must try to understand if the rival team has a clear mentality (offensive / defensive), or if they prefer to adapt their attitude to the circumstances. There are not many teams, in fact, which play in the same way both at home or away and against all kinds of opposition, strong or weak.

In order to evaluate whether our opponents have a clear and decided mentality or whether this tends to be modified, we must have a look at their performance over many matches, because one single game will not be enough in this context. The task of summing up their mentality is based on:

- ☐ Their interpretation of the system.
- ☐ The line from which they go into pressing, and the consequent balancing point of the team.
- ☐ The number of players that participate actively in the attacking and defending phases.
- ☐ Their will to control play for the whole duration of the match, keeping their attitude constant.
- ☐ Their possible adaptation of these various tactical components during one match and from one match to another. Even in the course of a single match we can watch to see if our opponents change their reaction depending on the result. It can happen that apparently offensive teams become defensive if they go into advantage, or that closed teams bring up their point of balance when they are losing, trying to take play in hand in order to overturn the result.

If after having analyzed a number of matches, we still think the team does not demonstrate a clear mentality, we must attempt to imagine how they will behave in the face of our own characteristics. If we are stronger on paper, we can expect them to play in a defensive way. If we are theoretically weaker, it is logical to think that they will play an attacking game. All this will also depend on whether they are playing at home or away. If they are playing at home we can expect them to be more courageous, and if they are playing on our field we can imagine they will be more prudent.

If from the studies we have made we deduce that they have a well defined mentality, we must expect them to use it even when playing against our team.

What effect will the rival team's attitude have on us during the match we are to play? The first thing to say is that their attitude will not cause us to make important changes in our set up, and the coach should only give some advice and make some recommendations to his players. It is always important for the whole team to be as aware as possible about who they are facing, and the first thing is to be conscious of the opponent's philosophy of play.

If we are expecting our opponents to interpret the match in an offensive way, we must consider the fact that, unfortunately, for a good part of the match we will be defending in our own half. The coach must urge the team to try seize control of play in any case, breaking off the opponent's maneuvers at their outset. Then he will have to counsel his players about how to behave when the opponents are dominating and crushing them in their half. The team must remain compact and the mid fielders must try to press the rival players in the same section, without ever being forced to keep too far back. The coach must insist that the team is not to panic when they are being crushed in defense, waiting in a tactically regular way to get back control of play. Even when we are in possession, and are undergoing our adversary's in-depth pressing, we must be careful about how we manage the ball, guaranteeing various passing solutions to the player in possession.

If we foresee that the opponent will be playing a defensive match, the coach must give his team indications about how to manage the tactical situation. The players must carry out encircling maneuvers, making good use of the flanks. When facing a closed team, it is important to exploit the sidelines as much as possible, using the cross from the base line as the principle finishing touch technique.

It will be difficult for the opposing defense to avoid mistakes in marking our attacking players as the crosses are piling in, and we can take advantage of any loose balls in the area if our players are correctly placed to cover the 'bounces' (Fig. 1).

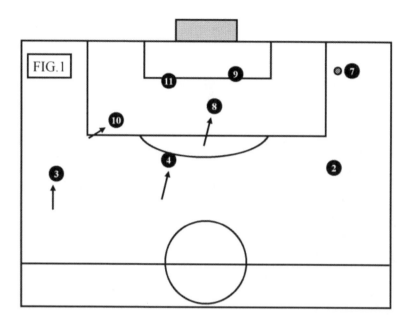

FIG.1

The team must be patient in attack and not get discouraged if they cannot create opportunities to score or even if they fail time and time again. If the team begins to panic, thus losing cohesion and tactical organization, we risk making too many mistakes in managing our phase of possession, and this will lead to easy counterattacking moves. Remind the team that the match lasts 90 minutes and that the goal(s) will come sooner or later if we continue to attack with order and intensity, varying our playing solutions all the time. The players must attack in a block, but they must always be ready to reposition themselves at once and carry out pressing when they lose possession.

THE PARTICIPATION OF THE PLAYERS IN THE VARIOUS PHASES

It is not difficult to evaluate how many players participate in the opposition's attacking and defense phases, and it is important for us to understand if we will be in numerical superiority or inferiority during these two phases.

When he is watching the opposing team's previous matches, the coach must determine how many players take an active part in the attacking and the defense phase. In order to do so, he must have a clear idea about what is meant by 'active player' in a playing phase.

A player is active during the possession phase if he is positioned in such a way as to permit him to carry out the aims of the sub-phase that he is interpreting. In the post-conquest and ball maintenance sub-phases (i.e., when the team has just regained possession and must now consolidate the situation, or when, as a result of having risked losing possession because of the opponent's heavy pressing, it is necessary to make a change of play or at least to put the ball in a safe place), we define the active players as those positioned in such a way as to allow the teammate in difficulty to dump the ball on them - above all the ones who are placed behind the line of the ball.

In the build up sub-phase (i.e., the sub-phase concerned with moving the ball forward towards the opponent's goal), the active players are the ones who allow play to develop in the direction of its target. Here, the active players are positioned in front of the ball line, even if the teammates behind the player in possession can come in handy for changes of play and for dump shots to be rebounded vertically on a player who is in even greater depth.

In the finishing touch sub-phase (putting a player into a position which will enable him to shoot at goal) the active players are those who are creating numerical superiority on the offensive side and are freeing themselves of marking so as to receive the final assist from the player in possession.

Apart from deciding which opposing players are active in these sub-phases, the coach must also make a classification of the roles played by the opponents in the offense phase. There are three roles that a player can assume in the attacking phase.

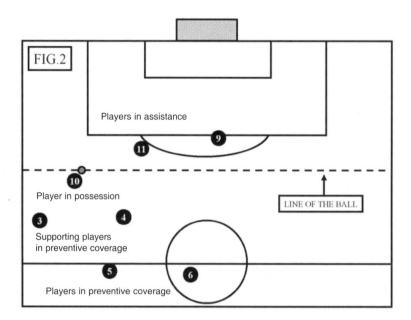

Player in **preventive coverage**: player under the ball line, positioned in such a way as to be able to intervene should the opponent regain possession.

Supporting player: player under the ball line and near the teammate in possession so as to allow for a back dump. Such a player is also in preventive coverage.

Player in **assistance**: player positioned in front of the ball line, allowing for the development of the maneuver towards the opponent's goal.

Generally speaking, we can say that the players participating actively in the maneuver are those that do not always remain in preventive coverage, but who frequently move over the ball line (e.g., an overlapping side back is to be considered an active player in the attacking phase). You should pay particular attention to the opposing defenders' behavior, seeing as it is only too clear that the mid fielders and the strikers will be participating in the attacking phase.

The coach should consider *the number* of players that always remain in preventive coverage and how many are positioned beyond the ball line - and not *limit* himself to deciding who these players actually are.

During the defense phase, the active players are those positioned under the ball line who can intervene on the opponent in possession, mark their rival supporting players and cover the open spaces in which the opposition can build up their play. We must also say that even the players above the ball line, very often the strikers, can be useful during the non-possession phase, placing themselves so as to cover the back pass lines that the rival player in possession might decide to use.

In order to simplify things, we must make a mental note of how many players belong to the defense and mid field block, because these will generally be the ones taking active part in the non-possession phase; but we will also have to observe the strikers' behavior with special attention.

How will all this influence our own set up. We will have to weigh the numerical situation in both phases, comparing the number of our active players in each phase with their active players in the same stage of play. However, this is only a theoretical calculation, respecting the initial placement of the team on the field and the typical movements of the players. The important thing is that we have to be able to create numerical superiority in both phases by moving without the ball. As a consequence of that, the situation facing us will always be dynamic, never static.

If we are in numerical superiority in the offense phase, we will have to decide whether the fact that their attacking players outnumber our defense is dangerous enough to force us to keep a player in preventive coverage. It is the same if we are in numerical equality and are particularly worried about our opponent's counter attacks. If our team is very strong in the attacking phase, there is nothing wrong with asking one of our players not to drive forward, but if we are having trouble building up play we will have to make a difficult choice based on the comparison between our ability in the defense phase and the danger the opposing team represent when counter attacking.

What we have just said is valid even if we are in numerical inferiority in the attacking phase. Once again we will have to measure up our team's attacking ability, the opponent's defense and their ability to hit us in counter attack.

As far as the defense phase is concerned, if we are in numerical superiority we could risk keeping one less player under the ball line, or keeping our set up unchanged so as to be sure that we will be getting the better of things in the phase of non-possession. That will depend on the quality of our opponent's play, the reliability of our defense phase and the difficulty we foresee in building up our play against the opposition.

My view is that it is not a good idea to change the defense mechanisms if they are well-oiled because we want the players to have the same points of reference on the field, getting them to move in situations that are always alike.

If we are in numerical inferiority in the non-possession phase it might be a good idea to ask the strikers to work even harder, integrating themselves with the mid field line. At least one player, however, should remain beyond the ball line as a point of reference on whom to direct an in depth pass should we recover possession. If we consider that the opposing team is not a real danger (even in relation to our ability in defense), and/or that we are the ones that will be finding it difficult to build up play, we could risk maintaining the situation of numerical inferiority in defense, which, however, entails us outnumbering the opponents in preventive coverage.

PRESSING AND DOUBLING UP ON MARKING: WHEN, WHERE, HOW

When compiling your 'identikit' of the rival team, one of the most important facets is an analysis of their pressing and doubling up on marking. Their pressing is also a fundamental marker for evaluating the opponent's mentality and the way they are applying their system of play.

As far as pressing is concerned the coach must assess:

- ☐ The level on the field from which it commences.
- ☐ The zones of the field in which it is applied (the flanks, the center, both)
- ☐ The circumstances in which it is applied.
- ☐ If there is any invited pressing.
- ☐ Its effectiveness.

We must explain the difference between pressure and pressing. Pressure is an action carried out by an individual so as to limit the space and time at the disposal of the opposing player in possession. One player goes in to close off the player in possession while the rest of the team covers the space, guaranteeing closure - by the use of the defensive diagonal - if the opponent dribbles past their teammate (Fig. 3).

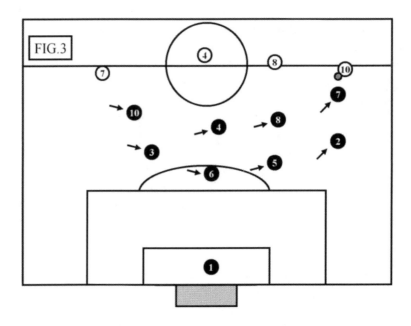

Pressing, on the other hand, is a collective action aiming to reduce the opposing team's space and time (one or more players go in to close off, while the rest of the team is in anticipatory marking on the opponent's supporting players but still guaranteeing coverage for the teammate who is defending the ball) (Fig. 4). Pressing is made up of two phases: a stand by phase and an aggressive phase. The first of these could be thought of as an individual action during which the player is standing by, though of course the player in possession is already being marked.

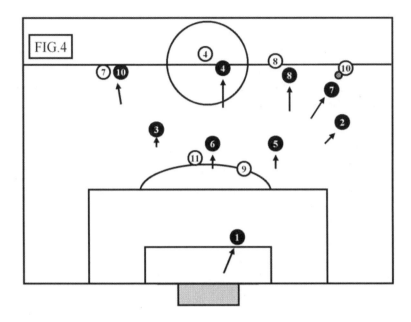

The second is the real pressing, the players showing aggressive behavior with double teaming on the ball and tight anticipatory marking on opponents without the ball.

When we are looking to see on what level of the field the opponents start pressing we must not be too strict about our parameters, but should include the stand by phase of pressing (pressure). We have to decide where the opponent starts to defend. If a team starts to interfere with its opponent's maneuvers in its opponent's half, this action will almost certainly be pressing in the strict sense. A team that begins to defend itself in the opposite half will almost always do so in a collective way - by anticipatory marking on the opponent's players in support. We can say that, strictly speaking, pressing is applied in situations where the opponent is in difficulty (when he is about to receive the ball, when he controls the ball badly, when he has to stop a high ball, when he is being double teamed, when he insists on an individual play, when he lowers his head ready to kick) - and being put under pressure in your own half is surely to be included in this list. It should be pointed out that a team requires a good ability to move collectively in order to be able to carry out pressing and close off the spaces. You can often find situations where pressure is being brought to bear in a disorganized way - aggressive actions created by individual initiatives even in the opponent's half.

We can distinguish three zones of the field where a team will begin to disturb the opponent's play, and therefore three types of pressing: ultra-offensive pressing (carried out from beyond the opponent's three quarter line), offensive pressing (carried out around the half way line) and defensive pressing (carried out in the team's own half).

We must also keep in mind that pressing is often carried out only in certain parts of the field and in certain circumstances.

Tight pressing is often brought to bear only on the flanks, where because the strong and weak side is well-defined, the opponent is forced to play in basically half the space. The result is that it is easier and safer to double up on marking here, as there will be limited solutions open to the player in possession. That does not mean the opponents will be left free in the center, where we simply prefer to carry out stand-by pressing, putting the player under individual pressure, with the rest of the team keeping short and concentrating on covering the spaces.

The circumstances calling for this type of pressing are those we have already listed when speaking about difficult situations for our opposing players.

Connected with the two phases of pressing (stand-by phase and aggressive phase) there is also the concept of invited pressing.

Invited pressing is carried out by the player positioning himself in the stand-by mode in order to force the opponent to the play the ball in a way that will be to our advantage and that will permit us to carry out the aggressive phase of pressing. A team that uses invited pressing is usually aiming to open up the opponent's play onto the flanks (which, as we have already explained, are the best zones to go into aggressive pressing), or to get the opposition to play the ball onto a less technically gifted player or one who suffers psychologically from being pressed.

Double teaming comes about as a result of aggressive pressing. When our opponents are undergoing those negative situations of play that we have described above, we must try to attack the player in possession with at least two players. When double teaming takes place the rest of the team will be covering the nearest passing lines so as to put the player in possession under even greater difficulty and so we will automatically get a situation of aggressive pressing.

We must, therefore, assess the type of pressing carried out by the opponent we are to meet (ultra-offensive, offensive or defensive); and at the same time whether they prefer to do it on the flanks or if they make no distinctions about the sidelines or the center, always applying pressing in every part of the field. We must then decide in what circumstances - among those we have listed - they carry out aggressive pressing, and whether, how and where they make invited pressing or double up on marking. In connection with this last element, we must try to foresee, on the basis of the psycho-technical characteristics of our players (and in particular the defenders), whether the opponents will be attempting to force our play onto a particular member of our team. Also, we must look to see if our opponent's pressing is effective -i.e., if it is carried out in the right way and with the right timing without committing errors and always succeeding in its aim of regaining possession.

If we conclude that our opponents always carry out pressing in more or less the same way against any other team, then we must expect them to do the same with us.

If we see that they change the 'when, how and when' of their pressing in reaction to their opponent, we will expect them to behave according to our own characteristics.

Another thing to keep in mind is that teams that adapt their pressing to the opposing team prefer to use ultra-offensive pressing if they feel that their opponents are inferior, offensive pressing if they consider the other team equal to themselves and defensive pressing when they consider the opposition to be superior. We must therefore compare the strength of our own team with that of the one we will be meeting; at that point, we will be able to deduce what type of pressing our opponents will be applying against us.

Let us now have a look at the countermeasures that we will have
to take in relation to the sort of pressing the opponents will be
carrying out.
If we expect them to be doing ultra-offensive or offensive pressing it is important that:

- ☐ the mid fielders place themselves in such a way as to
  create triangles and rhombi of play, which will give the
  player in possession more passing solutions;
- ☐ the attacking players move to meet the defenders so as to
  give them points of reference in front;
- ☐ the defenders place themselves so as to cover for each
  other in order that they can intervene should the opponent's pressing be successful. Also, the ball must never be
  moving parallel to the mid field line;
- ☐ we change play as often as possible because there will be
  a lower density of players on the weak side and the pressure will be less. The player in possession dumps the ball
  on a supporting player situated behind, who will be able to
  change the playing front more easily (Fig. 5);
- ☐ in cases where we are in difficulty we should not simply
  make a long forward pass to take off the pressure and
  then go to press in the zone where the ball falls.

We must give precise tactical instructions to the defense concerning the best ways of moving into depth to get over the
opposing strikers' pressing. We must compare the number and
the lay out of their attacking players with those of our defense.
This will make it easier for us to decide which are the safest outlets for the third line when setting up the maneuver. For example,
a 4-man defense against 2 strikers must make the ball converge
on the side backs who should have considerable space around
them. Instead, a 4-man defense against 3 strikers should be
looking for a way out through the center with combinations
between the two inside defenders, who are in numerical superiority against the opposing center forward, while the two side backs
are under pressing from the wings.

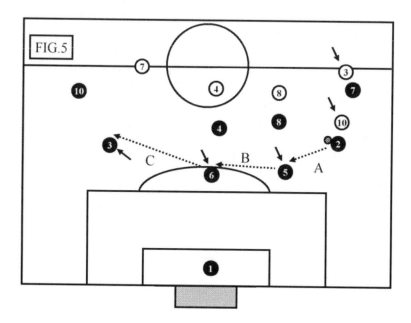

If you are expecting the opponent to use defensive pressing it is necessary that:

☐ you open play onto the flanks as much as possible in order to get around the opponent's pressing;

☐ you try to use crosses as the main finishing touch technique because the central zones will be blocked up;

☐ the whole team is ready to intervene in cases where you lose possession;

☐ the maneuver is collective, quick, fluid, intense and varied.

What it all boils down to is this: when our opponents are carrying out defensive pressing we behave as we would against a team that has have a defensive mentality.

As concerns the invited pressing that our opponents will be applying to make us play the ball in particular parts of the field or to certain players, we will have to make sure that the player we think may be undergoing such aggressive action will have a wide range of passing solutions open to him at all times.

The coach must insist that whenever there is a situation favorable to this type of pressing, the whole team should behave in a rational way, giving assistance to the player in difficulty.
The coach must also give psychological support to those players he thinks will be pressed in this way by the opponents, telling them to keep calm and to think, and advising them to go for a change of play or to dump the ball or, as an extreme solution, to make a long pass.

Lastly, if we consider that our opponent's pressing is not very effective, the coach should tell the team to look for the strikers at once, sending the maneuvers into depth to make the best of the good chances they will have to counterattack on account of any mistaken application of pressing by the opposing players.

ZONAL DEFENSE OR MAN MARKING - OR A MIXTURE OF THE TWO

Summing up the opponent's defense system is very important and at the same time simple to do.
Teams change completely in the non-possession phase on the basis of their defense system, and that has a great influence on the general 'picture' that we are making of our opponents.
We get an instant idea of a team's defense system the first time they are forced to defend. We will then be able to see whether the defense players take on the opposing men themselves, or if they are covering the spaces and moving in reaction to the ball.
What is more difficult to analyze are all those grey intermediate areas between the zonal defense system and man marking.
There are defensive set ups that adopt a mixture of elements between the two systems, and these defense forms, which can be defined as 'mixed defense systems', are the following:

☐ Man marking defense with a zonal set up in the mid field;
☐ Zonal defense and mid field with some man marking (generally on the opposing attacking mid fielder);
☐ Man marking on the opposing strikers, with a detached sweeper and all the other players zone marking;
☐ 'Man marking in the zone': each defender covers a certain zone of the field, in which he carries out man marking on the striker present in his space.

In preparing the match the coach must pay special attention to whether or not one of the defense systems listed above applies. Here he will need to make a deeper analysis, not limiting himself to his initial perception but watching carefully from the beginning.

Attacking the man marking defense system

Once he has established what kind of defense system the opponents will be using, the coach will have to give precise indications to his players, in particular the strikers.
If the opponents are man marking, the team must:

☐ Move even more persistently without the ball;

☐ Carry out a counter movement to free themselves of marking before making their real movement - that is, they must dummy so as to put the player marking them out of phase;

☐ Build up play by using short triangular passes (both give and go, give and follow) so as to accelerate past a great number of opposing marking players;

☐ Try to make the best of the fact that the opponent's defense is not in line (the sweeper is detached): the strikers should get themselves free of marking by moving into depth more frequently without having to worry about finishing up in an offside position. In other words, the strikers should try to exploit the spaces between the markers and the sweeper (Fig. 6);

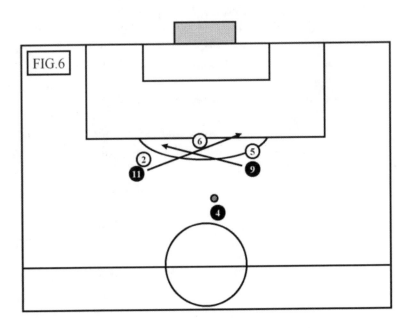

FIG.6

□ Constantly attempt to break into play from behind, both on the flanks and in the center so as to put the opposing defender who is marking into numerical inferiority (1:2) (Fig. 7);

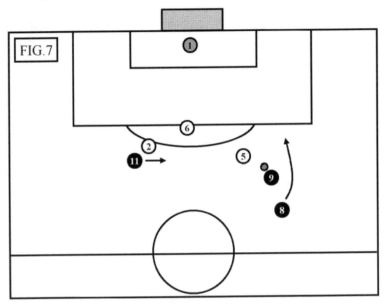

FIG.7

□ Always remember that it is important to create numerical superiority around the ball in order to upset the opponent's marking;

□ Get the defenders to move into depth to create numerical superiority against the rival backs. Because they are marking the man, the opponents will not be able to shift onto our defenders who are breaking in, and who will therefore be unmarked. The only solution our opponents will have is to ask their strikers to mark our defending men as they break in. In this way, their strikers will not be ready when there is a counter attack.

Our strikers' most important job is to create spaces by opening up this man marking defense system. The movements they will have to carry out most frequently are the following:

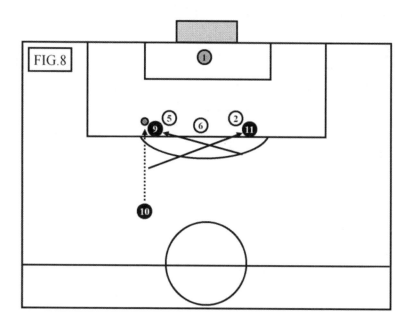

☐ Crossovers (Fig. 8). The two attacking players have to put their bodies between the teammate in possession and the man who is marking them so that when the ball arrives their bodies will act as a shield.

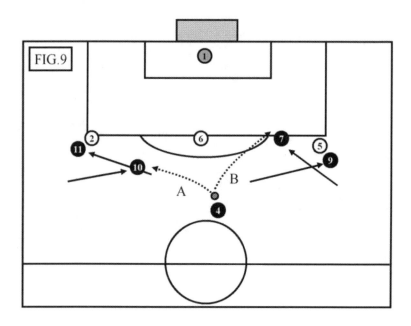

☐ Deviating movements towards the flanks (Fig. 9). This movement will attract the markers towards the sidelines, and space will be created to be attacked by the mid fielders (if possible the side players).

☐ 'Diagonal' movements (Fig. 10). Diagonal movements have the same aim as deviations. The difference is that now both strikers are moving towards the same flank.

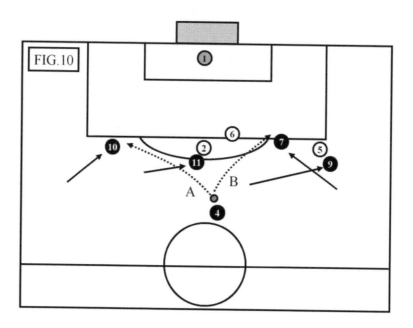

Attacking the zone

If our opponents are defending zonally we must make continuous changes of play because a zonal defense tends to be attracted towards the strong side, leaving the weak side unguarded with wide open spaces where we can create numerical superiority. We must also attack along the flanks because the central zones will be crowded.

Another thing to do is create numerical superiority in every part of the field by getting players to break into play from behind and going to meet the player in possession.

We will attack our opponent's defense on the blind side by having our side mid fielder break in behind the last man in the row on the opposite side (Fig. 11).

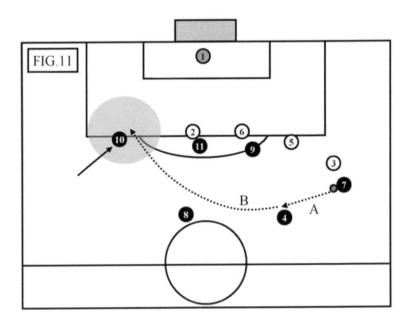

Above all the strikers must:

☐ Carry out 'one goes, one comes' movements (Fig. 12). The two strikers sprint into depth, making the opposing defenders move back and so creating distance between them and the mid field line. At this point, one of the strikers comes to meet the player in possession, receiving the ball in the neutral zone between the opponent's two lines that has just been widened out. Another 'one goes, one comes' movement is the following: one of the strikers comes immediately towards the player in possession, while the other cuts behind him into the space that has been created. In this way the player in possession will have two different solutions open to him.

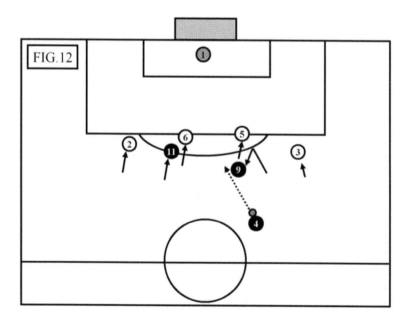

FIG. 12

- [ ] Carry out tight combinations, putting the opposing defense in difficulty.
- [ ] Carry out in-depth cuts, making the most of the spaces between the defenders.

If our opponents are using a mixed system, we too must mix the types of countermoves used to face either a zonal defense or one that is marking the man. Our choice of combinations must vary on the basis of the opposing defense's specific mixed conformation.

Returning to the opponent lined up in the zone, in order to make full preparations for the match we need to consider the specific mechanisms of that defense system.

DIAGONALS AND LINES OF COVERAGE

The defense diagonal can be divided into various types (Fig. 13):

- [ ] With one covering line;
- [ ] With two covering lines;
- [ ] With two covering lines in a curve.

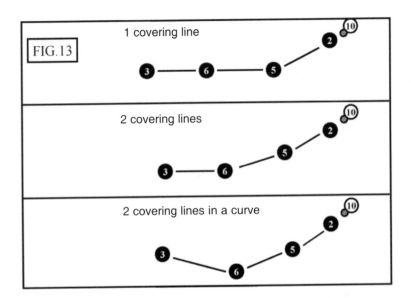

You very rarely find three covering lines. The mid field diagonal is usually made up of two covering lines.

If our opponents use one covering line in the diagonal, we must make the best of the fact that the center defenders are not covering each other. The nearest striker must cut between the two inside defenders to dodge the first central defender's anticipation of the pass. If the ball gets through it will be difficult for the other central defender to recuperate because he was not in a position to cover for his teammate (Fig. 14).

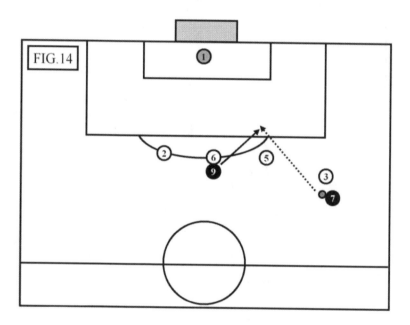

If the opponents are using the two-line diagonal, we must make the best of the fact that their defense is not aligned and will concede space in depth.

The strikers should 'throw themselves' into depth as much as possible without worrying about finishing up in offside. In particular, the nearest striker must cut towards the existing space at the side of the defender who is furthest back (Fig. 15).

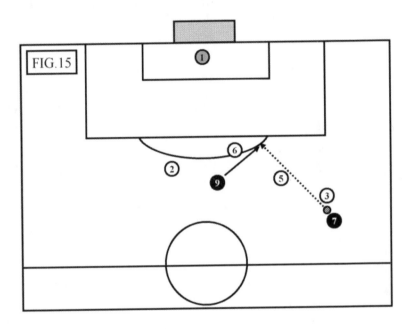

In cases where the opponents use a curved diagonal we must only tell the team to be careful during changes in play because the advanced position of the fourth player in the defense will give him good chances of intercepting. If that happens, the opposing team is better positioned than we are for a counter attack.

ELASTIC AND OFFSIDE TACTICS

☐ We must evaluate the vertical movements of the opponent's defense. The first thing to understand is if the rival defense line limits itself to moving up to meet the ball (i.e., do they go into depth only to meet a ball coming back so that they can maintain the distance from the mid field section going into pressing?) or do they advance on other occasions as well, applying offside tactics in an active way. The situations in which a team can apply offside in an active way are the following:

☐ When the mid field section passes from the flanks to the center;

☐ When the defense makes a long pass away from the area; when a rival striker makes a back pass;

☐ When the opponent in possession looks down in order to carry out a pass or to sprint with the ball;

☐ When the mid field section has been cut out of play, and the defense is forced to intervene on the player in possession;

☐ When, after having moved back and detached themselves from the mid field in order to absorb the strikers as they are breaking in, the defense moves back into depth because the player in possession has missed his moment for the play;

☐ When the strikers, after having sprinted into depth, line themselves up with the defense;

☐ When they are in numerical inferiority and there are no opponents breaking in from behind.

In the same way we must assess the tactical ability of the opposing team to carry out the defense shift in the correct way (the guiding lines are to move back when the opposing player in possession is in a position to play the ball into depth and to move up when he is no longer able to play it forward). A well-organized defense should already be mentally prepared to move back as they are moving up and ready to move into depth when they are moving back.

If we have seen that our opponents move up in a prudent way only when the ball is moving back to keep the right distance with the mid field, then we should try to play the ball forward immediately, hoping to catch them unprepared. The strikers should move back in order to not end up in an offside position, but be ready to sprint into depth as soon as they get the chance.
If our opponents are making use of offside tactics in other circumstances, the following are the countermoves we should be trying to make.
As they move back, the strikers should carry out crescent movements to create difficulties in the exchange of marking for their opponents who are moving vertically. By making such movements, the strikers will also be in a position to sprint into depth as soon as their mid field teammates have controlled the ball (Fig. 16).

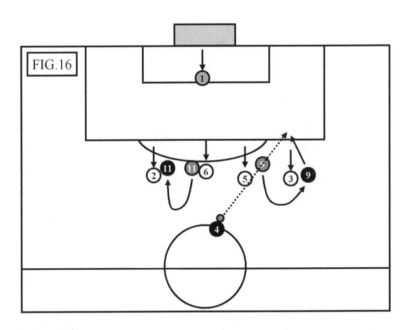

A defense using offside tactics tends to tighten up, and so our side players must immediately break in along the flanks so that our player in possession can pass to them in the free spaces alongside the defense (Fig. 17).

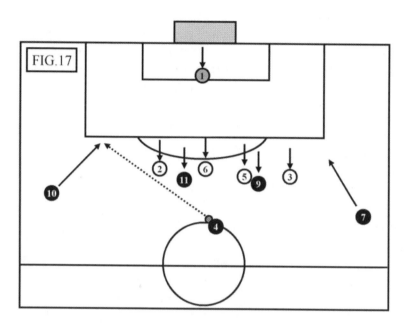

If the player in possession has his back turned to the goal and is being pressed, he must have teammates at his side and in front of him who are ready to receive his dump. In any case, when the opponent's defense is moving up and one of our players is able to play the ball into depth, the mid fielders must immediately break in from behind.

To make the best of the fact that the opponent's defense moves back when our player in possession plays the ball into depth, the two strikers should sprint forward first of all, after which one will return to meet the ball, attacking the wide open space that has been created between the opponent's lines (c.f. Fig. 12).

SECTION DOUBLING UP

For double teaming, what we said in the paragraph dealing with pressing still holds good. Here, we are talking about doubling up within the section - when two players belonging to the same line double up on marking. This kind of doubling up is generally carried out when the section is in clear numerical superiority, or when the defense line has to close off an attacking player in the area who is just about to shoot at goal.

If our opponents make the mistake of doubling up in the section when their line is not in numerical superiority, our player in possession should immediately make a change of play onto the opposite side of the field where there will be wide open spaces. Either that or he should pass to a teammate breaking into the center - if the opposing section have opened space there on account of their bad shifting move.

THE RELATIONSHIP BETWEEN COVERING THE ZONE AND MARKING THE MAN

Another important thing for us to assess in the opponent's defense system is the relationship between covering the zone and marking the man. A zonally placed team can present variations on the theme. There are zonal defense systems that take no interest whatever in the opposing players without the ball, closing in on the opposing player in possession every time and covering the spaces with great attention. But there are also zonal defense systems in which the backs mark the man without the ball whenever he enters a particular zone without worrying about covering the spaces. This last case is defined as a mixed defense system.

When preparing a match to be played in such terms, the coach should advise his players to carry out collective movements, creating and attacking space, in addition to the other countermoves we have already talked about for facing a defense that marks the man, especially if the system will be marking very tightly. Instead, if the opposing defense is concentrating on covering the spaces, the advice is to pass the ball around constantly to create problems for the opposing sections when they shift to close us off. Also, the whole team must move without the ball, making the most of the fact that the opponents will not be following our movements. We must also try to create situations of numerical superiority around the ball so that our opponents will have trouble positioning themselves.

SHIFTING MOVEMENTS

For a complete analysis of the opponent's defense system, it is a good thing to assess the way in which they shift and the effectiveness of these mechanisms. Naturally, the ways in which they shift depend on the playing system they are using.

As regards their effectiveness, look to see if the opponent makes the mistake of shifting on a 'stationary' ball or whether they are shifting correctly when the ball is being passed. It is to our advantage if the opponent shifts when the ball is stationary, and we should tell our players that in such cases they should make immediate collective movements without the ball. In this way we will be able to exploit the spaces that are created and, above all, some of our players will be unmarked for a moment or two. We can advance with the ball with speed and effectiveness, creating serious problems for the opposing defense system, which will risk finding itself in numerical inferiority in parts of the field.

Another thing to consider in connection with shifting movements is the opponent's ability to slide the back section over to close off a player of ours who is free of marking. If the opposing defense shifts badly in such circumstances, our strikers should take advantage of the situation by sprinting into depth and making the most of our rival defenders' moment of difficulty.

Lastly, it is important to know whether the mid fielder on the opposite side is aware of the fact that he should shift to protect the defense line's blind side when their diagonal is too short (this happens principally in the area when the defenders tighten the marking). If the opponents do not protect the weak side of the defense when it is necessary, we should tell our side players to make the most of such a situation by using cuts to enter and attack this unguarded part of the field (Fig. 18).

THE FLANK ON WHICH THE OPPONENTS FIND THEMSELVES IN GREATER DIFFICULTY

In this in-depth analysis of the opponent's defense system, we must decide which flank will be giving them most trouble. It very often happens that a team's defense is weaker on one flank on account of the fact that the side players there are less diligent. These difficulties defending a flank will become even greater if it is the side back on that flank who is not very good during the defense phase.

From our point of view that is very important indeed. Of course, our play must be 'symmetrical', by which I mean that what happens on the right of the field must also happen on the left. But it is reasonable to ask the team to insist more on the flank where our opponent is weaker, so as to make the best of a situation favorable to us. Clearly, the other flank must not be neglected, but there should be more play on the flank where we find ourselves in a stronger position.

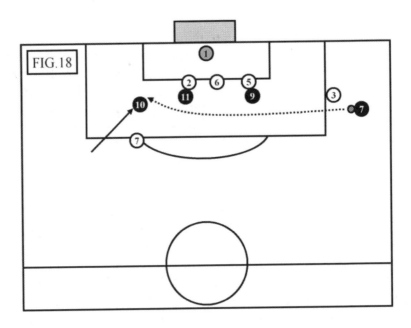

FIG.18

BUILDING UP PLAY AND WHAT FINISHING TOUCH TECHNIQUES TO USE

When delineating our opponent's offensive phase we have to look at how they are building up play and what finishing touch techniques they will be using.

We can make a classification of three types of build up:

Elaborate build up. The team moves forward in a block with the ball towards the rival's goal, alternating horizontal and vertical passes so as to make the most of the width and the depth of the field.

Immediate build up. When the team has regained possession they overturn the action at once, especially using long passes for the strikers.

Maneuvered counterattacks. Even though they mean to overturn the action at once, the team does so by passing along the ground, involving a great number of players in the action, not only the strikers.

We must also say that during the course of a single match the team can alternate between these three ways of building up play, using the elaborate maneuver when the defenders regain possession in their own half; immediate build up when they get the ball in the opponent's half and the maneuvered counterattack in cases when the opponent is off balance or badly placed on the field at the moment we regain possession.

As we have seen, the way we build up play will depend on the part of the field where we regain possession in the defense phase, which is a demonstration of the fact that the two phases of play are strictly connected to each other.

A team will always try to build up play in a certain way and so one of the three ways of doing so will predominate over the others. Our job is to understand which is the form of build up most frequently used by the opponents and whether, when and to what extent the others are used as well.

Having summed this up, we must now give our team precise indications as regards our defense phase.

If our opponent is making most use of the elaborate build up, we must try to close off and double up on the opposing player in possession as much as we can, but above all we must cover the passing lines so that the opponents cannot pass the ball around too much. Also, our defenders will be able to push into attack more often because the opponents will not be counter attacking at once. Keeping in mind that the opposing team will be trying to open play out on the flanks all the time, our defending players should carry out the diagonal onto the sidelines with the right timing, doubling up the marking on the opponent's player in possession as quickly as they can.

With reference to the opposing team's width of play, we must establish which flank they prefer attacking from. It very often happens that a team's attacking play is not symmetrical, and so once we have established which flank they prefer to exploit, we should try to create numerical superiority there in the defense phase by doubling up the marking with the intervention of the mid fielders (if necessary also moving a center player to the side).

If our opponents are using immediate build up most of the time, the whole team must be ready to go into pressing as soon as we lose possession. The defense line must be good at using the shift, so as to get the better of the opponent's long passes. The defense must always be ready to move up or back depending on the tactical situation in order to take away depth from the rival players. However, if we think the opponents are particularly good at counterattacking, we must tell our defenders to advance a little less.

If our opponents are mostly using the maneuvered counterattack, it is more or less as if we have to face the immediate build up, with the difference that instead of worrying about long passes, our defense will be trying to annul the rival strikers, who will be the advanced points of reference for their team's plays. Our defenders must be quick to follow them when they go back to meet their teammates to try to anticipate and not to let them turn when they receive the ball.

We will now define the finishing touch techniques. A shot at goal can be a result of:

- ☐ Cuts
- ☐ Crosses
- ☐ Dump and rebound passes
- ☐ Overlapping
- ☐ Combinations
- ☐ Dribbling

One of the things we will be looking for during the analysis phase is what kind of finishing touch techniques are most frequently used by by our upcoming opponent. Keep in mind that a team that plays varied and unexpected soccer will be using the whole range of finishing touch techniques during the match. To assess things in the right way you must decide the average number of times each technique is used during the course of the matches you have watched, remembering also that figures like these can be influenced by a particular opponent's defense system.

Once you have established the finishing touch techniques most frequently used by your opponent, you must instruct your players in what they should try to do.

If the most frequently used technique is the cut, our defense should reduce the opponent's depth by the correct use of the defense shift. If the opposing player in possession is able feed the strikers the moment they sprint into depth, our defense should behave in different ways depending on their position in relation to that of the strikers:

If the defense is aligned to the strikers, our backs should move up in order to put them in an offside position. They must be careful, however, that there are no other opponent's nearby who could break in from behind (Fig. 19).

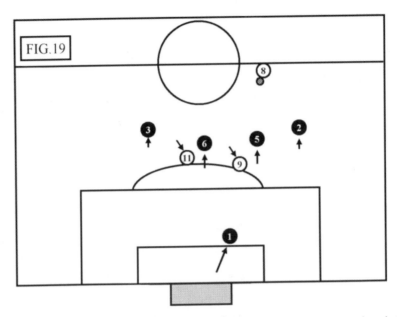

If the defense is not aligned with the strikers it must move back to absorb their in-depth movements, ready to move out again as soon as the attacking players get in line or the player in possession has lost his moment (Fig. 20).

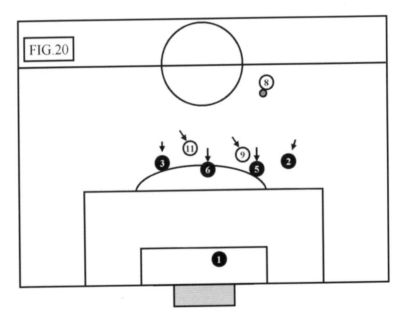

If the striker's cut is carried out above the defense line (cut to receive) the defenders must be quick to exchange marking.

If the cut is made into the gaps between one defender and another, the defender from whose zone the striker has set up his movement must follow him, putting his body between the goal and the striker himself so as to close him off the moment he receives the ball. The defender towards whose zone the striker is directed must move up a yard or two, placing himself on the lines of the probable vertical pass in order to anticipate it (Fig. 21).

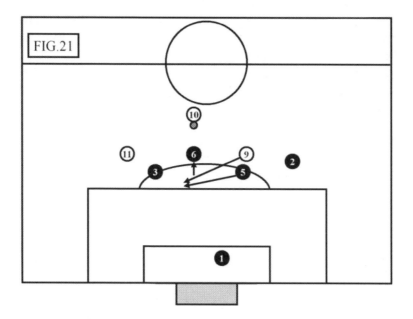

If they are using the cross as their principle finishing touch technique, we must make sure first of all that our opponents cannot get into position to carry it out. The cross from the base line is the most dangerous because our defenders will be at a disadvantage to their strikers. In fact, their strikers can see where the cross is coming from as well as the goal, which they are facing. Our defenders are the ones who will be badly placed when the cross arrives from the base line.
Crosses from behind are less dangerous because now our defenders can see the ball, while the opposing strikers cannot.

To stop the opponent from getting into position for the cross, we should always close off the player in possession moving up along the flank. The defense line must make the correct diagonal while the side mid fielder must come over quickly to double team. When the opponent manages to make the cross, the defenders in the area must be ready, tightening up the marking on the players in their zone. Also, the mid fielders must come back to the edges of the area to mark the attackers positioned there and, in any case, to increase the density of our team in the zone to which the cross is arriving.

If the opponents are making principle use of the dump and rebound pass as a finishing touch technique, the defenders must follow the striker that is coming to meet the ball, trying to anticipate the pass but being careful not to move too far into depth, for otherwise they will be leaving their zone free. If the striker manages to carry out the rebound, our defense must quickly tighten up and get compact to close off the new player in possession. Because all plays with a rebound by a striker are carried out by three players in collaboration (the initial player in possession, the striker and the player breaking in), the mid fielder must put the first in this series - the one who starts off the action - under great pressure.
Remember also that shots on goal coming from a dump and rebound are often made from the edge of the area. The defense must be ready to move up and close off the player who has just broken in and is about to take the shot.

If the finishing touch technique most frequently utilized is overlapping, the first thing to decide is whether this is carried out in the central zone or on the flanks. In both cases we will be in need of close collaboration on the part of at least two players. When the player pressing the opponent in possession sees that he is about to undergo overlapping by another opposing player, he has to move back at once on the opponent coming up. The nearest mid fielder must then immediately come in to mark the player in possession, who will be free for a moment or two (Fig. 22).

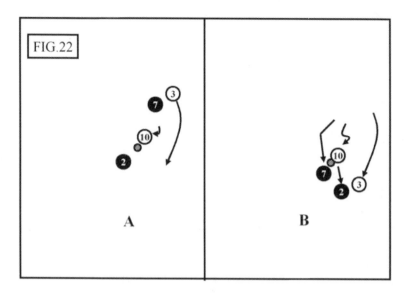

When our defense has good numerical superiority against the opposing attacking players and the ball is on the flanks, the defender who is on the ball can continue marking the player in possession as the overlapping takes place, while the other members of the back section must shift over to mark the player who is breaking in.

When the opposing team is making great use of combinations between the strikers as finishing touch techniques, we must first of all make sure that they are not playing in numerical equality against our central defenders. If we are in numerical equality, we must tell the whole defense to keep tight. The defender who closes on the striker in possession should not get too near him. He must carry out 'wide' marking so that, as soon as the striker passes the ball to his teammate coming to meet him in order to carry out the triangular pass, our contrasting defender will have a couple of yards advantage and will be able to make sure that he is not sidestepped. Our other central defender must try to anticipate the more advanced striker, who is the hinge for the 'give and go'.

Another equally dangerous combination is the give and follow. In this case the striker originally in possession follows the passing line, then cuts in to receive the ball instead of sprinting into depth. Our defenders must be ready and quick to exchange marking without forcing the third defender to intervene, which would create a dangerous situation of numerical inferiority in other parts of the field.

Finally, if individual dribbling is our opponent's most frequently used technique we must first pick out the players who seem to be best at jumping the man. As we will see later, we have to arrange for systematic doubling up on such players.

CHANGES OF PLAY AND CREATING NUMERICAL SUPERIORITY

Another thing about the opposing team that we should keep in mind is their ability to make changes of play, and, more generally, to create numerical superiority around the ball during their attacking phase.
We have to assess to what extent and in what way change of play takes place. This will depend to a great extent on the way play is being built up. A team that is used to building up play in an elaborate way will look for a change of play more frequently than one that prefers the immediate build up.
When making a change of front we can use one or more sections of the team.
What you are doing when making a change of front is trying to create numerical superiority so that the ball will always be played into the part of the field that is short of opposing players.
The change of front is the best way of creating numerical superiority. This can also be obtained by getting past the opponent using dribbling, overlapping, by breaking into play or by shifting more players to the vicinity of the ball to help the teammate in possession.
We will have to see if our opponent tries to get numerical superiority by exploiting these situations.
When the opponent is making a change of play we must tell the team to tighten in less towards the ball zone, keeping the defense and even the midfield triangle looser so that we are lined

up to face the opponent on the weak side of the field.

If our opponent prefers to look for numerical superiority by using the other solutions we were looking at above, it is a good idea to ask the team to tighten in towards the strong side to create a good concentration of our players in that zone. When a team tries to create numerical superiority by dribbling, we should organize double teaming on those players who are particularly good at sidestepping our men.

SPECIFIC CHARACTERISTICS OF THE ATTACKING PHASE: EFFECTIVENESS, SPEED AND UNPREDICTABILITY

When we have a clear idea how the opposing team will be building up play, and the techniques they prefer to use, we must also have a look at the effectiveness of their moves, and the other important factors concerning this phase of play. During the offense phase, every team presents particular characteristics that make it different from all others even when they are applying the same type of build up and the same finishing touch techniques. In order to assess a team's effectiveness during the attacking phase, we must look at the number of occasions they create as a result of the continuity of their play. You should also make out the approximate percentage of their good passes with respect to the total number of passes they have made.

At that point, we go on to analyze the specific ways in which they are putting the attacking phase into effect. What we mean is:

☐ The number of cuts generally made during the maneuver (one, two or three touch plays - or even more).

☐ The speed with which the offense phase is normally carried out. In order to be fluid and effective, play must develop fairly rapidly, and the ball must circulate quickly both in the vertical and the horizontal sense (this is connected also with the number of touches made by each individual before he frees himself of the ball). Maneuvers must always be quick, not only when we are talking about immediate build up, but also when we are constructing in an elaborate way.

☐ The rhythm and intensity of play. This is connected to the two preceding points. If you want the rhythm to be sustained, both the ball and the entire collective must be on the move at all times so as to put the opposing team in serious tactical, physical and psychological difficulty.

☐ Unpredictability and variety of play. An organized and therefore an effective team must be able to carry out a wide range of plays and movements, and they must also regularly alternate between looking for width and going for depth.

When you have set down the specific characteristics of your opponent's play, you must explain things to your team and set them on their guard about any difficulties they will be meeting during the match. If the opposing team has shown itself to be fast and unpredictable and capable of developing effective, intense play, then you must recommend that your team concentrate at all times and remain compact and orderly as they carry out the defense movements without panicking and falling into the opponent's traps. When the opposition's play is very fast, it is important that the man going in to press the player in possession does not allow the opponents to pass the ball around too easily, but can count on his teammates' collaboration as they take away the supporting players' time and space.

As concerns the variety of the opponent's plays, our players must interpret the phase of non-possession in a situational way, facing all opposing action by making well-ordered, rational movements, always choosing the best possible solution.

PLAYS AND MOVEMENTS CARRIED OUT MOST FREQUENTLY

Taking an even more detailed look at our opponent's attacking phase, you must study the movements and the plays deriving from a more personalized application of the playing system.

You must establish the movements most often used by the different players covering the typical roles of the system:

The center defenders: are there any plays that foresee them breaking into play down the center?

The side back: how and with what regularity do they most often go into attack (overlapping towards the center or along the flanks)?

The side mid fielders: do they prefer to receive the ball widening out along the flanks, or do they go into attack alongside the strikers? Another thing, do they play the ball out on the flanks or are they inclined to cut in towards the center.

The center mid fielders: do they play in a static way acting as hinges for the action, or are they more dynamic, i.e., do they break into play in a vertical or diagonal direction (attacking the spaces created by the strikers or the free spaces along the flanks)?

The strikers: do they prefer to come and meet the mid fielders or set up passing opportunities by moving into depth, and do they carry out movements attempting to free space for the mid fielders, above all by making deviating cuts towards the flanks?

It is very important to establish which are the more static and more dynamic of the opposing players. Usually at least one of the center mid fielders plays in a static way acting as a hinge and a point of reference for the maneuvers.

The strikers and the side mid fielders are usually the most dynamic players.

We must put the static players under pressure, destroying the opposing team's points of reference, while the dynamic players must be managed as well as possible by keeping the team compact and exchanging marking in the right way.

More than anything else we should be watching the movements of the strikers. All those particular schemes of play characterized by synchronous movements of groups of players without the ball depend on the movements of the strikers.

It is these collective schemes of play that we should be studying. We must understand how the movements of single players are put together into a collective chain.

At this point we must integrate the single movements delineating the range of collective schemes used by the opposing ream, keeping in mind above all the movements made to create and attack space.

However, we must distinguish between actions resulting from applying schemes of play that have been practiced in training from those that come out by chance or from a single individual's improvisation. Thinking about that, we will be better able to understand the opposing team's degree of organization. In any case, we must keep in mind only those playing schemes that are part of the opponent's organization, without worrying too much about chance movements.

When we have an overall picture of the schemes deliberately applied by our opponents, it is our turn to take the necessary countermeasures, instructing our players how they are to behave. For example, against overlapping we should tell our side players to close off the player breaking in, while another player must run up to press the player in possession, who will be left free for a moment. Against the space creating movements of the strikers, we must insist that the central defenders do not follow their movements.
We must illustrate the collective schemes of play in detail to our team so that the players can memorize their opponents' movements. While we are explaining the opponent's specific schemes we must explain how to face up to these particular movements so that our players are not unprepared.

TAKING UP POSITION DURING A CROSS, INACTIVE BALLS AND COVERING BOUNCING ZONES

In making an assessment of the opposing team, you must not neglect a number of important particulars: the players' position during a cross, solutions regarding various inactive balls (both active and passive) and the ability to cover bouncing zones after the shot.
As regards the position of the players during a cross, you must evaluate:

- ☐ The number of players positioned inside the penalty area.
- ☐ The number of players dislocated on the edge of the area.
- ☐ Each of the strikers' ability to take up position near a goal post, maybe even after making a crossover in order to free themselves of marking with perfect timing.
- ☐ The possible presence of other players on the opposite side of the field, ready to carry out another cross if the first is too long.

❑ The possible presence of another player in support of the one carrying out the cross.

In any case, you must remember the distinction between a cross made from the base line and one carried out from behind.
With the first type, the player will be searching out the head of one of the players present in the area, while those placed at the limit of the area will be attempting to shoot from far out if the ball comes to them.
With the second type, what happens is that a striker searches out the player slightly behind but breaking in with a high ball behind the defense (Fig. 23).

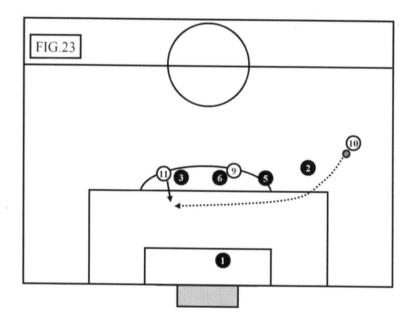

FIG.23

We have to establish if our opponents prefer to cross from the base line or from behind.
The ability to cover the bouncing zone is connected with that.
This particular ability consists of the correct ranking of the players present in the penalty area, other teammates positioned at its limit and a man supporting the one making the cross.

We will now see how all this can influence our own team.
Firstly, if we realize that the opponents keep a fairly large number of players in the penalty area, we should ask our mid field line to move far back when the other team brings the ball to a position from which to cross, principally in order to control the players present at the edges of the area. Above all the side mid fielder on the other flank must be told to integrate himself on the weak side of the defense because the backs will be tightening in their positions (Fig. 24).

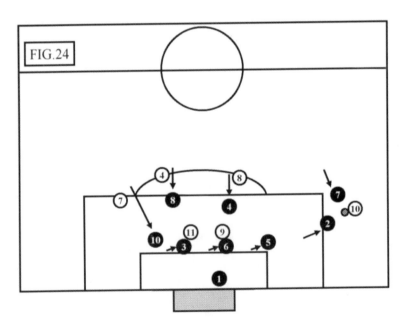

FIG.24

Also, we must set up an immediate counter attack if we regain possession because there will probably not be many opposing players in preventive coverage.

If the rival strikers are good at freeing themselves of marking and positioning themselves correctly, we must tell our defenders to tighten up the marking in the penalty area, trying to anticipate the opponents and arrive on the ball before they do. As we are using a zonal defense system, we must be able to make the correct exchange of marking when the attacking players move into a teammate's area.

If the opponents bring a player into the weak side of the field, our side back there must be quick and ready to close him off when he receives the ball, and the entire defense must concentrate on marking the players present in the penalty area.

As for the possible presence of a player supporting the one making the cross, we must point out that as soon as such a player receives the ball he will usually cross at once from a position slightly behind.

In that case the whole defense and mid field block must move up as soon as the initial player passes the ball to his supporting player. In that way we will put all the opposing players in the penalty area into an offside position (Fig. 25).

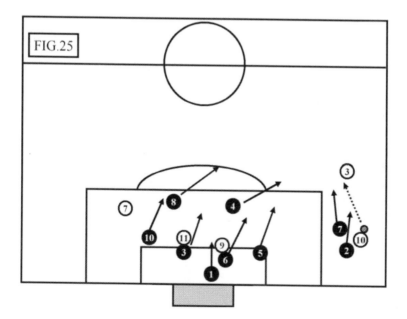

FIG.25

Generally speaking, the defense is at an advantage during a cross from behind. However, we must tell the defenders to try to anticipate the player acting as the target and to use tight marking against the other attacking players about to receive his rebound as well as being ready to absorb any other players breaking in. If the opponents try to cross the ball behind our defense line, we must ask our defenders to move back just as the cross is about to be made, or to move forward should the opponents make the mistake of sprinting into depth too early. The goalkeeper must position himself a yard or two in front of his goal, ready to intervene if the cross is too long or if the defense makes a mistake in their application of offside.

In any case, as far as crosses are concerned, we can apply the same general consideration that we made in the paragraph about finishing touch techniques. We must insist in particular that the defense diagonal must be rapidly carried out on the opposing player in possession, just as we must be quick to double up the marking on the nearest mid fielder.

Concerning the opponent's ability to cover the rebounding zones after the shot, we must ask the defense and mid field block to stay compact inside the penalty area, creating numerical superiority there so as to have more chance of intercepting the ball. Whoever gets back into possession after the shot must not hesitate to send it away from the penalty area without making dangerous internal passes. After having sent the ball away you can apply offside, moving up collectively to press the point where the ball has fallen, leaving the opponents inside the area in an offside position (Fig. 26)

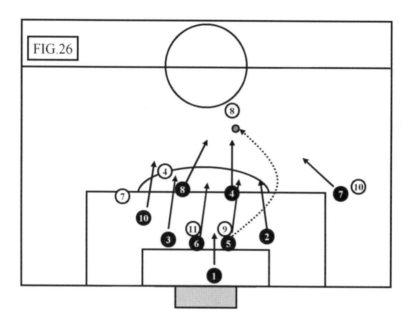

FIG.26

At this point it is a good idea to make some suggestions about how to exploit offensive crosses. Basing ourselves on our opponent's behavior and characteristics, we must determine what type of cross to go for (high, low, tight, behind the section, into the center of the area, to the limits of the area, on the near post, on the far post, from behind, from the base line).

If our opponents usually keep the defense high and in line, our own team should insist on crosses from behind that go beyond the section. If their defenders are not good at aerial play, we must go for high crosses from the base line into the center of the area. If they are good at marking in the air, we should be making low, tight crosses so that the strikers can shoot while on the run. Crosses directed at the center of the area are useful against opponents who leave this zone free, and our mid fielders should immediately break into play there. Choosing between crosses on the near or far post will depend principally on the aerial characteristics of our strikers (on the near post if they prefer to deviate with the side of their head, on the far post if they are better at hitting the ball with their foreheads). The peculiar characteristics of the opposing team are important as well: you can decide to cross onto the post where the defender weakest with his head is placed, but of course this will depend on the side the cross is coming from.

Clearly, however, as far as crosses are concerned the first things to consider are our own attacking characteristics, particularly those of the strikers, remembering that we must make the best possible use of their particular characteristics. Consequently, when deciding what instructions to give the team about how to carry out crosses, we have to keep both our rivals' attitudes and our own characteristics in mind.

Now we will have a look at set plays, starting from those that are favorable to our opponents.

We will have to evaluate the following:

☐ Corners
☐ Free kicks
☐ Throwing in
☐ Putting the ball back in play from the base line
☐ The kick off

Corners

As concerns corners we must have a look at the typical positioning of the opposing team, in particular:

☐ The number of players present inside the penalty area and at its limits.
☐ The possible placement of players around the goal line or to block out the goalkeeper.
☐ The possible presence of a player ready to come and meet his teammate for the 'short' corner.
☐ We must evaluate the opposing players' typical movements to free themselves of marking and the way the corner is kicked. In particular:
☐ The creation of blocks favoring those players especially good at aerial play.
☐ Movements to create and attack space in the penalty area.
☐ Sudden movements by players initially situated on the edges to break into play.
☐ Whether they free themselves of marking collectively or individually.

❑ Whether they prefer to cross in the direction of the players in the area or to those at the edges, or whether they carry out the 'short' corner.

If we are using zonal defense on corners these things will not give us particular problems, because our players will be concentrating on the trajectory of the ball rather than on the opponents' movements.

If we are marking the man, we must first of all establish the marking. We must then make sure we are in numerical superiority in the penalty area, if necessary asking the strikers to move back so that we can keep a player on the near post and others in different strategic positions (on the far post, in the zone near the near post, along the horizontal line of the goal, in the wall set a few yards from the player taking the corner). if our opponents are blocking the goalkeeper with a player, he should try to get free, possibly with the help of a teammate, protecting him.

For the opponent's blocks, it is a good thing for our defenders to exchange marking quickly during play (Fig. 27).

Another very dangerous thing is when the opponents originally placed on the limits of the penalty area suddenly break into play. Our men marking these players usually breaking in from behind must wait for them in the area, ready to intervene. They must not make the mistake of marking them tightly when they are still at the edge of the area.

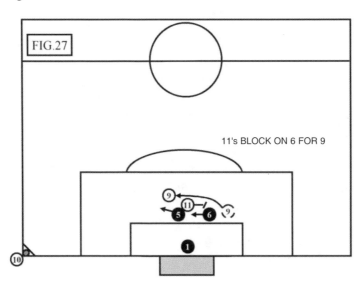

FIG.27

11's BLOCK ON 6 FOR 9

If the opponent usually crosses towards the inside of the area or even near the goal line, our defenders must be waiting fairly far back, ready to intervene by trying to anticipate. It is also important for the goalkeeper to be ready to step in by coming out and catching a high ball. It is useful to place two players on the goal posts to protect the goal when the goalkeeper comes out.

Lastly, if our opponents are in the habit of making short corners we must first of all position one of our players in the barrier so that we will be two against two after the corner has been kicked, keeping in mind that the player going to meet the ball must be followed at once. Also, the defense must be ready to move up when the ball goes back, watching out for any players breaking in from behind.

Free kicks

Speaking about free kicks from near our area, from the tactical point of view we will not be worrying so much about the ballistic ability of the opponent's specialists, but rather about the placement of the rest of the team in the area, and any movements they might make.

Both the attacking and the defending team's behavior will change depending on how near the free kick is to the area. The nearer it is to the goal the more likely the attacking team is to shoot directly and the defending team to tighten the coverage until the players are marking the man (unless they mark the zone even on a free kick). The further it is from the goal, the more likely they are to play the ball in front by crossing into the area, or to build up along the ground while the defending team worries more about covering the spaces than about marking the man.

As with corners, our job is to understand how the opponents are positioned during free kicks in connection with how near or far away they are to be.

You must be very careful about using offside on free kicks - and not do so in a systematic way but to catch the other team by surprise. It is a good idea to use offside on the first occasion to put the opponents in difficulty at once. Zonally placed teams can carry out offside on free kicks by getting the defense to align themselves with the opposing strikers and then move up together just before the player kicks the ball.

Free kicks taken from the crossing zone are like corners. Once again, if the opponent carries out a horizontal or back pass, we must make the best of the situation by applying offside.

Throwing in

As far as throwing in goes, we need to see if the opponent's tactical organization is so detailed as to foresee specific plays for such situations.

When throwing in you usually carry out 'one comes, one goes' movements to create and attack space to give the player at least three options for his pass in different directions.

If our opponents are carrying out schemes of play connected to such principles, the first thing you must recommend to the team is that they do not let these movements take them by surprise, but remain in position without following the opponents too much as they move. The team must also tighten the spaces around the point where the opposition is throwing in.

Also, it is not only right to double up on whoever receives the ball because he has to stop and control it and thus might find himself in difficulty, but also because it is a great help to prepare invited pressing situations by leaving another opponent free of marking, who, as he will be receiving the ball with his back to the goal, will have even more problems controlling it and turning. As soon as this player receives the ball we double team him as well, at the same time carrying out anticipatory marking on the supporting players, reducing the possible solutions for the player in possession under pressure.

Putting the ball back into play from the base line

In these cases, you must look to see whether the opposing goalkeeper starts off the maneuver with the ball on the ground, sends it to a defender or makes a long pass seeking out the head of a particular player.

In the first case, we must tell our players to be ready to tighten up in front in order to press their defenders; in the second, we can send our best aerial player to the zone where the goalkeeper usually sends the ball. If we think that the player to whom the goalkeeper passes is so good in the air as to be unmatchable for any of our players, we should tell the team not to challenge him so as not to leave other important parts of the field undefended.

We must decide how our opponents line themselves up on long passes, paying particular attention to how many players place themselves in depth near our defense line.
If we are in dangerous numerical equality or inferiority in defense, we must ask one or two of the mid fielders to shift back temporarily and make up the numbers.

The kick off.

Many teams apply special playing schemes at the moment of kick off. Most of these foresee the players starting play passing back to the center mid fielder who directs play. He will them immediately pass into depth to the side mid fielders who have sprinted ahead.
Our job is to realize this, and then to analyze these schemes of play if they exist, illustrating them to our team together with all necessary advice and recommendations.

We can now move on to the opponent's defense of set plays.
What we must look at are above all corners and free kicks.
Fundamentally, we will be trying to understand whether the team will be zonally placed in these situations or whether they will be marking the man.
In the first case our players should behave in this way: the men in the penalty area start out a couple yards behind, then sprint forward, beating the defenders in speed so as to take them by surprise. Also, our best players in the air should place themselves in the zones controlled by the weakest opponents with their heads.
If the opposing team is marking the man, it is a good idea to come up with schemes using blocks to free our best players with their heads; we must also make movements to create and attack space.
When kicking the ball back into play from the base line, we must see if our opponents are good at placing themselves to tighten up the spaces, and which players are having more difficulty with aerial play. Our best headers should position themselves near those

players. We can also try to create numerical superiority against the defense by bringing up the side mid fielders.

When throwing in, look to see whether the opponents are careful about closing off space in the zone in which the ball is being put back into play, and if they are doubling up and carrying out invited pressing. If we think our opponents are good in such situations, it is best to ask the team to help the player throwing in by sending more men to give him a hand, telling them that they should immediately make a change of play towards the weak side of the field.

There are no particular elements to evaluate concerning the kick off.

ABILITY IN BREAKING FREE OF PRESSING AND OFFSIDE TACTICS

If our team applies ultra-offensive pressing and uses active off-side tactics, it is important to consider our opponent's ability at eluding these tactics.

We must see if our opponents manage to break away from our pressing by making changes of play and by the correct placement of the whole team. In cases where their defenders are obliged to make long passes towards the strikers to resolve the problem of our pressing, we must see whether they are able to make the best of such plays, creating difficulties for our defense. We must also judge whether they are able to make the right countermoves against our use of offside tactics. We have already listed these countermoves in the paragraph about the type of defense system.

If we see that our opponents have problems when they are pressed and cannot find a solution against offside tactics, this will be an incentive to use them with even greater intensity. However, if we see that they are able to face up to these things, we must make some comparisons. The first thing is to measure up our own ability in applying pressing and offside tactics with the similar ability of the teams our upcoming opponents have faced in the matches we have been watching.

If we feel that these teams are inferior to us in the application of such tactics, we must then compare our ability with that of our opponent in eluding them. If we think that we are better at applying them than our next opponents are at escaping them, we can allow ourselves to apply these tactics in our coming match.

If we get the impression that our opponents are better at eluding than we are at applying them, we should ask our team not to apply offside in an active way (still making use, however, of the shift), and to apply pressing from the half way line (in any case, a team should never close itself in its own half, assuming a defensive attitude).

The same thing goes, naturally, for those cases when in our first comparison we have decided that the teams faced by our next opponent are even better than we are in the application of pressing and offside.

In cases where we have been forced to think twice about the application of these tactics, we should make a mental note to improve our own team's ability in carrying them out. We should aim at arriving at such a level of ability that we can use them against any other team.

THE TRANSITION PHASE

Because there are three phases of play we should have a good look at the third as well, the one considered least important, but which plays a very important role in the organization of a team: the transition phase, i.e., passing from the defense to the attacking phase or vice versa.

The transference from the defense to the attacking phase (positive transmission) is a sub-phase of the phase of possession: often called the post conquest phase. We must carefully watch the opponent's ability to carry out fast, incisive counterattacks. The type of counterattack being used (immediate or elaborate, created by the defense line's management of the ball) depends on what part of the field they have regained possession and the finishing touch techniques they prefer. For positive transition you should look back at the paragraph concerning the different ways of building up play.

As regards going from the attacking to the defense phase (negative transition), you should make an analysis of the sharpness and the speed with which the whole opposing team manages to reposition themselves and go into immediate pressing on their opponent's player in possession so as to gain space and time for teammates.

If it comes out that the opposing team is particularly good during negative transition, we should tell our team not to go for immediate counter attacks when they regain possession in their own half, but to build up calmly: the defense should manage the ball first of all, moving it onto the flanks to consolidate possession, and then making a change of play onto the far side. Also, we must assist our player who has regained possession by giving him support and players to pass to, according to the logic of the triangles and rhombi of play. It goes without saying that when you regain possession near the opponent's goal you should play it into depth at once.

If we get the idea that our opponents have some trouble with negative transition, we must ask our players to send the ball immediately into depth in order to turn the action upside down even when we regain possession a long way from the goal. The strikers' work is important in this context because they will be acting as their teammates' points of reference. The strikers should not move in the same way: one must come to meet the ball and act as a safe support for the player in possession, helping his teammates to break in by the use of dump and rebounds, while the other should sprint into depth. If the opposing defense leaves a lot of space at their sides, the two strikers can widen out one on each side to receive the ball in the easiest way possible. The one who receives the ball can serve the other, who will immediately have cut towards the center (Fig. 28).

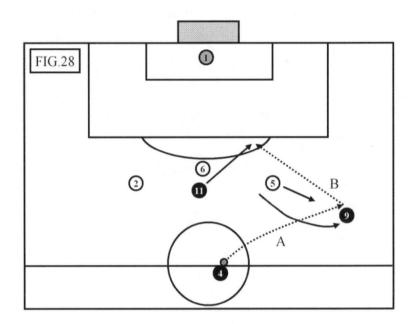

However, the strikers should wait before carrying out their movements if the player who has regained possession is not able to
pass to them (covered ball). When the player supporting the one
who has regained possession has received his pass, the strikers
can free themselves of marking.
It is also important to make the best of any situations of numerical superiority that can come up on the attacking front. In particular, when we outnumber the defense, our attacking player in possession must make directly for a defender forcing the opponent
to close him off; at the same moment, the other strikers must be
making movements aimed at 'carrying away' the other defenders,
leaving our extra player unmarked (Fig. 29).

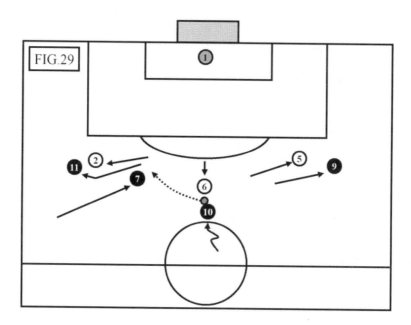

TACTICAL DISCIPLINE

We must also have a look at our opponent's tactical discipline. You can often see very well-organized teams that for one reason or another do not seem to be able to keep up their coordination for the whole 90 minutes.

Teams with little tactical discipline tend to lengthen themselves out, to lose cohesion, concentration and rigor in their application of the attacking and defense schemes. A team that has not assimilated the coach's instructions begins at a certain point of the match to play as comes natural to the players - that is in an individual way. By looking at these things we can see to what extent the opposing team has assimilated the tactical and behavioral elements required by the coach.

What we want to establish is whether the opponent succeeds in following what the coach is expecting for the whole length of the match or if the players tend to lose concentration.

Another thing is to assess in what moments of the match the team loses concentration. Generally speaking, teams tend to lengthen out during the second half, while there is good tactical concentration in the first part of the match.

This is due to reasons of a psychological character which we will be looking at later on: we can say, therefore, that tactical and psychological discipline are interconnected.

Once we have established in what moment of the match the opponent will probably lose concentration, we have to ask our players to make the best of this situation, stepping up on pressing, rhythm and the intensity of play.

RELATIONSHIP BETWEEN COLLECTIVE ORGANIZATION AND IMPROVISATION

It is pertinent to assess the degree of organization of the team you have to meet. All the tactical elements that we have been looking at lead us to the formulation of this analysis. In particular, we will be trying to conclude whether the opposing team is on the whole building up play in a collective way, using the pass as its principle technical element, with the clear consciousness of what they are doing, or whether the players count more on individual plays, putting dribbling and the creativity of the individual player as the first priority.
Teams very often rely on an inside mid fielder to build up play (in systems with a three man mid field, the 'director' will be the center mid fielder placed behind), while the attacking mid fielder (when foreseen by the system) will have freedom of movement.

When we have singled out such players who are their team's points of reference, we must make sure that they are being pressed and double teamed when in possession, and that we mark them in anticipation (but zonally) when they do not have the ball.
If our opponents have good tactical organization all the counter-moves and advice we have called attention to in the various paragraphs still hold true.

DEGREE OF ADAPTABILITY:
FIXED AND VARIABLE FACTORS

It is very important to work out which of the opposing team's factors never change from match to match and which ones vary depending on the circumstances. In this way we can assess the team's degree of adaptability.

This type of analysis must be made by considering various different matches played by the opposing team.

What we are really after are the fixed factors. When we have made out which are the variable elements of the opposing team, we must carry out some good deductive work to foresee the choices the opposing coach will be making against us.

We have to put ourselves in his shoes, imagining how we would prepare the match if we were about to meet our own team.

To give an example: if we know that our opponents tend to vary the way they apply pressing, and our team is objectively speaking superior to theirs, we must expect that they will carry out defensive pressing. As a consequence, we will try to get by their defense system by making the most of the flanks. If we are sure that our team is weaker than theirs, we must expect them to be using offensive or ultra-offensive pressing. We should then try to resolve this situation by using changes of play and by the whole team attempting to free itself of marking all the time, as well as using the space behind the rival defenders by getting the strikers to cut into depth.

NORMAL MODIFICATIONS DURING A MATCH AND THE COACH'S ABILITY TO READ THE GAME

Here we are concentrating on the rival coach's usual behavior during the course of a match.

In order to get a full idea about the opponents, it is useful to know the changes the coach usually makes to his team's set up during the match, particularly in the second half. The best coaches prepare a number of solutions in advance to apply if the match is not turning out in the right way for them, and it is our task to understand if he has considered these possible changes. If he has predisposed alternative tactical plans, we must identify them in detail and prepare the right countermoves.

The usual changes to make in order to improve your team's performance during a match are the following: change of system, inverting two or more players' positions on the field, bringing up or bringing down the line on which pressing is initiated, modifying the build up or the finishing touches, and substituting players with reserves. It can happen that some solutions have been resolved from the beginning, and will take place even if the match is going well. This happens in order to save the energy of certain players.

In any case, we will be looking to understand if the rival coach is good at reading the match. When we are looking at our next opponent's previous matches, we must put ourselves in the place of their coach. At this point we will have made a personal evaluation of how the coach works during the match. It is important to know these things, but they will have no effect on our set up.

CHAPTER 4

ANALYSIS OF THE TECHNICAL PARAMETERS

PLAYERS GOOD AT DRIBBLING

From a technical point of view, the first thing to look for is the presence on the opposing team of players good at beating their man by dribbling. When the opposing team makes heavy use of such individual play and we succeed in neutralizing it, the balancing point of the match will surely move towards us.

It is not difficult to pinpoint such players. One of the clearest things to see in a match, even if you have no particular tactical knowledge, is the presence of players drawing attention to themselves by getting past the opposing markers.

We must point out immediately that dribbling is different from running with the ball. Both concepts involve the individual moving with the ball, but while dribbling entails 'conducting the ball in order to get past one or two opponents', by running with the ball we mean 'conducting the ball without getting past opponents, but filling up the space between you and the first marker that you meet, with the ball at your feet'.

When you have established which of your opponents are good at dribbling, you must have a look at how it is carried out.

There are two types of dribbling:

Technical dribbling, in which the player in possession makes a tight movement wide to sidestep his marker, usually going around him on the weak side (the side on which his foot is placed in a more advanced position) by making a sudden change of direction, supported naturally by excellent ball control.

Physical dribbling, in which the player in possession gets past his marker by sending the ball ahead towards his strong side (the foot placed behind) and then sprinting to reach it, counting on beating the opponent in acceleration, and also by taking him by surprise.

Also, you must establish whether the opponent makes use of one or even a second dummy before carrying out the dribbling itself. The most self-confident and technically gifted soccer players often adopt personal techniques, like for example the 'double step'.

You must pay particular attention to the favorite kicking foot of every opponent good at dribbling.

Another thing to look at is whether the team gives tactical support to the individual play of their teammate who is good at getting by opponents. Some teams move in such a way as to create numerical superiority in the zone where the player doing the dribbling happens to be, making it impossible for the opponents to double team. Overlapping is very often the movement made to avoid the double team.

Lastly, we must see in what zones of the field our opponents carry out dribbling. Some teams (the least organized) will try dribbling in their own half, others not until just inside the opponent's half, but the best organized teams allow it only in or around the opponent's penalty area. Furthermore, some teams try dribbling after a change of play to make the best of the free space and the opponents' slow shift from the former strong side to the new one.

Having made an in-depth analysis of the players good at dribbling, we will have to explain to our players how they should react.

We must tell the players, and in particular the defenders, how the opponents good at dribbling usually apply it.

Generally speaking, we should ask the defenders to play for time as much as possible against these opponents, giving them a couple yards (especially if no teammate is guaranteeing diagonal coverage), and then intervening only when they are in difficulty or when a teammate arrives to double up. The position of their feet must be such that they force the opponent to make for the flanks (a less dangerous zone) and to give the chance to follow him into depth (Fig. 30).

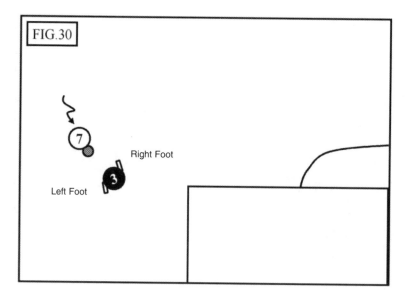

FIG.30

Right Foot

Left Foot

We must also carry out fast and effective double teaming every-where against these players. If the opponent is using technical dribbling, we must ask the player doubling up to stay very close to his teammate closing off. This player should 'invite' the opponent to move towards his helping teammate (Fig. 31).

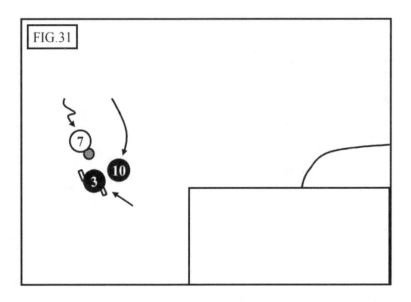

If our opponent's dribbling is of the physical kind, the player doubling up must take up position fairly far away from his teammate closing in, who, for his part, should concede a few yards to the player in possession.

In cases where the opponents insist too much on individual plays, taking no interest in their teammate's movements, we can tell the team to tighten in on the player in possession with more players while at the same time carrying out offside tactics.

We should of course show and explain any possible use of dummies by our opponents so that our players can memorize them and not be taken by surprise during the match.

We must also explain which is the kicking foot of those players good at dribbling so that our defenders can place their own feet in such a way as to close the opponent off on his best foot (Fig. 32).

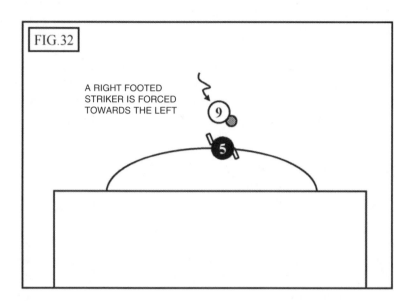

FIG.32

A RIGHT FOOTED
STRIKER IS FORCED
TOWARDS THE LEFT

This is the rule regarding the depth of the defense diagonal: the faster the player in possession is or the more capable he is at getting around his man, the tighter and closer together the covering players must be (above all in the central zones).

The aggressiveness of each single player closing in will change depending on the part of the field in which the opponent is trying to carry out the dribbling: the nearer you are to the opponent's goal, the more you must be encouraged to tighten up the marking on the player in possession; the nearer you are to your own goal, the more you must play for time conceding space to the player in possession (remember though that whenever an opponent is about to shoot at goal, you must close on him aggressively even if you have no cover). Also after a change of play you must carry out wide marking, waiting for your teammates to run up and carry out the diagonal or double team.

Lastly, as concerns overlapping and other movements aimed at creating numerical superiority in the ball zone and making it difficult to double up, we must tell our defenders to tighten up the spaces on the strong side and quickly exchange marking when there is overlapping.

You should not ask your players to carry out tactical fouls when they have been sidestepped because that is false and unfair play.

PLAYERS GOOD AT PASSING

It is not as easy to pinpoint players good at the prince of all techniques, the pass, as it is to find those good at dribbling. But an observer with just a little experience will soon notice technical ability in dealing with the ball: stopping it, controlling it and sending it to the best placed teammate with precision and the right force.

The ability to pass the ball is strictly connected with soccer intelligence, quick thinking and decisiveness as well as with strong personal elements like charisma and self confidence. Choosing the teammate you will send the ball to and the ability to read the tactical situation are the first things to be strictly connected with passing. The most intelligent players make sure when possible that they send the ball not directly onto the teammate's feet but into the space in front of him or, in any case, beyond the opponent who is marking him.

The most technically skilled are able to carry out medium or long range passes in the air, speeding up change of play or the crossing over of the attacking front.

Our job is to make a list of the players responding to such characteristics.

The best passing players are normally the mid field directors or the attacking mid fielder, and because our opponents will be depending on them in building up play, we must try to reduce their space and playing time.

We must ask our team to carry out continuous pressing against them, not letting them turn around when they receive a ball from a teammate behind, and not allowing them to raise their heads when they are facing our goal.

As regards passing into the space beyond the marker, we must insist that our players give a few yards to the opponent in their zone to take away his chances of sending the ball in a dangerous vertical direction.

On long passes, the defense must be able to carry out a good defensive shift.

Lastly, it might be a good idea to put our best defensive mid fielder in the zone where the opposing attacking mid fielder tends to play - still using a zonal defense system if we are operating such a system in its integral form. In this way, if their attacking mid fielder plays in and around the center-left of his offensive front, we must put our man to stop him on our center right. However, this can take place only if the quality of our attacking phase does not suffer negative effects. If our inside mid fielders do not feel good in inverted positions, it is better not to do it - or, as in every choice you make, you must balance the advantages and disadvantages.

If the attacking mid fielder plays in the center and further back, he must be closed off by an inside mid fielder moving up or by a striker shifting back.

PLAYERS GOOD AT AERIAL PLAY

As with dribbling, it is easy to find the players good in the air. These are often the first striker and the center defenders.

It is important to decide which are the best players with their heads for various reasons. They can be incisive on crosses from the base line, on corners and on long passes (even when the keeper is putting the ball back into play). This regards both the defense and the attacking phases.

If the opponent has one or two strikers good at aerial play, they will presumably try to make the best use of such players by finalizing their play to arrive at finishing touches using crosses from the base line. Either that or they will build up by making long passes for the strikers who will rebound onto the mid fielders breaking in.

If there are good aerial players on our opponent's side, it may be difficult for us to get the best of things on crosses or long passes.

In this connection, we must decide whether our defenders are capable of challenging the opposing strikers in aerial play during the defense phase . If they are not, the best solution is to tell the defenders not to challenge the striker good with his head on long passes, allowing him to jump alone so as not to uncover their zone for no good reason. It goes without saying that as soon as the opponent has put the ball on the ground, we must close in on him. Yet, it is better to tell the defenders to challenge him in any case, so we are not making life too easy for him. When the goalkeeper kicks the ball back into play directly towards the first striker, we should bring a mid fielder back to cover the space left free by the defender and to make it easier for his teammates in the defense section to take up position. Lastly, we must create a 'cage' around the striker and tighten up the space on every side so as to catch the ball when he slices it.

Try to give away as few crosses as possible using the methods we have already looked at in the section about tactical parameters. Here, we want to underline the fact that we must tighten up the marking in the area, trying to anticipate the opponent's strikers.

In the attacking phase, if we think that their central defenders are better than our strikers in aerial play we must tell the team not to use long passes, even when they are kicking the ball back into play from the base line. Rather, we must limit even our play along the flanks and crosses in general in favor of more vertical maneuvers so as to put our attack in a position to beat our rival markers in acceleration.

As for defensive corners, if we are marking the man we must assign their best players in the air to our best players in the same sense.

Lastly, in order to limit our opponent's aerial play, create more balance and be able to make the best of any situations favorable to us, we can invert the positions of the strikers and the central defenders.

If their best heading striker plays in the zone of our weakest defender in this sense, it stands to reason that we should change the positions of the two central players. In this way, we are also making sure that their fastest striker is facing our defender specialized in acceleration.

If we see that our tallest striker is in the zone of their best heading central defender, we should invert the strikers' positions, creating a situation where their shortest defender will find himself in difficulty.

In the same way, we are making sure that our fastest striker is set against their slowest marker. Yet, all this can take place only if the general effectiveness of our offensive phase remains unaltered: we should make sure, in other words, that the strikers do not have problems playing in a different part of the attacking front.

PLAYERS GOOD AT DEFENDING THE BALL

Defending the ball can be considered an individual tactical element rather than a technical one. In fact, when defending the player in possession, the choices made on the level of your behavior are what really count in taking the ball away from your opponent or, in any case, reducing his playing space and time. It is important for us to decide which players on the opposing team are good from this point of view. It is also to be pointed out that we should not be looking out only for the defenders, but for their mid fielders and strikers as well.

When you have pinpointed the opponents good at turning on individual pressure, we must explain to the team what to do with them.
If we think that the opposing strikers and mid fielders are good at putting on pressure, we must tell our players not to risk making individual plays against them. Instead, they must get rid of the ball as soon as possible.
The same goes for those defenders particularly good in this respect, even though you can take more risks in the last fifteen yards. However, for the most part the strikers should get rid of the ball immediately after they receive it, not insist on taking on the strong defender.
If you judge that their strikers and mid fielders are not good at putting players under pressure, we can manage the ball more calmly when setting up counter attacks.
In cases where their defenders are not much good at defending the ball, we should advise our best players from a technical and a physical point of view to have a go at dribbling against them.

Lastly, if we notice that our best mid fielder at setting up maneuvers and managing the ball is playing in the zone of their best contrasting mid fielder, we can invert his position with another player from the same section.

BAD PLAYERS FROM A TECHNICAL POINT OF VIEW

We must also assess which of the opposing players are the weakest technically (at stopping, controlling, passing the ball

quickly) and which have trouble when they are pressed. Constant pressing will give you even more results against these players. Another thing is to pick out those players who, though they are technically good, are nevertheless weak from a psychological point of view (for example because they lack self-confidence), and lose possession easily, making banal mistakes.
Generally speaking, such players are often center defenders and blocking mid fielders.

Once you have established which are the players of this kind, you should ask the team to:

☐ Press more frequently and with greater intensity.
☐ Double team them wherever they are on the field.
☐ Prepare situations for invited pressing, even on throw ins.

Initially you must leave the opponent unmarked, inviting the thrower to give him the ball, and then double up on him, marking all the supporting players in anticipation to take any outlets away from him.

It can turn out very useful to make the most of the individual weaknesses of the opponent. Ultra-offensive pressing on opposing defenders can be especially advantageous if these players are technically weak.

Connected with this is our analysis of the opposing goalkeeper's technical ability in passing and putting the ball back in play from the base line. Our choice of whether to carry out pressing beginning with the opposing defenders or to press their goalkeeper as well will depend on his technical ability.
If we think that the opposing goalkeeper has difficulty managing the ball with his feet and tends therefore to get into a panic when pressed, you should ask the strikers to bring up even further the level of their pressing.
When the defenders dump the ball on the goalkeeper, at least one of the strikers should go to press him, exploiting the transmission period of the pass. If the opposing goalkeeper is good with his feet, it is futile to press him and leave the defenders free to receive the ball.

PLAYERS GOOD AT FREE KICKS

One of the factors that deserves special attention is the study of the opposing specialists' ability in kicking penalties, free kicks and corners.
Sometimes all these are taken by the same player, but it can often happen that a team has a specialist for penalties, one for corners and maybe even more than one for free kicks. We usually find a left-footed player kicking a free kick from the center right and a right-footed one from the center left.
For penalties you must establish.

- ☐ Where the specialist prefers to send the ball.
- ☐ With what force he kicks the ball; whether he prefers precision or power.
- ☐ The type of run up (crossover or in a line; long or short).

This study should be carried out in the presence of our own goalkeeper so that he is aware of everything. We will discuss with him how to behave in order to neutralize the penalties.

Concerning free kicks from the edge of the area, we must decide:

- ☐ How many specialists on the opposing team prepare to take the free kick.
- ☐ Which of these actually kick the ball as a rule.
- ☐ If the single specialists prefer to kick with power or precision.
- ☐ If the specialist in question prefers to kick over the barrier or send the ball along the ground under the feet of the players in the barrier as they jump.
- ☐ In cases where he prefers to send the ball over the wall, if he directs it on the goalkeeper's post or on the one covered by the wall.

Here also our analysis should be carried out in the company of the goalkeeper and of the members of the wall. If the specialist prefers to kick powerfully, we should ask a member of the wall to detach himself to make a wall against the shot.
If the specialist prefers to aim precisely just where the crossbar

meets the posts, the first thing we must do is ask the players in the wall to jump as high as possible. In order to do so, the best advice to give is that the players should make little on the spot jumps as they are waiting for the opponent to kick, so that they will have more impulse when carrying out the real jump. The goalkeeper must be ready to fly towards one of the two posts. And here we must establish which post the player normally directs the ball to. Some players prefer to aim at the post covered by the wall in order to put the goalkeeper - placed on the other post - in difficulty. Others prefer to aim at the goalkeeper's post, counting on the fact that the goalkeeper - thinking that he will be going for the other one - will leave his own undefended. Leading on from there, if we know that the opponent prefers to aim for the post covered by the wall, we should tell the goalkeeper to place himself more or less at the center of the goal, so that he has to cover less space before arriving at the first post. But we must sternly recommend that he not move towards the first post until he is sure that the ball will be directed there. The goalkeeper must move only when the ball has just taken off going towards the first post - because an intelligent opponent might try to surprise him on his own post.

When the specialist prefers to send the ball onto his post, the goalkeeper must be ready to catch it, but also to fly towards the other post should the opponent decide to make a change.

It must be said that players rarely make free kicks along the ground, and then only to surprise the wall who let the ball go under them as they jump. The players in the wall should jump with their feet pointing down so the tips can slow the ball (in any case, they should always jump with their feet pointing down).

As for corners, we must establish:

- ☐ if the player kicking is gifted with precision
- ☐ if he prefers giving the ball a spinning effect towards the inside at the goal, or, on the contrary, towards the limit of the area.

If the player prefers to direct the ball towards the goal, it is better to put a player on guard at each post as well as one in front of the near post (Fig. 33). In addition, the goalkeeper must be prepared to come out and catch high balls, with a teammate ready to help him, placing himself in front to shield him.

If the opponent prefers to send the ball towards the limits of the area (out swinger), we must position a couple of players in that zone, ready to challenge the players taking up position there. Also, the entire defense must be ready to move up and 'wall off' the players preparing to shoot from the limit of the area.

As far as precision on corners is concerned, there is nothing particular to say, except that our players must keep their concentration.

In any case, for other aspects regarding free kicks and corners we refer you to the paragraph on the tactical aspects of set plays. One last piece of advice might be to send a player to disturb the player taking the kick in cases where the field is particularly restricted and the player usually kicks with great precision.

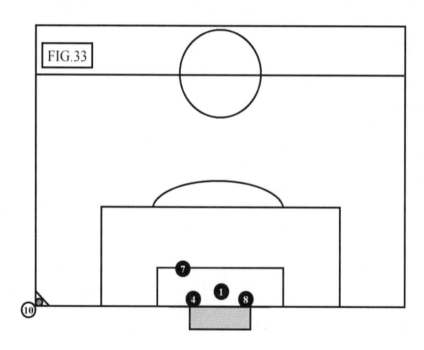

GENERAL TECHNICAL ABILITY

Having spoken about the technical ability of the individual, it is a good idea to make a comment on the opponent's degree of general technical ability.

This is useful in order to decide whether they will be able to get around our pressing by passing the ball tightly and precisely to each other.

In cases where we judge the opposing team so technically skilled as to get past our in-depth pressing, we should ask our team to move the starting line back to the mid field, applying offensive instead of ultra-offensive pressing. At the same time, of course, we will have to tell ourselves that we need to work on this aspect more intensely in training because our pressing needs to be effective enough for us to use it against any other team.

When we think that the opposing team is weak technically, above all in relation to our ability in pressing, we should clearly ask our players to apply it with even greater intensity.

CHAPTER 5

ANALYSIS OF PSYCHOLOGICAL FACTORS

APPROACH TO THE MATCH

The first thing to think about from the psychological point of view is the rival team's approach to the match.
Kicking off with the right drive, with intensity, determination and conviction is quite an unusual thing in fact. It is no use having good tactical organization and a high degree of individual technical ability if you begin a match by underrating the difficulties you are facing - and yet, that very often happens.
Mistakes are often made in the approach to a match when our opponents are inferior to us on paper, or when the match itself is not an important one in terms of the league standings. When following our opponent's performances in the days leading up to the match, we must therefore keep in mind and evaluate these psychological factors.

If we reach the conclusion that they generally have a good approach to the match, all we have to tell our team is that they must do the same.
If we think that they do not always approach the match in the right way, we must insist that our own players should enter the field with determination and conviction, if only to make the best of the fact that the opponents might not be in the same condition.
In any case, presenting yourself on the field with greater intensity than your opponents can be crucial, because the first few minutes of a game often condition the rest of the match. It is therefore important that you get command right from the start.

We must also make a similar type of summary regarding their approach to the second half, on the same lines as those set out above.

GENERAL MENTAL ATTITUDE DURING THE COURSE OF THE MATCH

If you wish to get your opponents fairly in the picture you will also be looking out for their mental approach during the course of the match.
The elements to consider here are the following:

- ☐ Their level of concentration.
- ☐ Their level of determination.
- ☐ Their level of conviction.
- ☐ How discouraged they tend to become when they allow a goal, or when they are at a disadvantage.
- ☐ How optimistic they tend to become when they are one goal up.
- ☐ General level of their motivation.

We must establish if our opponents manage to keep their concentration for the whole match, or if there are periods when their level of attention drops. Teams sometimes start off the two halves with a high level of concentration, which they then lose with the passing of time.
In cases where our opponents cannot keep hold of a good level of concentration for the whole 90 minutes, we should establish when their attention tends to drop most evidently. Generally speaking, teams tend to lower their guard when play gets going again after an interruption (throw ins, putting the ball back into play from the base line etc.).
Clearly, our team should increase the intensity of their pressing and their playing rhythm in such moments.
As far as determination and conviction go, we can refer back to what has already been said concerning the approach to the match and the players' concentration.
It is fairly normal for a team to get dejected after giving up a goal, especially if it happens at the beginning of the match. A team can also get discouraged if they are down by a goal or two even though they have been playing well - particularly near the end of the match.
If our adversary seems to become discouraged in such situations, once again we must ask our team to increase the intensity

of their pressing and the rhythm of play, above all after having scored a goal. This will clearly put the opponents - already shaken by having given up a goal - under even greater psychological strain.

As far as optimism is concerned, it often happens that a team feels they are on top just because they have scored a goal or because the game is nearly over and they are one goal up. In cases like this you get two different attitudes: either their determination increases because they are galvanized by having scored or because they wish to bring home the points they are winning, or their concentration diminishes because they think they have already won. If the up and coming team have shown that their optimism leads to an increase in determination, all we must do is tell our players not to get discouraged in their turn, so as not to open the way to the opponents. If their optimism leads the opponent to a loss of concentration, that will help our team get back into psychological control.

As for motivation, when a team loses a match or plays badly everybody always says that it is the players' fault, that they have no drive and were not even trying. The fact of the matter is that it is rare to find players who do not try. Or rather, the players try hard in most matches that they play, but not always as hard as they can. There is a clear difference between their drive in an ordinary league game and in a cup final, just as there is a difference in the importance of the match itself. The players may not be giving everything they have, but they are doing so unconsciously and not because they do not care. Having said that, however, we must add that all the other psychological attitudes - their determination, conviction, concentration etc. - evolve from the level of motivation in the players.

Apart from the opponent's motivation, proof of which we will find in the matches we have been watching, we must also try to establish the level of importance of the actual match we will be playing. If it is an important one, we must conclude that the opponents will unconsciously be trying even harder; of course if it does not have much importance, we can expect them to be playing with less drive.

In either case, we must make sure that our own unconscious drive is the same or greater than that of our opponents. And in order to pave the way for that, we must prepare the match in a suitable way from the mental point of view, using the methods we will be illustrating below.

PARTICULAR PSYCHOLOGICAL CONDITIONS

Apart from the principle psychological conditions illustrated in the previous paragraph, it is a good idea to see whether there is any sign of the other particular mental states that sometimes appear in a soccer team.
These particular emotional states are:

- ☐ Group harmony and team spirit.
- ☐ Tension.
- ☐ Anxiety
- ☐ Calmness and belief in their ability .
- ☐ Unity of intent.
- ☐ Selfishness

Group harmony, team spirit and unity of intent are the most effective weapons you can have. When everyone is 'rowing in the same direction' and playing with altruism, half your problems have been resolved.
On the contrary, when selfishness is the basic element of a team, everything becomes more difficult for the coach.
Tension and anxiety can appear in any team, no matter how good the group spirit may be. You get tension and anxiety when the team does not think they are good enough for the opponent, or in cases where the match is very important. Needless to say, these are negative states of mind, in that they 'block' the team, who will then have more difficulty than they should in getting results.
What allows the team to express itself in the best possible way, making the most of its qualities, is the calmness that comes from thorough confidence in their potential.

You will need special ability in catching hold of what are often subjective sensations in order to evaluate these psychological factors. At the end of a match, everyone must be allowed to reach their own conclusions without claiming any are definitive. Concerning the direct match against our team, we must try to imagine, on the basis of the theoretical ability of the two teams, whether our opponents will be presenting themselves with symptoms of anxiety.

If we think our opponents will be tense as they come out on the field, we must try to make the best of the situation, asking our own players for even more determination, which will then create more intense pressing and a high rhythm of play.

As for our opponent's team spirit, which, let us suppose is very strong - we must work still harder to make sure that of our own team is even stronger.

If we think they have little team spirit, we should ask our players always to put the opposing player in possession under pressure. The fact is that from a tactical point of view a team shows itself to be selfish by basing its play on the individuals. If our opponents are selfish, everything will be that much simpler for us - as long as we ourselves are gifted with good team spirit.

PLAYERS IN DIFFICULTY WHEN FACING PRESSURE OR PRESSING

It is very important to single out those players in psychological difficulty when facing pressing so as to make our actions of disturbance more effective during the defense phase. Getting into a panic when you are being pressed does not necessarily depend on the player in question being technically weak.

Finding out which players in the opposing team are "panickers" is not difficult at all. Central defenders often fall into this category.

Once we have pinpointed them we must find a way of exploiting the situation. We must not only ask the team to put pressure on these players, but we must also prepare invited pressing situations.

When carrying out the stand-by phase of pressing we give momentary freedom to the opposing player who suffers most from such situations - in this way the player in possession is more likely to pass the ball to him.

When that is happening, we bring immediate pressure on the new player in possession, who must also find it difficult to pass to any nearby supporting players. In order to do this, the whole team must place themselves in such a way as to mark and antici-

pate any opponents without the ball near the player in possession - so closing off all the passing lines.

Another thing about psychologically weak players is that they
tend to get more and more depressed the more balls they are
losing as a result of pressure. Thus, our intelligent invited pressing could become more and more effective with the passing of
time, making it still more worth our while.

Other weak players are those that tend to lose their tempers
when things are not going well. These players will often look for
fights or seek revenge after taking hard fouls or even when they
are continuously frustrated on either the defensive or offensive
ends.

Even if it may be useful to pick out such players - it is important
to know as much as you can about your rivals - it is not correct or
fair play to exploit these defects of character by provoking them
verbally or physically.

CHAPTER 6

ANALYSIS OF PHYSICAL AND ATHLETIC PERFORMANCE

CONDITIONING LEVEL OF THE OPPONENT

Determining the conditioning level of the opposing team is not a simple thing to do because you will have to take various factors into consideration.

First of all, you must compare the type of play the opponent wants to carry out with what the team has effectively shown in the matches you have watched. If, for example, the team sets out to play hard and tiring soccer based on pressing and the rhythm of play, but in the matches we have seen them only manage to do so for ten or twelve minutes - that can only mean that the conditioning level they have reached is still low and as a consequence they do not have much stamina.

We must say, however, that the team's imperfect conditioning can sometimes hide the real nature of the soccer the coach wants to play. It could be that the coach intended to apply aggressive and offensive soccer but, on account of the poor conditioning level of his players, he is forced to adopt stand-by tactics.

In the analysis phase we must be good at establishing the relationship between the tactics being applied and the athletic condition of the players, because every team's attitude is strictly connected to its physical possibilities. We must try to catch all the clues and traces we can of the tactics selected by a team and the moves made by its coach.

When, for example, a team takes to the field with a very aggressive attitude, that might be a sign that it has a good level of conditioning. Or again, if during the course of the second half the coach does not carry out substitutions (or delays in carrying them out) that means that all his players are in good physical form.

Obviously, the level of physical preparation reached by a team will also depend on where we are in the season. If the match is at the beginning of the year, the level of conditioning is often not yet at its best, while the team will usually be giving more from a physical point of view during the winter months. Some coaches prefer a type of preparation that gives as much as possible in the short term, so as to get off to the best start possible. Other coaches want their team's preparation to be at the top in the medium or long term so as to finish the championship with a bang.

Nevertheless, we can say that teams normally finish off the season completely worn out from the physical point of view.

Other clues to the physical state of a team are the number of challenges they are winning and whether the players are getting cramps towards the end of a match.

From our own point of view, if we think our opponents are not in good physical condition, we must ask our team to play with rhythm and speed, for the simple reason that when the players' legs can hardly even hold them up, they begin to lose out on mental clarity and the ability to elaborate. We can also ask the strikers to go more often for dribbling in the last twenty yards because the defenders will have less force to put into their challenges.

On the contrary, if the opposing team seems to be in good athletic condition, we should ask our team to play with less rhythm and intensity so as to deal out their stamina, bearing up physically to the other team for the whole match. Also, we must tell the strikers not to try out individual plays all the time, because the opponents will be fully ready at all times to challenge.

However, more complete treatment on how to behave in relation to the physical condition of the adversary must also keep in mind the athletic state of our own team, which will probably be different from that reached in any particular moment of the season by the opposing team. We will be speaking about our own physical state in the part of the book regarding the study of factors related to the condition of our own team.

ABILITY TO DOSE OUT YOUR ENERGY

Apart from the physical condition reached by the team, another thing to keep in mind is our opponent's ability to administrate their stamina during the whole course of the match.

You can often see teams that, even though their physical preparation is good, dose out their energy badly, and arrive at the end of the match practically running on empty. There are also teams which, though their athletic preparation may not be particularly good, manage to arrive at the end of the match with enough energy to finish off in a competitive way.

It is not easy to evaluate a team's ability to dose out its energy. It is difficult to know whether a team has arrived at the end of the match with energy to spare because the players have been able to dose it out efficiently or because it is in excellent physical condition.

Generally speaking, if a team starts the match off strongly but finishes it with no energy left over that is a clear sign that they have not used their energy efficiently. On the other hand, if a rival team begins slowly and concludes the match with no energy all the same, that is due to poor physical preparation.

Very often, however, the situation is not so clear and any judgments about this specific capacity are only subjective.

From our own point of view, all this does not have any real influence on our own set up. If our opponent does not seem to be able to dose out its energy, we can ask our team not to begin all-out, saving energy for the second half, when we can 'press on the gas', playing with greater intensity and rhythm.

If the opponent seems able to use its energy wisely, we must insist that our players do the same, so as to keep on a level for the whole match.

Another important thing to be looking for is when the opponents have a drop in energy, and when they are at the maximum in terms of rhythm and intensity of play.

You have drops of energy in teams that are not able to dose out their energy, and these generally come out towards the end of the match.

On the other hand, the moments of the match played with most intensity are usually the first few minutes of the game.

In any case, when the opponents tend to have drops in physical force, we must tell our players to accelerate the rhythm.

In their moments of strongest competitiveness, the players should be told to double their attention and the effort they are making.

FAST PLAYERS AND PHYSICALLY STRONG PLAYERS

From the individual physical and athletic point of view, we must establish which opposing players are faster when running with or without the ball, and which have particular physical or athletic strength.

When summing up the speed of the rival players, do not let yourself be taken in by the fact that one player gets past another as they are running. Everything is relative, remember; and if the player being passed is very slow, then the one who is doing the overtaking may not actually be so fast. We have to try to judge the speed of the players without giving too much consideration to their 'overtaking'. It is easier to get an idea about the physical strength of players, because their sheer size is a fairly good sign from that point of view.

Generally speaking, the fastest players are the second strikers and the wings, while the center defenders or the center mid fielders tend to be the strongest.

When you have pinpointed these players you need to indicate them to your team, as well as the behavior to adopt.

Players who are fast with the ball are generally good at physical dribbling, which is something we have seen in the relative paragraph.

Players who go mainly for the sprint into depth so as to get past their marker before the ball gets to them are really dangerous for our defensive set up. In situations where the player in possession is free to launch the ball to such players moving into depth our defense must immediately move back to reduce their space, then move out again as soon as the player in possession has lost the moment for his play.

Particularly the defender in the opposing 'fast' player's zone must carry out fairly wide marking, so as not to be taken in by his dummies. Players whose greatest strength is their speed will often first make a counter movement to free themselves of marking by coming towards the half way line, and then attack their marker into depth, taking him by surprise.

If we foresee that one of their wings will be putting our side back into trouble, we should consider substituting him right from the beginning with a faster player.

If the strongest players are the center defenders we cannot make too great a use of crosses or long passes because players like these have an advantage in aerial play. Also, when our striker is closed off by one of these players, he must not waste time with the ball but should pass it immediately to a teammate because big players are usually good tacklers.

At the same time we have to pick out the opposing players that are slow in running and those that are physically smaller. Of the first type we often find central defenders, while the wings and the second striker are often smaller players.

Thus, we can say that slow players are often physically powerful, while the fast players are smaller and thinner.

We must therefore make the best of the presence of slow players in the opponent's defense section by positioning our fastest striker in one of their zones, being careful, however, that the striker himself does not lose effectiveness by playing in a position different from his usual one.

If we think that one of their side backs is particularly slow, we could consider putting a faster side mid fielder than usual on the field.

If there are any small defenders, we might think about putting our first striker in their zone.

CHAPTER 7

OTHER FACTORS LEADING TO THE BEST MATCH STRATEGY

OUR OWN TEAM

Naturally, the preparation of the match must also keep its sights on the state of our own team, evaluating the level of tactical preparation we have reached and the athletic and psychological condition of our players.

We must put any consideration that we make about our own team in comparison with those that we have come up with concerning our opponents.

It is very important to contrast the state of the two teams because this in itself could bring about changes in the countermoves we were thinking of making.

The following are the elements to be considered from a tactical point of view:

- ☐ Level of tactical preparation reached.
- ☐ Assimilation of required tactics and playing schemes.
- ☐ Situations in which the team finds itself in difficulty.

From the physical athletic point of view, what you want to be analyzing is the following:

- ☐ Level of athletic preparation reached.
- ☐ Minutes of self-sufficiency on the part of the team in terms of stamina, above all at high rhythm.

Lastly, you must consider these aspects from the psychological point of view:

- ☐ General psychological state of the team (enthusiasm, serenity, depression, anxiety, tension, crisis point, etc.).
- ☐ Conviction and confidence in their ability.

If you think that the whole potential of the individual players has been reached from the technical point of view, then you should give pre-eminence to the tactical aspect of play during coaching sessions, carrying out only a couple of fundamental revision exercises. If you think that there are any more or less serious deficiencies on your players' technical side, you must dedicate more time to looking after the basics.

The only thing to say in relation to a single match from the technical angle is that you must make comparisons between:

- ☐ The aerial ability of our attacking players and that of their defenders.
- ☐ The aerial ability of our defenders and that of their attacking players.
- ☐ Our attacking players' ability in dribbling and that of their defenders in defending the ball.
- ☐ Our defenders' ability in defending the ball and that of their attacking players in dribbling.

From making these comparisons, we can see whether it is possible to invert the positions of pairs of players as we explained when looking at the technical factors regarding the opposing team. As we will see, these comparisons also give us the information necessary to decide what players to put on the team for this particular match.

Let us now make an analysis of the implications to be derived from the tactical, physical and psychological information we have been gathering about our own team.

As regards the level of tactical preparation reached, we must decide - keeping in mind our opponent's characteristics - whether it is a good idea to apply certain tactics that the team has not fully assimilated as yet.

Even the system we are using may have to pass this exam. It will have to do so, for example, when we have just taken the team on hand and we want to teach the players a playing and/or defense system which is different from the one they are used to. To give an example, if our predecessor applied a 3-5-2 man marking system, and we now want to use a zonal 4-3-3, it would probably be a mistake to put the team on the field with this line up right from the first match, above all if the opponent has shown itself to be well-organized. We should continue with the old playing system until the new one has been sufficiently assimilated.

The choices which will always have to undergo rigorous examination are relative to pressing (above all whether or not to use ultra-offensive pressing) and to offside tactics. As we saw in chapter 3, these two particular tactics must be compared to the opponent's ability in getting past them.

To sum up, if the opponents demonstrate that they are able to get past our ultra-offensive pressing (either on account of the technical quality of their play or because of the tactical solutions they adopt) better than we seem to be able to apply it, it is probably better to tell the team to bring back the zone where we are pressing to the mid field. If the opposite is true, we will be encouraged to apply it with even greater intensity.

If our opponents are eluding our offside tactics better than we seem able to apply them, the team should limit themselves to carrying out the defensive shift to reduce the risks. In the opposite conditions, of course, they will be able to apply offside. It sometimes happens, however, that a team manages to get past the offside trap only in certain situations. We should, therefore, try to assess in what moments the opponent is good at getting past our trap, and consequently we can tell our team not to apply it in those particular situations.

Of the two tactics we are looking at, it is above all offside that will undergo modifications. With pressing we should be a little more rigid in terms of tactical adjustments.

From the tactical point of view, another thing is to assess carefully where our team seems to be having trouble. In order to decide whether or not to adopt changes to the tactical set up you must compare these difficulties with the opponent's ability in the same situations.

For example, if we are in trouble when facing counter attacking moves and one of the particular strengths of our opponents is counter attacking, then we must make precise adjustments. We might decide to keep more players in preventive coverage, or we could lower the level where we start pressing.

Perhaps our team has trouble with play along the flanks; if our opponent makes the best of this part of the field, we might consider asking the inside mid fielders to widen out during the defense phase (above all if we are applying a system that foresees a single side player on each flank).

There are many situations in which we might be having trouble (vertical passes, crosses, in-depth pressing, changes of play, etc.) and it is up to the coach to judge whether and in what way to apply any tactically corrective moves.

From the physical point of view, it is very important to assess the degree of athletic preparation reached by the team, and consequently, its stamina under speed and duress.

From such an assessment, we will be able to make any necessary tactical adjustments.

If we are behind in our conditioning program, we must see whether it might be a good idea to adopt a less physically tiring match conduct. We should ask our team to lower the initial level of pressing and reduce the general rhythm and intensity of play so as to dose out their energy in a better way because they are low on stamina.

If we are ahead with the conditioning program, we can afford to put on a team that will have as its points of force the rhythm and intensity of its play. There are naturally intermediate conditions between what we have just spoken about, and these will lead to more moderate solutions and tactical changes.

The elements to be considered from a psychological point of view have nothing to do with the other team.

The only effects the psychological state of our team will have on our tactics is that it will help us to resolve any doubts we might have had about our countermeasures relative to our analysis of all the other factors.

If it is a positive moment for our team, and there is serenity and enthusiasm in the group, we should modify our tactical set up as little as possible.

If, on the other hand, the team is going through a moment of crisis, and tension and anxiety have the upper hand in the group, we should first of all adopt aggressive tactics. In that way, and through pressing, the players can get rid of tension, and they will have the feeling that they are overcoming their unsatisfactory performances.

Furthermore, we should consider the possibility of ignoring the tactics and the playing schemes that the team has not been able to make their own in order to simplify the players' tasks on the field.

From the point of view of our players' confidence in their ability, we should say that the more self-assurance they have, the more we should vary our play to give them more feeling of being in control of the movements and the basic tactics.

If the players are not convinced about their ability, it is not a good idea to change too much because when we take away precise tactical points of reference from our players we will create even more problems of identity for them.

From the psychological point of view, there is a special mental preparation for matches, which we will be looking at in the following pages.

WEATHER CONDITIONS AND THE PLAYING FIELD

Have no doubt about it, the weather conditions have a great effect on a soccer match, to the point where they can completely upset everyone's expectations.

Depending on the weather, any prediction about the match can go completely haywire, because strategy and tactics can become more or less effective in relation to the state of the day and of the field.

For example, play based on ball possession with short passes and on elaborate build up will be effective only when the field is in good condition. With a heavy field after a lot of rain, a team that usually plays in such a way will be forced to change their normal style.

Then again, play based on immediate build up, and so on the long pass, has a good chance of being extremely effective when heavy rainfall has softened the ground, and when in particular you are meeting a team that uses the elaborate build up.

We could go so far as to say that the weather can have more effect on tactics than any other element regarding the opposing team.

The weather conditions also have an effect on the excitement of a match. When it is raining, beautiful soccer is heavily penalized, and the match will not be so spectacular. Even when the temperature is too high the match will not be very enjoyable, because in order to save energy, the players will have to run less, lowering the rhythm of play.

The very best conditions for the spectators are when the weather is good but it is not too hot, because in that case the teams that play spectacular soccer will be at an advantage.

In any case, the weather conditions have an effect on the playing field, making the ground more or less difficult and heavy. The heavier the ground, the more difficulty the players will have in using the basic techniques; the more regular the ground, the easier the players will find it to use their individual techniques. The coach will have to make the necessary changes to the team's tactical set up to adapt things to what the playing field will allow the individual to do.

The weather conditions also have a great effect on the players' stamina: the hotter it is, the more energy they will need during the course of the match.

Lastly, we can also say that the weather has an effect on the morale of the players. Players perform with more enthusiasm and confidence when they can express themselves to perfection, both on the level of individual technique and on that of team tactics; in bad conditions they tend to be tense and uncertain.

One of the problems from this point of view is how to predict the weather conditions for the day of the match. It is important to know what the weather will be like in advance in order to prepare the match as well as possible from a tactical point of view. If we suddenly realize that the conditions are unfavorable to us on the actual day of the match, it will be too late to prepare all the tactical countermeasures with any effectiveness, because there will be no time to do theme exercises with the players. Sometimes then, you will be preparing some countermoves during the week that you will not be able to use in the match on account of the weather.

We must add that if the coach is forced to revise his tactical decisions on the day of the match, he must try to make sure his final modifications are the least drastic possible, explaining what he wants from the team in his own words and with simplicity.

With the help of the table below, we will now analyze the effects that certain particular weather conditions can have on the state of the playing ground, and how that can influence our tactical set up.

WEATHER CONDITIONS	GROUND CONDITIONS	TACTICS TO SUGGEST	TACTICS NOT TO USE	OTHER ADVICE
HIGH TEMP	DRY	ELABORATE BUILD UP, SLOW CIRCULATION OF THE BALL	IN DEPTH PRESSING, COUNTER ATTACKING AT ANY COST, HIGH SPEED PLAY	RUN AS LITTLE AS POSSIBLE, SAVE YOUR ENERGY
RAIN	HEAVY	LONG PASSES, IMMEDIATE BUILD UP, PRESSING, SHOOTING FROM OUT-SIDE THE AREA	ELABORATE BUILD UP, SHORT TIGHT PASSES	TRY NOT TO PLAY WITH THE BALL ON THE GROUND
FREEZING	ICY	IN DEPTH PLAY, LONG PASSES	PASSING THE BALL HORI-ZONTALLY	RUN AS LITTLE AS POSSIBLE, (THE STATE OF THE GROUND MAKES RUNNING DIFFICULT)
SNOW	SNOWY	LONG PASSES, IMMEDIATE BUILD UP, SHOOTING FROM FAR OUT	ELABORATE BUILD UP, PLAYING ON THE FLANKS	DO NOT PLAY WITH THE BALL ON THE GROUND, DO NOT LET THE OPPONENTS SHOOT FROM OUTSIDE THE AREA

As you can see from the table, when the ground is heavy you must not insist on short passes and horizontal play, but rather on immediate build up and shots from far out because it will be more difficult for the opponent's goalkeeper to get hold of the ball in these conditions.

In muggy weather, you should use tactics permitting you to save energy so that your team's performance will be constant for the whole 90 minutes.

THE IMPORTANCE OF THE MATCH

Another thing to consider when you are preparing a game is the importance of the match itself. Coaches who do their job with passion, enthusiasm and professional sense will never underestimate any match, putting everything into their work and expecting their team to behave likewise. But there is no doubt that preparing a friendly is something different from preparing a cup final. In the same way, the preparation carried out for the first match of the championship is not the same as when you are facing a decisive game for the whole season - because, of course, the psychological implications will be totally different.

Everyone's approach to the game changes on the basis of its importance. The more important the match, the more the spectators will be looking forward to it and the more excited they will be. The players will go onto the field in a state of greater tension and concentration for the all important matches. And lastly, the coaches will have to adapt their preparation of a match in relation to its importance.

The first thing the coach must do is to handle any particular psychological situations that might occur.

When the match is not very important, the negative tendency of the players is to go on the field with less concentration and 'wound down' from a competitive point of view.

When they feel the importance of the match, the players will be split between their great determination and the tension that the event creates.

Concerning the studies we will be making of the opponents: when the match in preparation is a friendly, the coach can clearly afford to be less obsessed about all the details and concentrate on giving his own team the best preparation possible.

When preparing an important match, we need to analyze even the most insignificant of details, not limiting ourselves to watching again and again the other team's last couple of matches.

As far as the tactical countermoves are concerned, the more important the match, the more flexible we should be. It is inadvisable to carry out particular tactical countermeasures for a friendly match because in those kinds of situations you want the players to concentrate on perfecting their general tactical organization. On the contrary, you must not hesitate to apply modifications to the set up for an important match - if you think that they are necessary.

Lastly, when playing a friendly match you should ask your players to save their energy; little by little as the matches grow in importance players must be told to put greater physical energy into what they are doing.

As you can see, the most important thing about preparing matches of different levels of importance is to administer to the changing psychological states of the players.
The coach must make sure that the team takes to the field with the right approach, with concentration, determination, and free of particular states of mind like presumption or fear.
It can be useful to bring the team to a place of seclusion before an important match in order to find the right concentration.
But for further information on this subject, see the part of chapter 8 regarding the mental preparation for a match.

THE DIVISION YOU ARE PLAYING IN

The division your team is playing in has its importance when preparing the match.
Preparing a match in the top division is different from preparing one in the third category. First of all the coach of an amateur

team has only a couple of hours a week in which to train his team. He will dedicate most of the little time at his disposal to teaching the players in a generic way and to perfecting their universal tactical organization, and so he will have very little time indeed left over for the real preparation of the next match. Sometimes such coaches will only be able to give verbal advice to his players about how to play the coming match because it is impossible for him to carry out adequate specific training sessions complete with their relative theme exercises.

On the contrary, the coach of a professional team, lucky enough to have more time at his disposal, can dedicate a large part of it to the preparation for the next match.

Another problem is that getting hold of the data regarding the next opponent might be more or less difficult depending on the division in which our team is playing.

In professional categories the coach will be able to prepare the coming match on the basis of a great deal of information about the opposing team, but in amateur sections he risks not knowing anything at all about his next opponents.

When his club has little or no resources, the coach will not have enough material to inform him about the other team and he will be able to make little or no specific preparation. He will have to carry out 'blind' countermeasures, very often basing himself on what he has heard about his opponents through the grapevine.

Also, in amateur divisions the coach has another job and would not have the time to study his opponent even if he had the opportunity to do so.

Again, the relationship with the team is less direct when you are playing in the lower categories. As a result, it will be more difficult to prepare your players mentally for the match.

We can add that when the team is playing on an amateur level, you cannot load the players with too much responsibility, keeping in mind that, as far as they are concerned, the sport is not a job but a hobby. You cannot expect a high level of tactical discipline from them and, above all, you cannot bring the players to a place of seclusion a few days before the match.

Nevertheless, the coach of a non-professional team must try to put all he can into his work, using his free time to the best of his ability in order to study the opponents. The little information he has about his opponents must be exploited to the maximum, in the same way as he must make the best use of the time at his disposal for the training sessions.

The coach of an amateur team must not exaggerate with tactics, keeping in mind that his players do not have much time at their disposal to learn the countermeasures that he has chosen.

He must illustrate these 'soft' countermeasures to his team during training sessions, finding time to train the players by using simple but effective theme exercises.

He must try also to psyche up his team, forcing them to shoulder their responsibilities within the limits of good sense.

There is no point in underlining here how a professional coach must manage the preparation for the match. He will have to make the best use possible of his potential, both as regards the time at his disposal for training sessions and the material he has to work with. His responsibilities are much more serious and he must carry them out to the best of his ability.

THE PREVIOUS MATCHES

In preparing for the next match, we must remember that it is never a one-off thing, independent of the context that characterizes the two teams. Every match is closely connected to the 'recent history' of the two teams that are disputing it. But you could also say - and the contradiction is only apparent - that each game is unique and unrepeatable because the preceding matches condition it to a great extent.

The two teams approach each game in a different way depending on how they have played in the matches before.

The questions a coach will have to ask himself are these:

- ☐ In terms of the play expressed and the results, how did our team get on in the last few matches, and in particular in the one that they have just played?
- ☐ What were the reasons and the tactical and psychological errors that led to the team not expressing itself to perfection, or, in any case, what can we do to correct the situation?

☐ How has the opposing team been playing in the last few matches?

☐ Where are the two teams in the standings?

Our last few matches will have an effect on us above all on the psychological plane. If the team has been performing in a positive way, it will probably go into the next match with enthusiasm and self confidence in its abilities. The risk in such cases is that the players are so psyched up that they can not keep their feet on the ground and will enter the field with negative presumption (over-confidence).

On the contrary, a team that has been playing badly could present itself on the field in two different ways. Either the players will be full of the desire to make things up or they will be oppressed by negative feelings like the tension or the fear of losing again.

When preparing the match then, we must analyze how our team has been playing in terms of results and performance. The last match played is particularly important for the way it influences the players' morale.

Let us now have a look at all the possible psychological implications, remembering that the coach will be working on these mental attitudes so as to make use of the positive ones and eliminate the negative.

If our team has hit on a positive series, both in terms of the results and the actual performances, which has been confirmed by the last match played, the mental attitudes that you will find in the players are the following.

☐ Enthusiasm.

☐ Greater confidence in their abilities.

☐ Serenity.

☐ Presumption.

The coach must try to keep the group's enthusiasm high right up to the day of the match, avoiding at the same time those feelings of presumption that can unfortunately come up in such situations. In this serene, stimulated atmosphere, the coach can increase the amount of work the team must do, asking them to show more concentration and tenacity. In this kind of situation the players will be more predisposed to listening to the coach and carrying out what is asked of them. When things are going well 'the ground to be sown is always fertile.'

If our team is on a hot streak, both in terms of the results and the play, but have lost the most recent match - this might create a moment of difficulty to be crushed immediately. The coach must remind his players of the positive matches, getting them to keep their heads and sustaining the group serenity formed over the last few weeks. This in cases where the last defeat has been caused by bad luck or other variables, and is not the direct responsibility of the players.

If, on the other hand, you are convinced that the team lost the last match on account of their over-confidence, you should take a sterner attitude towards the players. You must try to put their feet firmly back on the ground, without hesitating to take all the necessary measures to bring them back to a more modest stance.

If our team has won most of its recent matches without playing in a particularly convincing way, we are facing a potentially dangerous situation. The team is bringing home results but we can not expect to keep winning, especially if our next opponents are stronger. We must hope, of course, that the positive results will be the right medicine for the team's play, allowing them to improve as a result of the enthusiasm that has been created in the group, but we will also have to work hard at rectifying our play and eliminating the tactical flaws that we have noticed. Also, we must try to make the team understand the danger of continuing to play in this unconvincing way without dampening their enthusiasm. In fact, their enthusiasm will permit you to ask them to increase their effort in training to express more convincing play.

If the last few matches have been negative from the point of view both the results and the play, then we are without doubt in a period of crisis.

Here the whole thing becomes more complicated because the coach must try to understand the psychological reasons at the base of this difficult stretch.

From the mental point of view, the principle reasons could be the following:

- ☐ The players are not putting everything into the matches.
- ☐ The players are finding it difficult to keep their concentration and determination for the whole course of the match.
- ☐ The players are short on confidence and conviction in their ability, and these two things are even further reduced with every match we lose.
- ☐ No serenity and group harmony

The coach must try to understand if one (or more than one) of these factors is responsible for the bad performances of the team, and he will have to take suitable measures. If the players are not working hard enough, the coach must give them a brushing down that will make them see that they need to be more serious.

If the team cannot manage to keep its concentration for the whole match, the coach must come up with training sessions in which, along with carrying out the exercises, the players will also need to sustain their attention. In order to do this, the exercises must be based on an incessant intensity of execution.

If the reason that things are going badly for the team is that they have no confidence in their ability, the coach needs to talk to his players and convince them of the contrary.

If the lack of serenity and group harmony is the reason for the crisis, the coach should make internal inquiries in the locker room, trying to smooth out the conflict between the players, perhaps even asking that those who are creating ill will should be sent away.

In any case, the team must nurture a positive desire to get back on top, never giving in but, on the contrary, continuing to struggle.

A particular situation is when our last matches have been negative only from the point of view of the results, but the team has been playing well and has often deserved to win. Even if we try to convince the team that the important thing is to play well and that sooner or later the results will arrive, the players will have trouble recovering the right spirit. As far as they are concerned, the results create morale, and the fact that they are defeated while deserving to win will cause despondency.

The coach must convince the team to continue playing well because in the long run they well get on top of their adversaries. You should build up the players' confidence and their hopes, putting them in a position where the want to get on top of their difficulties and not simply give in.

In cases like these the coach must show that he at least is calm and he must give back confidence to his players.

If the team's performances have been up and down, you must encourage the players to go ahead in the right way and to abandon their negative attitudes.

You must keep reminding them of what they are doing right so as to increase their confidence in their ability. At the same time you must show them what they are doing wrong to make them aware of the mistakes they are making so that they will be able to correct these with your help.

Apart from these psychological motivations, you must also see whether the team's bad play is arising from any tactical or physical factors.

Regarding tactics, perhaps the team just cannot assimilate some of the moves and / or playing schemes proposed by the coach. You should ask yourself whether it might be a good idea to change them, considering the possibility that they may be incompatible with the players' characteristics.

Whatever the problem may be, we will have to study our team's preceding matches (using video recordings if possible) in order to understand all the tactical errors that have been made, and correct them with suitable training exercises.

Lastly, from the athletic and physical point of view, the reason behind our team's crisis may be that they do not have enough energy either to take the heat against their opponents for the whole 90 minutes of a match, or to apply the tactics required by the coach.

The solution to that could be to make them carry out tactics that they will find less tiring or to enact an in-depth turnover of the players.

When you have looked at how our team has been playing, you need to do the same for your opponents.

If they are going through a positive stretch, we must expect a very difficult match. Our players must be made aware of that, and put on guard against the difficulties they will be facing so that they can double their concentration during the match. However, if our players tend to become anxious and afraid, the coach should use a 'softer' approach to keep them calm.

If the opposing team is in the middle of a bad period, we must first of all tell our players not to underrate the match. It often happens that a team breaks its moment of crisis thanks to the simple fact that a presumptuous opponent has made the wrong approach to the game.

We have to ask our players to make the best of their opponent's moment of difficulty by going on the field with strong determination, concentration and also respect for the rival team.

Lastly, we should consider the position in the standings of both teams.

The better placed team in the standings will usually be at a psychological advantage.

If your team is ahead in the standings, you must tell the players not to feel they are the favorites because otherwise they might be underestimating the opponent.

If your team is further down the tables, the players must be told that they are not worth less than their opponents, especially if they put everything they have into the match.

You must establish which of the two teams will show more determination on the basis of their position in the standings, but it is also important to know which of the two has less to lose in case of a defeat.

For example, if one of the two teams is fighting to win the championship and the other is floating around half way down the table, the first will obviously be more determined (even unconsciously), but the second has the advantage of having less to lose. The coach of the first team will have to eliminate his players' possible fear of losing, and turn it into the determination to win. The coach of the second team only has to make his players aware of the positive conditions in which they will be playing.

Such situations usually come to light at the end of the season when teams that are fighting to win the championship meet teams that are fighting in order not to be relegated.

PLAYING AT HOME OR AWAY

Have no doubt about it, there is a great difference between playing at home or away, and these can be decisive variables in determining the performance of a team.

It is true that all playing fields are green and always of the same dimensions, but because the psychological angle is of primary importance in soccer, having the public with you or against you is something that can decide a match.

When a team is playing at home, supported by its own fans and immersed in a friendly atmosphere, it will have all the incentives it needs to attack, taking play into its hands and keeping possession.

On the other hand, a team playing an away match is facing a hostile atmosphere. This is not only because the crowd is supporting the opposing team, but also because every time our players get possession they will be undergoing the shouts and choruses of disapproval on the part of the local supporters. In such an environment, it becomes very difficult to attack and keep ball possession. When a player on a team facing an away match gains possession, he will have the feeling that he must free himself of the ball as quickly as possible in order to return to the preordained attitude typical of a team that is playing in a hostile atmosphere: staying in defense.

When preparing an away match, many coaches simply align themselves to this role, instinctively adopting stand by tactics.

Instead, we should try to convince the players not to change their mentality and their playing style when facing an away match. It is not easy because the team will naturally tend to button itself up. But we must make the players understand that it is not necessary to accept this one sided sort of play, and it is by using an active attitude even during an away match that we increase our chances of winning. The team playing at home will not be expecting to face an active opponent and will find itself in difficulty carrying out its preordained role of controlling the match.

So, when you are preparing a match to be played away, you must not make the smallest change either from the point of view of mentality or from that of the tactical set up.

You must prepare the away matches from a mental point of view, making sure that your players enter the field convinced that they can impose their own play without being frightened and trying to keep the adverse environment at arm's length.

You must above all work on the first minutes of the match, those in which a team playing away will normally appear most unstable and irresolute.

Also, the tiniest tactical change made to protect the team in view of the fact that they are playing away would be a negative sign for the players.

In time, by making suitable mental preparation for the away matches, we will be able to apply the same type of play there as that which we develop when we are at home (though it will be difficult for us to get the same positive results), eliminating the players' tendency to stand by in a passive way.

When preparing home matches, on the other hand, we should have a look at the opponent's usual attitude when playing away. If they normally apply stand by soccer, we will only have to ask our team to be careful about counter attacks and not to get frustrated if they cannot unlock the situation at once.

If our opponents play active soccer even during away matches, we must make sure our players are aware of that so they do not find themselves unprepared.

Coming under attack when you are playing at home is without doubt a nasty surprise, but if it has been foreseen, that will make things easier for us.

After having analyzed all these things and having listed the possible implications for our team, we must conclude this part of the chapter by saying that the subjects we have treated are the result of interpretations that are sometimes very subjective, and there may be others which would be completely different.

Those who do not see soccer in a spectacular and therefore offensive light, but who always try to be pragmatic, must not hesitate to adopt more utilitarian methods when they consider them necessary.

To clarify, here is an example: a coach may believe, contrary to what we have been saying above, that when we meet, perhaps even in an away match, a team that is superior to us on paper, the most useful thing is to adopt a defensive, stand by attitude. He will bring back the initial line of pressing, insist on immediate build up or, in any case, on counter attacking, with only a few players participating in the possession phase while having almost every player involved in the defense phase.

Lastly, for those coaches who prefer to man mark, it is necessary as you are preparing the match to establish the individual markers, especially in connection with the opponent's attacking players.

To do that you will have to make a careful study of the rival strikers. In a nutshell, the fastest striker must be marked by the fastest defender, while the strongest one, who most excels in aerial play, must be taken up by the marker best in these two aspects. When the opponents are fielding an attacking mid fielder, a team marking the man must pay particular attention to him. The biggest problem concerning such a player is to decide if he should be marked by a defender or a center mid fielder. This must be established on the basis of the depth of the field at which the attacking mid fielder usually plays, keeping in mind, however, that it is better to put a mid fielder on him so as not to unbalance the team and create other problems in the defense

To conclude our remarks on marking the man, we must say that the original system will undergo significant changes in the defense phase. When a team defends by man marking, its system adapts itself like a mirror to that of the opponents who are attacking because the position of the players carrying out their offense phase will be copied by the markers who are following them.

Lastly, when preparing a man marking system we must make sure that the defenders are in numerical superiority over the rival strikers to keep the sweeper detached from the rest of his section teammates, ready to intervene if need be. To do this, you sometimes have to adopt a different system in the defense phase from the basic one, perhaps even asking a mid fielder to integrate himself with the backs when necessary.

To speak in a more detailed way about man marking, we would have to keep in mind all those grey areas between man marking and zonal defense - analyzing all the different types of mixed zones that can exist. This would be followed by indications regarding the behavior of the single marker: at what distance do we mark the striker? In what zone of the field should we take him on? In which zone should we let him go?, etc. However, this is not the place to carry out such an analysis.

CHAPTER 8

EXERCISES AND PRACTICAL PREPARATION
FOR THE MATCH

Once you have established what tactical changes to make to the team, you must then make sure that the players are acquiring them as well as possible.

During our training sessions, we must carry out a specific program of preparation for every countermove that we have decided to make, and for every attitude that we are expecting from the players.

This practical preparation will have as its main points of reference:

☐ Technical and tactical exercises aimed at teaching the team what attitudes to take and the most important themes to be developed during the match.

☐ Exercises (in the form of training matches) simulating the tactical situations which will come up during the next match, aiming above all to penetrate the opponent's defense system and to block their typical attacking moves.

Before giving a list of the most important exercises, we will make an analysis of how the coach should behave in order to manage the training sessions dedicated to the upcoming game.

First of all the coach must get his ideas together about the strategies he will be using, after having analyzed all the factors that we have been looking at in the preceding sections of this book.

At this point, the moment has arrived to make a definitive outline of the strategy to be used in the next match. We have to decide whether to confirm the tactical countermeasures foreseen in the analytic phase, or whether to eliminate some of them. Also, we must see if these countermeasures counterbalance each other, and then bring up anything new if we see fit. For example, maybe we have established, on the basis of our study of the opponent's defense system, to use elaborate build up, but we now foresee that the weather will be bad. This will now become the prevailing factor of our preparations and as a consequence we will choose more aggressive defense strategies in order to make better use of our counter attacks.

In drawing up the final strategic set up for the match , we must remember not to get obsessed by tactics, and above all not to put the teams' points of reference out of all proportion.

All the tactical moves we have established for the match should be jotted down on a prospectus, in which we should also list our advice and recommendations to the team.

As far as advice and recommendations are concerned, these should be given to the team during the course of the week running up to the match, especially in the specific training session we have fixed.

Considering all the time on hand for the training sessions, the coach must decide how much space to dedicate to the strict preparation of the match.

It is important, however, not to make too clear a distinction between normal training sessions and specific training for the next match.

For the whole of the preceding week you will be working on the players' minds so that they will have an adequate approach to their next match. You must give them constant advice and direction about how to behave, and you must also supply them with all the necessary information about their upcoming opponents.

In any case, the tactical exercises aiming to make direct preparations for the next match must be fixed at the beginning of the week.

In deciding these things, you need to keep the following factors in mind:

- ☐ The importance of the following match.
- ☐ The level reached by the team in their general tactical preparation.
- ☐ The number and complexity of the tactical counter measures the team will have to take.
- ☐ The time on hand for training.

If we have to play an important match - as for example a decisive match for the championship or a final in some competition or other - we will have to dedicate a lot of the time we have on hand to preparing the match.

If, on the other hand, it is an unimportant match - a friendly for example - then clearly it will be a good idea to dedicate the majority of our time to perfecting our general tactical organization. In other words, the time we have on hand must be shared out as well as possible between improving our tactical organization and preparing for the match itself.

At this point, things connect in with the general tactical level we have already reached. At the beginning of the season, for instance, when we are just getting underway with the tactical itinerary, we must dedicate a higher percentage of our time to that aspect of things, limiting our direct preparation of single matches. At the end of the season on the other hand, at which point we will have finished actually teaching the basics, we will have to spend much more time preparing for the up and coming match.

Naturally, we will also have to spend some time revising the tactical principles connected with the general organization of play.

The higher the number of tactical countermoves we wish to make, and the more complicated they are to learn, the more time we will have to dedicate to preparing the match. In cases where we do not have much time we will not be able to devote a great deal of it to training sessions that directly concern the match.

Basing ourselves on the four factors listed above and keeping in mind the number of days we can spend in training, we should fix the (approximate) amount of time to dedicate to the preparation for the next match.

For example, if a professional team trains five days a week for a good number of hours every day, you should dedicate two of them to the specific preparation of the upcoming match, or perhaps only one, or even, at the end of the season, three days or more.

If an amateur team only trains three days a week or even less, and then only for a couple of hours at a time, you will have to decide whether to dedicate one whole day to the preparation for the match, or two (above all if we are at the end of the season), or even less than one (if you are behind with the learning process).

The next step will be to decide which of these days to dedicate to the preparation of the match. The end of week training sessions are usually chosen for this (particularly the day before the match, in which we carry out what is called 'polishing up'), so that the team goes on the field with their match preparation fresh in their minds. If you teach the players the countermoves that you have chosen at the beginning of the week, you will be running the risk that they will quickly forget what they have learned.

It is not advisable to carry out intense training sessions the very day of the match because you want the players to go on the field with their legs strong and ready, and all their energy eager to go.

The last thing is to give the best organization possible to the training sessions fixed for the specific preparation for the match. The first thing is to introduce the team to the opponents we are to meet, telling them all we know about the information we have been gathering. This should take place by giving them real lessons even using a blackboard if we have one, and allowing them to see some of their opponent's most significant plays, which we will have selected from their last few matches. This will help our players to understand not only the team they are to meet, but also the plays that we have decided on, which we hope will put them in difficulty. It is easier to explain the counter measures we want to adopt if that is done after we have shown our players the characteristics of the rival team.

If possible we should prepare an audiovisual summary composed of the most significant highlights answering our particular needs. This will save us time, because the players will not be able to have a look at entire matches.

When we have shown them the characteristics of the rival team, we must explain the countermeasures they will be applying. You must also give the players reasons for everything they have to do, which will help them to understand in an active way.

So that the team can acquire the attitudes we are expecting of them, we must propose technical and tactical exercises aimed at teaching them the themes that we consider fundamental.

Here is a list of the most meaningful:

Exercise 1 (Fig. 34)

Tactical attitude: Elaborate build up
Specific aim: Change of play, ball possession
Nº of players: 9 against 9
Size of the field: 40 x 40
Objectives: 10 small goals placed around the field
Touches permitted: 2 or 3
Rules: You must pass the ball through the goals and take it up again on the other side.

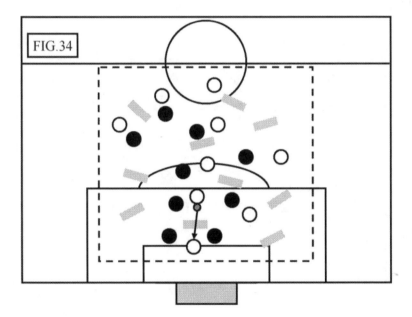

Exercise 2 (Fig. 35)

Tactical attitude: Elaborate build up
Specific aim: Width, change of play, ball possession
Nº of players: 4 against 4
Size of the field: 40 x 40
Objectives: 6 small goals placed along each base line (3 on each line)
Touches permitted: 2
Rules: A goal in the central net counts 2 points, one the side 1
Variations: Two goals in each side placed at the corners of the playing field

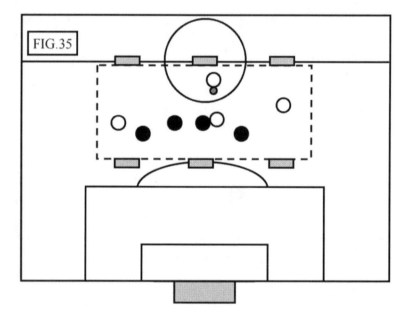

FIG.35

Exercise 3 (Fig. 36)

Tactical attitude: Elaborate build up
Specific aim: Change of play, using overlapping on the flanks
N° of players: 11 against 11
Size of the field: 80 x 40 + 2 external corridors 10 x 80
Objectives: 2 goals
Touches permitted: 2 or 3
Rules: A goal is valid only if it comes about following overlapping on the flanks. On each external corridor you can have only one defender and one attacking player. Only when this attacking player has received the ball can overlapping take place.
Variation: No attacking player can remain on the flank before receiving the ball (he must receive it as he is widening out to free himself of marking).

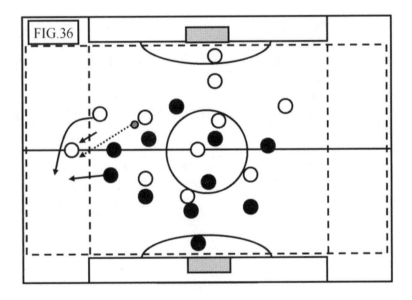

FIG.36

Exercise 4

Tactical attitude: Elaborate build up
Specific aim: Width, change of play, crosses from the base line
Nº of players: 8 against 8 (or 11 against 11)
Size of the field: Half the field (or 80 x 60)
Objectives: 2 goals
Touches permitted: 2 or 3
Rules: You must try to cross from the zone at the side of the penalty area (the so called 'crossing zone'). A goal will be considered valid only after a cross. Another important rule is that after you have regained possession, you are obliged to make a change of play. After that any changes of play can be carried out at discretion.
Variation: You can cross only from the opposite side to where you regained possession.

Exercise 5 (Fig. 37)

Tactical attitude: Mixed build up (both elaborate and immediate)
Specific aim: Ball possession, change of play, penetration
Nº of players: 8 against 8
Size of the field: 40 x 40 plus two neutral zones at the two ends
Objectives: None
Touches permitted: 2
Rules: 1 point for every 10 consecutive passes; 1 point every time you free yourself of marking and receive the ball in the neutral zone

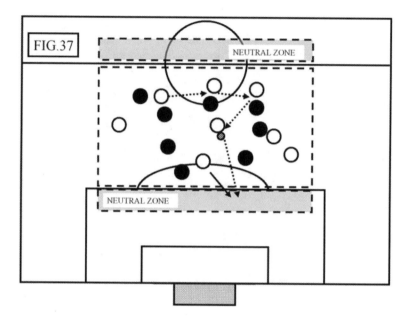

Exercise 6 (Fig. 38)

Tactical attitude: Elaborate and immediate build up
Specific aim: Width, change of play, ball possession, penetration, speed of maneuvers
Nº of players: 8 against 8 + 2 side players (one on each flank)
Size of the field: Half field with two side flanks of 10 yards each and 2 neutral zones at the bases of 10 or 15 yards
Objectives: None
Touches permitted: 2
Rules: You have 5 passes to penetrate into the neutral zones in depth or to open up play on the flanks. 2 points for every penetration, 1 when you open up onto the flanks. One of the side players cannot touch the ball until the other has done so.
Variation: 1 point for the penetration, none for opening up onto the flanks.

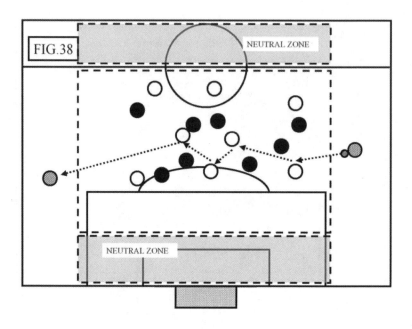

Exercise 7

Tactical attitude: Immediate build up
Specific aim: In depth play, speed of maneuvers, counterattacking
Nº of players: 7 + 7 plus 2 goalkeepers
Size of the field: Regular half field
Objectives: 2 goals
Touches permitted: 2
Rules: You must shoot within 5 passes
Variations: You must shoot within 5 seconds

Exercise 8 (Fig. 39)

Tactical attitude: Aggressiveness in defense and immediate build up
Specific aim: Ultra-offensive pressing and counterattacking
N° of players: 6 against 5 + goalkeeper
Size of the field: Regular half field
Objectives: 1 goal
Touches permitted: 2 or 3
Rules: The play is started off by the goalkeeper. The 5 players must bring the ball over the half way line, the other 6 must press and counterattack, shooting within 5 - 6 seconds.
Variation: You must verticalize after 3 passes so as to speed up play to the maximum.

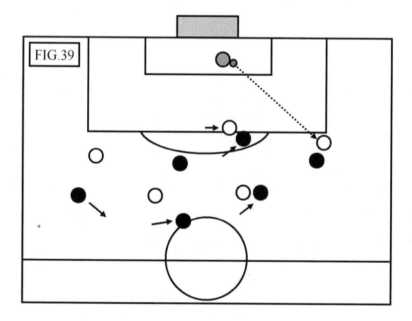

Exercise 9 (Fig. 40)

Tactical attitude: Aggressive defense, getting through pressing
Specific aim: Offensive pressing around the half way line, getting past pressing and counter pressing
Nº of players: 11 against 11
Size of the field: Regular field divided into three zones
Objectives: 2 goals
Touches permitted: No limits
Rules: Players setting up the action in the defense zone cannot be disturbed. All the players must wait in the central part of the field, in which the struggle between the players will take place. You must arrive to the attacking zone by getting past your opponents' pressing, ball on the ground (long passes are forbidden). Players who have arrived in the attacking zone cannot be contrasted but must shoot within 5 seconds.

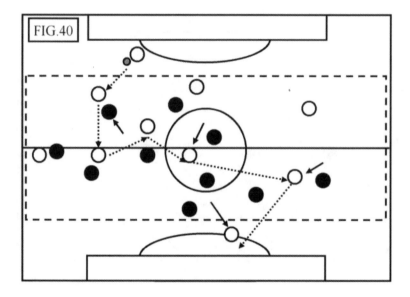

FIG.40

Exercise 10

Tactical attitude: Aggressive defense in our own half
Specific aim: Defensive pressing
Nº of players: 8 against 11
Size of the field: The defending half of the field
Objectives: 1 goal
Touches permitted: Free
Rules: The eight defenders must protect their goal using defensive pressing, doubling up, the defense elastic and offside tactics. They must pay special attention to shifting movements.
Play starts off from the attacking players or from the coach himself who gives them the ball.

Exercise 11 (Fig. 41)

Tactical attitude: Long counter attacks, getting away from the opponent's in depth pressing.
Nº of players: 8 against 8
Size of the field: Half field + a neutral zone of 10 yards
Objectives: None (even if the goalkeeper of the team directly connected in the exercise concerns starts off the action from his goal, it will not actually be in use).
Touches permitted: 2
Rules: The team in possession must get past the opponent's pressing and arrive in the neutral zone via a ground pass. No one is allowed to enter except by getting free of marking so as to receive the ball. The other team must apply constant pressing. One point for each time the attacking team reaches the neutral zone or carries out 10 consecutive passes. One point every time the defending team regains possession. Long passes are forbidden.
Variation: When the team in pressing regains possession they must set up a counter attack and shoot within 5 passes.

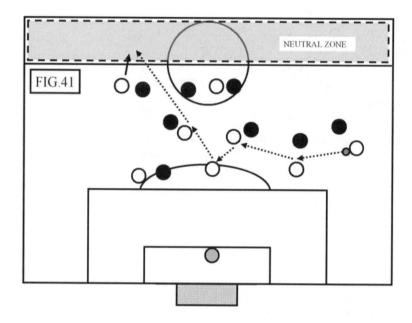

Having now given a list of the most significant tactical exercises to allow for a better development of the themes to put into effect during the match, we must now supply a couple of indications on how to prepare our team to face the opposing side.

Our players have to get past the opponent's defense system and face up to their typical attacking moves as well as possible, and so it is a good idea to prepare some training matches on regular-sized fields.

In these training matches our eleven starters will face eleven other players placed according to the system that the opponents will probably be using. These 'scout players' must also be asked to carry out movements typical of the team they are imitating both in offense and defense.

We must make sure that the eleven starters have to resolve tactical situations that they will find on the day of the match.

In this way the players will get to know their next opponents better, and they will have a clearer vision of what they will be called on to do during the match.

The first team must be trained in the following situations in particular:

- Getting past the pressing carried out by the opponents.
- Getting past offside tactics (if the opponent is applying them).
- Opposing the principal playing schemes applied by the rival team.
- Getting past the opponent's defense system by making adequate movements depending on whether they are using a zonal system or marking the man.
- Carrying out pressing, shifting moves and doubling up on the marking against the opponent's typical set up.

These training matches need not necessarily be fluid and uninterrupted. There is nothing wrong with stopping the play to show the players what mistakes they are making and to correct them. There is no point either in exaggerating the rhythm of play. The players must concentrate on the situations rather than on the intensity they will have to have during the match.
You must keep a careful eye on active and passive free kicks, following the ideas we have set out in the specific paragraph.
We must add that, since in training there should never be starters and reserves, there must be turn over between the eleven men included in the opponent's team, so that everyone can affront situations they will find during the match. Everybody must have the chance of playing in the 'picked' team during training.
You can if you want, but only in the last couple of training sessions, tell the team who will be starting and who will be the reserves for the up and coming match.
It is important, lastly, that the players carry out the exercises in an active way, concentrating to their limits as if they were really facing their next opponent.

MENTAL PREPARATIONS FOR THE MATCH

Mental preparations for the match are as important as tactical ones. As we have already said, psychology is vital to soccer. If a coach wants to have success he must also be something of a psychologist, which is not easy without knowing very much about the subject. In any case, you must know how to 'face' the group and you cannot always afford to behave in the same way. You must be authoritarian at times, permissive at others. There are moments when you have to criticize, others when it is better to encourage; sometimes you can praise your players and there are other occasions when you should be indifferent to them.

All this depends on the situation in which you find yourself, on the type of match you are facing and on the character of the single players. It is a mistake, in fact, to behave in the same way with the whole group: sometimes it is better to talk to the entire team, in others to turn to the individual player - always adopting a personal attitude.

The coach must act with great tact and in a rational way during the whole week, never improvising but always making programs concerning his daily attitudes down to the smallest detail.

Your concrete psychological preparation for the match comes about as a result of:

☐ Speaking to individuals and to the group
☐ Encouraging, praising and giving out to individuals and groups.
☐ Very good organization concerning training sessions

By speaking to the players - and you should prepare what you have to say in order to be persuasive - you will try to convince them that they must behave in a certain way - underlining the advantages of this behavior. Players often get carried away by unconscious emotions (it rarely happens that a player makes a determined effort not to concentrate on the game in hand), and we should base what we have to say on this.

Encouragement, praise and reprimands are very delicate measures from the point of view of behavior, and you must be very careful about when and if to use them, depending on the psychological state of the team and the character of each single player. If you think the team is not getting results because it is not putting enough into the match, then you must reprimand the players; if it is your impression that they are trying hard but just cannot manage to get results, then it is right to encourage them.

If the team is getting good results but these are not going to their heads, you should praise them, which is something you must not do if their good results are making them conceited.

It is the same when speaking to the single players.

You must also give the group the correct values of the sport (fair play, clean play, etc.) and a sense of responsibility towards their supporters and towards everyone's expectations. You must impress on your players a rigid sense of duty, so as to get as much as you can out of them.

Lastly, the careful preparation of the training sessions, their length and the difficulty and intensity of the exercises to be carried out are all things which will have a great influence on the team's 'mind'. Sometimes you will have to tighten the reins, at others let them go - that will depend on the psychological state of the team.

During the various sessions of the week, the coach must adopt the best approach possible in order to give the team all the psychological preparation they need.

The aim of the psychological preparation for the match is to make sure that the players' approach to the game is as good as can be managed. What we want is the following:

☐ The team must enter the field with concentration, determination, conviction and ready to give everything they have.
☐ Eliminate any possible states of anxiety and presumption.

The first thing is to create similar conditions during training sessions to those you will be seeing during the match. That means the players must get into the habit of facing the various training sessions as if they were playing a match - with concentration, determination, willpower and drive. Intensity must be the predominant element during training to keep the team under pressure and get them used to the rhythm that must be maintained during matches.

One of the biggest problems to resolve for a trainer is the gap between training and the match.

It can happen that a team gives its best in training, carrying out all that is required to perfection, but then does not succeed in doing the same during the match, building up high hopes and then letting everyone down.

That leads from the fact that the players are in the habit of facing the training sessions in a passive way, believing unconsciously that they are not so important on account of the difference between training and the match itself.

On the contrary, the players should get to a point where they consider the training sessions as the best means possible of presenting themselves at the match in full form.

Another connected element to keep in mind is the players' difficulty in really assimilating the movements required of them by the coach. It often happens that the playing schemes proposed during training sessions are carried out as asked, but then the players move as they see fit during the match. Why does this happen? The reason is quite simple: as we have already explained, the players are just not able to think calmly during the match situations, when they are being pressed by the opponents and under competitive tension - and they begin to move in whatever way comes natural to them. Clearly, too, their instinct tells them to move in an individual way and not as they have been required to do during training, and they will begin to rely on the actions of the single players, who will feel encouraged to keep the ball. But with the passing of time, if the coach is doing good work, it will come naturally to the players to move as they do in training.

To make sure that happens, the fundamental thing is to repeat the playing schemes and the general exercises. The coach must be as clear as possible in his various tactical 'lessons' as well as being good at correcting the mistakes that are being made.

Anxiety and presumption are particular states of mind that can precede the day of the match, created on the basis of the opponent's ability and the importance of the match itself.

As we have already explained, you get anxiety when the team does not think it is good enough for the next opponent or even for the next match (particularly if it is a final or a decisive match in the championship). In such cases, we get feelings of fear or negative tension that can compromise the result of the match.

Presumption on the other hand can come about when the team underestimates the difficulties because the players feel strong enough to defeat the next opponents without putting too much into it, or because they do not consider the match itself particularly important. In such cases, the players will enter the field without much concentration or determination, and when they realize that they have made a mistake it will be too late to resolve the situation.

Of these two psychological conditions, the first is undoubtedly the best, because you can in any case make the best of tension. Tension very often helps a team to find the right concentration and positive competitive drive.

What you have to eliminate from this psychological state is the fear, which is something that can block a team and end up by detracting from their play. You must tranquilize the players, getting them to concentrate on their potential and giving them the awareness that by playing to the top of their possibilities they are carrying out their duty in any case, and if the opponents end up by winning that is only fair. It is a healthy thing to 'know how to lose', and that in itself can be a great help in getting over any excessive anxiety and the fear you sometimes get in players, who will, at this point, become more courageous. You must convince your players of their capacity and that, thanks to the work they have been doing during training they will be able to face any opponent one to one.

To defeat their presumption, what you have to do is 'frighten' the players, talking to them about their opponent's qualities, maybe even magnifying them when they are really slight. As well as that, you must also make them understand the difficulties they will be meeting if they are defeated (above all as a result of a bad performance) - which will mean having thrown away the chance of getting points.

You must remind the players that the greatest enemy when facing a weaker opponent is of course presumption, because you must gain and deserve victory on the field. Their slogan should always be: 'conviction, not presumption'.

Another important thing connected with the psychological preparation for the match is that we must keep in mind the situation of the team.

If the players are going through a crisis we must try to give them encouragement. We must not insist too much on the mistakes that they are making but try to underline the good things they are doing, praising them whenever possible in order to build up their morale, without ever reprimanding, unless, of course, we notice that they are not giving enough effort.

It might be useful to show the team and the players pictures of their past moments of 'glory' in order to get out of the difficult period: great matches, wonderful goals, etc.

You must do everything in your power to make sure the team is not depressed.

If you are going through a positive period, you must be careful that they do not lose their heads, reminding them that you have acquired a winning mentality when you do not get too depressed in difficult situations, but also when you keep your feet on the ground in cases where things are going well.

You must not give them too much praise, insisting, rather, on correcting the mistakes they are making. You must keep reminding the group that the worst is yet to come, that what they have succeeded in doing until now is not enough and will be thrown to the four winds if they lose the next few matches. They must, therefore, take this as an occasion to double the work in training so that the players are not resting on their laurels.

The coach should give a good example, being the first to roll up his sleeves in the training session immediately after any victory.

Psychological preparation also regards the cohesion in the group in terms of the relationships between its various members.

Sometimes the team is united and everybody is working together, but it can also happen that you get internal tensions and the coach has to work in a difficult context. The first condition usually comes about when things are going well and the second when the team is not getting results.

When there is cohesion in the group, all you have to do is to keep things going that way.

When the atmosphere is not serene, you must firstly do all you can to bring the group together, trying to pinpoint and smooth over the internal conflicts.

The best medicine is to make sure the players see as much of each other as possible, because you get socialization when people share joy and distress.

If the situation is particularly serious, you will have to do something about it, picking out the members that are not liked and asking the club to send them away.

From this point of view, you might find it helpful to use those so called 'socio-metric' or 'sociogram' tests, in which, without comparing notes every member of the group must give a list of the team mates he likes and those he does not. These lists will help us make out a graph of the internal relationships in the locker room, and at that point we will understand the clans, factions and rivalries on which we can go to work in order to improve the situation.

In any case, the mental preparation for the match during the week must also include particular attention to the relationships in the group.

Lastly, when coaching a professional team you should consider the hypothesis of bringing the players to a secluded place in the days before the match. That will help them find the right concentration and the right competitive drive.

You can bring them away when:

☐ You have to play a very important match.
☐ The team is going through a moment of crisis.
☐ You want to tighten the relationships among the players.
☐ The team is not putting everything into the matches.

When you bring the team away on account of their bad results, you must tell the players that this is not a punishment. The period of seclusion must never have this character (except in cases where the players are not working hard), otherwise the players enter into conflict with the coach, and that would have more negative than positive results.

As we have already underlined, the psychological preparation for the match is an important thing. This kind of preparation should last right until the moments before the match. You can consider your match preparation over only when the game actually begins.

SELECTING THE TEAM

Those who know little about soccer, and in particular about the role of the coach, believe that his greatest responsibility and most important job is choosing the best team to put on the field.

Even those who are more expert think that selecting the best players for the team is one of the most important things a coach has to do. Entire TV programs are set up around the subject: 'if the coach had put on this player instead of that one ...', 'that coach is incompetent because he got the whole team wrong', 'that team won thanks to the ability of its coach in selecting the first eleven players', etc.

Clearly, the word 'if' doesn't make history, and it is entirely useless to put a coach under accusation after the facts because of the team he put on the field.

I am not trying to say that choosing the players is an unimportant task. On the contrary, selecting the players to send on the field is a job that must be carried out with intelligence. But there is no doubt, in my opinion, that, in comparison with the other duties of the coach, like looking after the general tactical organization of the team or preparing the match, selecting the side has only relative importance.

You could liken the duties of the coach to an iceberg, the greatest proportion of which is invisible to the eyes of the public. The tip of the iceberg is the choice of which players to put on the field and the coach's tactical moves during the match (the substitutions he makes) - and these are perfectly visible to the eyes of those that are interested.

The coach's real work - that which determines the performance of the team during the match - takes place during the day by day training sessions. The choice of the best side will have only a marginal effect on the performance of the team, just as it will make very little difference to the performance if his selection of the eleven players is not absolutely perfect.

It is clear, however, that a coach good at preparing his team is even better if he is able to choose his eleven men in a rational way.

Having said that, and in order to clear up the importance and the penetrating vision necessary to selecting the players for the side, we must give some indications and some advice about how to carry out this last task (in chronological order) connected with the preparation of the match.

The first thing to say is that the coach will often find himself faced with a real dilemma. As far as some of the roles are concerned there will be no doubts, but for others we will have to make a very tough choice based on the criteria that we are about to look at below. If everything goes well and the results are in line with the expectations, the coach will be described as a genius; if things go badly he will be accused of incompetence.

In choosing his side, and resolving his various doubts, the coach should keep in mind the following factors connected with his various players:

- ☐ Their integration in the play and in the schemes and their tactical ability.
- ☐ The work that they have shown during the week's training sessions.
- ☐ Their physical and athletic condition and their state of fitness.
- ☐ Their mental state.
- ☐ If they are suitable for the match to be played.
- ☐ Their technical ability.

In soccer, time and space are two fundamental specifics, and when you are deciding which players to send onto the field it is very important to keep in mind the players' integration in the play and in the schemes. It is better to bet on a player who is less flashy but who has assimilated the things that have been asked of him, rather than on one who is very gifted individually but who is still playing in an 'anarchical' way. This is connected with the fact that the tactical ability of the single player must always take first place, even with respect to the wonderful technical ability of the single player who shows that he has not integrated himself into the mechanisms of the team, but still appears an extraneous body.

The effort put into things is an important criteria in carrying out the arduous job of choosing the side. Only those who are working hard deserve to represent their team, guaranteeing the same application also during the match. It would never be right for a player who has shown little effort during training - even the public love him - to go onto the field in the place of another who has given all he has got during the week, even if he is not so famous. The players' physical and athletic condition determines their physical fitness. It is clear that the fittest players of the moment (and this will be determined by the most recent matches and the training sessions carried out during the last week) deserve to play the match because they guarantee greater results. This becomes even more important towards the end of the season, when the players do not generally have much energy left, and whoever still has should be put on the side without considering other factors.

It is the same thing for the mental state of the players: whoever is going through a positive moment and is therefore in a state of great confidence (as the result, for example, of having played great matches in the recent past) must be put before the others, above all those who are in a state of personal crisis. Again, all this is over and above any considerations about individual technical ability.

Suitability to the characteristics of the match to be played is another thing to be considered, even if it has minor importance to the other factors we have been looking at.

If we have to play a very important and difficult match it is better to put the 'older' players on the side. They will have more experience than the younger ones, who will likely be unprepared to face similar situations.

Suitability can also influence our choices from the tactical and technical point of view.

If we have to play a match in which it will be difficult to get a firm hold on the play, it might be a good idea to put on quick strikers in order to make the best of our counter attacks.

If the opponents have attacking players good at aerial play, it is only logical to consider putting on a defender who is better able to contrast this type of play.

These are only two examples to show how technical and tactical suitability can play an important role in choosing the side you will be using. Of course, there are innumerable others.

To conclude, also the individual's technical ability is a criteria to be considered in selecting the first eleven. However, this last case is something you should think about only when, after analyzing all the other factors, you are still in doubt about who to send on the field.

The problem at this point is how to integrate all these criteria.

And which of them should we consider most important?

The first thing is to make out a list of the players that correspond to the various requirements. Then the coach should numerate them in order of importance on the basis of his own personal convictions.

My own view is that the first four in the list are the most important and that they are more or less on the same level, the first two having perhaps a slight pre-eminence.

At this point your 'scientific' operation should follow on with the definitive choice of the first eleven and also of the reserves to be put on the bench - and again you will still be basing yourself in relation to the two lists we have spoken about. In cases where there is a 'ballot' between players you must consider the list if criteria, in order, until, if the situation demands it, you must decide on the basis of their individual technical quality. The various criteria must then be integrated as much as possible, keeping them all in consideration as if they were a united whole.

It is, as you will see, a complicated operation to be carried out in a rational way.

It is important to add that in choosing his team, the coach must not allow himself to be conditioned by anybody: players, club managers, fans, critics, journalists, etc.

A charismatic coach who wants to be successful must go through with his own ideas, courageously taking sole responsibility for his choices.

When all is said and done, it is better to have picked the team all wrong using your own head rather than that of another, because in that case your feelings of remorse will be even stronger.

You must also make sure that there are not eleven fixed first choice players: in general there should never be players whose place is guaranteed whatever happens. You must make sure that all the players are first choices during the course of training sessions because that will give them the incentive to face the week's program and it will also eliminate hierarchies of players within the group.

The coach should only make his choice for the match at the end of the week, and the players must know that if they want to be on the side they must earn their place.

The concept of turnover is connected with this. You must be sure to use continuous turnover so as to be in a position to line up the best side possible at every moment and also to dose out the energy of the group. Turnover will be fully used during the final months of the championship, and it is particularly important if the team is involved in several different competitions and must therefore play a large number of matches throughout the season. The basic idea is different players, selected according to the criteria we have already seen, will be playing in different matches but the essential playing plan will remain fixed and unchangeable.

However, players with particular experience, charisma and ability in guiding the group should be in a privileged position from this point of view and could even be exempted in some cases from turnover. Also the goalkeeper should be exempted from turnover because too much competition in his role can create tension. In order to perform as well as possible the goalkeeper must be confident and calm.

The selection should be communicated the day of the match if you want everybody to give their best until the last moment.
Of course, those who have not been lined up will not be happy and might even get depressed, and the coach must encourage these players reminding them that next week they will be able to earn their place by their effort, application in their work and perseverance.
Turnover is something that will guarantee equal opportunities for all the players and simplify this delicate task of 'consoling'.
In any case, a player who does not begin the match as one of the first eleven must know that he may be called on at any moment of the match, and that his contribution could be a determining factor.

When you have communicated the side, the match will begin. Now is the moment when we will see how good our work has been.

CHAPTER 9

THE ANALYSIS OF THE MATCH

By the time the match begins, the coach has carried out most of his duties, and it will be the game to decide whether his work has born fruit (both in terms of the general organization given to the team and as regards the preparation for the match itself).

Once again, the coach's task, visible to the public during the competition - inciting the team and calling them to order, carrying out variations, tactical corrections and above all substitutions of players - are part of that tip of the iceberg that we spoke of in connection with the choice of the side to send onto the field.

People who are not in the know wrongly judge the expertise of a coach basing themselves principally on these elements.

YOUR ATTITUDE ON THE BENCH

An important characteristic to bear in mind is the coach's attitude during the match.

Every coach assumes a different attitude, depending on how great an effect he thinks he can still have on the performance of his team. There are two attitudes he can take.

On one side, there are those coaches who are up in arms for the whole length of the match, convinced that in this way they can have a positive influence on how their team is playing: they give advice to their players, reprimand them, incite them, etc.

Sometimes they enter so much into the competitive climate of the match that they go so far as to attack the referee verbally, and consequently get sent off.

At the other extreme are those coaches who just sit quietly for the whole match as if they were any other spectator, limiting their communication with the players to the minimum. Naturally, they behave like this because they are convinced that they can have no effect on their team's performance and they want to concentrate on what is happening on the field.

These are two extremes, and there are, of course, many intermediate positions between them. There are coaches who speak, but only to give advice to their players, and there are those who only get off the bench to correct a player in difficulty and to give new tactical indications to the team, etc.

In my view, a coach must do all he can to improve his team's performance during the match, making the best use of the little improvements that can come about in the players thanks to the support of the trainer. In any case, everything you do must be carried out in full consciousness that most of the coach's duties have already been put into effect during the preparatory training sessions of the week before.

If we can call the training session during the week the 'laboratory', then the match is a 'test' of all that we have created. The coach must take his place on the bench with the right composure coming from the idea that 'what you put into things is what you get out of them'.

However, during the match the coach can have an effect both on the tactical side - by making changes if they are necessary - and from a psychological point of view, by giving support to the players, inciting them on, criticizing, etc.

It is particularly from the psychological point of view that the coach can and must manage his team during the match, above all in those moments of difficulty which, unfortunately, very often come about as the ninety minutes are going by.

What we have said about the preparation of a match holds true from the tactical point of view as well: any changes that are made can regard only the 'details' of the team, not the 'basic structures that hold it up'.

So the coach will not be able to have a great effect from the tactical point of view. He will have to concentrate on whether the opposing team is placed on the field and is playing in the way he had foreseen, and whether the tactical countermoves adopted for the match are really suitable.

He must be ready, therefore, to apply any of those tactical corrections that his analysis of the match in real time will make him think are necessary.

In order to be in a position to help his players and have an effect on his team's performance during a match, the coach must behave in a rational and reasonable way. It is important that he makes his presence felt on his players so that they do not have the impression of being alone, but also to make sure that they do not get too relaxed and lose concentration, which is something that can happen when he does not have an active attitude. He must also transmit to his players the right competitive drive, seeing to it that they do not rest on their laurels if everything is going well, and that they are not getting depressed if they are losing. You must not exaggerate in spurring on your players. Hassling them with continuous directives in the attempt almost to 'radio command' them will never give positive results because the players risk losing their nerve, getting irritated and, in any case, getting through the match in a stressful way leading to the so called 'fear of making mistakes'.

It is much more productive - and will enable you to improve individual performances in all the various aspects (tactical, technical, etc.) - if you correct their errors in real time without assuming an irritated outlook, but always using a calm, paternal tone of voice and approach so as to encourage them and influence them in a positive way.

Another thing to remember is that your attitude towards the players should be different depending on the character of each one:

- ☐ Encourage those that are putting a lot into play but are making mistakes, unable to express themselves to the top of their potential perhaps on account of the tension.
- ☐ Reprimand those who are playing badly because they are not putting enough effort into the match.
- ☐ Praise and commend those who are playing well but have little confidence in themselves and in their ability.
- ☐ Do not show too much approval to those who are playing well when you know that things tend to go to their heads and they might become complacent. In any case, tell them to keep it up.

To conclude this general treatment on the role and the behavior of the coach on the bench, it must also be pointed out that he should be a positive example to his players and also to the public. He should moderate his language, must never insult the players of the opposing team or even worse the referee or the linesmen (or the fourth man), and his behavior should reflect sportsmanship and fair play at all times.

It is not easy for a coach to observe a match played by his team. There are great differences between looking at such a match and watching one played by another team, or following a game on a video cassette.

First of all, the bench is by no means the best place from which to watch a match and observe the tactical behavior of the two teams. In fact you cannot see the movements of the players very clearly from the sidelines, and the perspective you have of the playing field is imprecise and deceptive both in terms of width and depth. You can get the best vision of play from the grandstand, where you can see and understand the layout of the two teams and the movements of the players with the utmost clarity (above all from the stands behind the two goals you get a perfect in depth prospective of the playing field and therefore of the two teams, catching at a glance also the shifting movements and the horizontal motion of the ball).

Another difference between watching the match on a videocassette is that you cannot stop and rewind and have another look at a single play. So it is difficult to bring out all the tactical implications connected with the various plays in real time.

Lastly, and this is an important factor, it is very difficult for a coach to follow his own team and its single players with attention, while at the same time observing the opposing team so as to confirm or vary his own tactical set up.

The more one-sided you are, the more you tend to neglect the opposing team, concentrating on your own. This is true above all for the all-out supporters: at the end of the match, for example, a fan may not even know who has been playing on the rival team. A coach who is not very good at following his match could risk doing the same.

In order to watch the match in the right way, the coach should behave as follows, which will help him resolve the three problems we have just set forth.

There is not much that can be done about the positions on the field. Deciding to go and follow the match from the grandstand would be the wrong move all along the line. The advantage of having the perfect vision of the match would be completely annulled by the extremely negative fact of not being able to guarantee the necessary psychological support to your players.

Coaches are often tempted to follow a match from the stands instead of from the bench, but their rationality gets the better of that idea and such situations never come about.

It might be useful, if you have the chance, to send one of your collaborators to follow the match from the stands, and then to consult with him during half time in the hope of getting whatever tactical indications you have not been able to pick up yourself from the bench.

It is very useful, if you want to make the best of your observation of the match as it is being played, to equip yourself with a note-book on which you will take down everything that appears to be of interest, including the mistakes made by your players.

Using notes will also help you to resolve a problem we have already mentioned: the difficulty in viewing the opposing team and the various tactical implications arising from the actions of play. Noting down what you see in real time permits you to rationalize your ideas and sensations, above all when a lot is going on and your memory does not allow you to keep them all in mind.

It is a good idea, however, to ask a collaborator to carry out this particular task of writing down on paper everything you notice. It is useful to take notes, but in order to do so you have to cut yourself of for a moment from the match, concentrating more on the words you are writing than on what you are watching. The final result of this operation could therefore be negative if it is carried out by the coach in person.

It is better, then, if the coach dictates out loud to his collaborator all that he notices from the tactical and technical point of view (both in their collective and their individual aspects), above all concerning the opposing team, but also his own. It is important, in fact, to note down all the mistakes made by our players so as to be in a position to explain things later, and you should also record any other tactical considerations that might be useful as the match goes on or for future games.

We can also say that dictating what he sees on the field out loud will help the coach to concentrate, allowing him to pinpoint each playing action in all its detail.

In order to resolve the problem of his difficulty in following the rival team, it is important for the coach to decide how he should behave even before the match kicks off. A coach must follow his own team with great attention, at the same time keeping an eye on the opponent's behavior, on their movements and their placement on the field. This must come about both in collective terms (following the opposing team as a whole) and from an individual point of view (following the performance of the single players).

A coach needs to be able instantly to catch the significant elements regarding the opponent's actions, maybe even trusting to his personal hunches.

In any case, the coach must not limit himself to looking at the good and bad points of his own team as they carry out the various playing schemes, but he must also consider how the strengths and weaknesses of the rival team have influenced those same plays.

For example, the moment the opponents score a goal, we must not only 'see' the mistakes and any ingenuity committed by our defense, but also the individual and / or collective ability of our rivals in this situation.

The coach must try as hard as he can to watch the match with 'open' vision. The fans' vision can afford to be 'closed' but the coach must keep in mind the highest number of factors possible, also making use of the help of his collaborators.

To end our treatment on how to observe a match, we must make sure to get hold of all appropriate material concerning our team's match so that we can study it carefully when the game is over. In order to prepare next week's match and to correct any mistakes that have been made, it is important for the trainer to study the match that has just concluded with care and tranquillity. In order to make that possible it is to be hoped that the resources of the club will permit you to get hold of a videocassette of the match. Otherwise the report made by the collaborator who has been sent to the grandstand will come in handy. During the match itself he will be able to help only during the half time break, but his chance of looking at the play from a favorable position will come in very handy when the match is over.

We will now have a look at the analysis of the match that the coach should be carrying out moment by moment. This analysis must concern every aspect, tactical, technical, physical and psychological of the two teams on the field, both during the defense and the attacking phase, both from an individual and a collective point of view. The factors are practically the same as those that we have been looking at in the preceding chapters, so there is no point in going into them over again and we refer you back to all that has already been written.

In order to make a suitable 'reading' of the match so as to carry out the necessary tactical corrections or to take provisions of any sort, the coach must keep all these elements in mind for the whole length of the game.

The coach must always be at the center of things, keeping a permanent monitor on the attitudes of the two teams on the field from all the angles that we have already analyzed.

You must never let your attention wander from how the match is going. It can often happen that the tactical situation of a match changes and the coach does not notice because he has convinced himself that he has interpreted the play in the right way. We must always be prepared to change the idea we have made for ourselves about how the match is going, ready at all times to intervene if need be.

This does not mean that the coach must completely transform the team's identity if the match is going badly, but you must always be sharp in order to those little but significant adjustments to the set up of the team that can then straighten out the result of the game.

It is not easy to analyze a match in real time because the coach, especially if he does not have much experience or is without this specific ability, does not have much time to think about what is happening on the field in a rational way. Sometimes the coach is concentrating so hard on the match itself that he neglects to decide what he should do in order to help his own team.

All we can say is that a good coach must follow his team and at the same time promptly put in act his tactical ideas concerning what he sees.

It is useful to consult your collaborators as often as possible concerning the analysis of the match because your reasoning will always be more constructive if it comes about through dialogue with a person that you trust. Thus, you can see things that had escaped your notice or look at considerations that are different from your own, but which may be interesting.

Very often your decision to behave in a certain way towards the team is based on the analysis you make during the match. This could be of a tactical nature, our could limit itself to giving advice to the players.

From the tactical point of view, these changes should above all be in connection with any countermoves that have already been established during the week, and never concern the general set up of the team, except in extreme cases.

We will now enter into the subject in question starting off with our analysis of the rival team.

HOW IS THE RIVAL TEAM PLAYING

In this phase of the coach's job, it is very important for him to make an analysis of the opposing team. Even if our studies of the previous week have been very carefully carried out, the opponent might still present itself on the field with unexpected variations. These modifications may be more or less significant, but in any case we must get to grips with them at once so as to decide if it is necessary to intervene on our own team.

The divergence between what we were expecting of our opponent and what is actually happening on the field could be due to:

☐ Mistaken evaluations concerning the opponent's characteristics in the studies we have carried out during the week leading up to the match.

☐ Our studies were correct but we have made a mistake concerning the opponent's possible adaptation to our own system.

☐ The coach of the rival team has decided to 'play his cards in a different way', going onto the field with a different set up or even different players. He might have decided to do this in order to take us by surprise or simply because, after a series of negative performances, he feels the need to change the tactical organization of the team.

In the first case, the coach can only blame himself for making mistakes in analysis which could turn out more or less momentous.

In the second case, the coach has less responsibility because it is by no means easy to enter into the head of his rival colleague, sensing when and how he will adapt his team to our own characteristics.

In the third case, it is not the coach's fault, in that the ability to foresee the future is not a human power. The opponents can sometimes put players unknown to us on his team, who we have not seen in the matches that we have been watching. The presence of such players can be an ugly surprise, especially if they are gifted with great technical ability, in dribbling for example.

In all three cases, however, we must do all we can to make sure that these surprises are managed in the best way possible.

Consequent to what we have set out above, as soon as the match kicks off the coach must immediately get to grips with any divergence there is between the opponent's actual tactical set up and the one that he has foreseen. All through the match he must be on the lookout for any changes there might be in this sense. Above all when the rival coach carries out a substitution, it is a good thing to think immediately if and how this will change the tactical set up of the team, the way they build up their play and the way they try and destroy our own. These changes in the two phases of play must be put into effect when the adversary is in difficulty, and we must keep an eye on the rival coach's moves when that is happening.

With the help of the following complete and sweeping table, we will now be setting out all the tactical, technical, psychological and athletic factors relative to the opposing team which must be evaluated by the coach. We will also give a brief indication in the table concerning the effects these elements can have on our own behavior. It must be clear that these things will have an effect only in cases where the elements taken into consideration give a different result from that which we forecast before the match, or if things have changed during the game itself.

ELEMENTS TO EVALUATE	DESCRIPTION	EFFECT ON OUR TEAM AND POSSIBLE CONSEQUENT BEHAVIOR
GENERAL ATTITUDE	OFFENSIVE / DEFENSIVE	If it is offensive, tell the team to reposition themselves immediately they lose possession, remaining compact and trying to get back control of play. If necessary, they can keep one extra player in preventive coverage when they are in attack. If it is defensive, they can attack with more men, give greater variation to the attacking solutions, be quicker with ball circulation, get in behind the defense by using the flanks, try shooting from far out.
PLAYING SYSTEM	VARIATION IN THE SET UP DURING ONE OR BOTH PHASES	If the variations regard the set up in the defense phase, give new indications to the team concerning the playing schemes to use most often. If they are connected with the set up in the attacking phase, give new indications about the doubling up of marking, pressing and the shifting mechanisms. Have a good look at the numerical situation in all parts of the field, being careful to make the best of those that are favorable to us, and find a remedy for those that are unfavorable (by using suitable shifting movements.
LINE FROM WHICH TO START PRESSING	ULTRA-OFFENSIVE, OFFENSIVE OR DEFENSIVE PRESSING	If it is ultra-offensive pressing, ask the mid field to furnish escape routs to the defense, who should not hesitate to kick the ball ahead if they are in trouble. If it is offensive pressing, carry out continuous changes of play and move around without the ball. If it is defensive pressing, see what has already been said regarding the defensive attitude.

BUILD UP MODE AND FINISHING OFF TECHNIQUES USED	EVALUATING HOW THE OPPONENT BUILDS UP PLAY AND HOW HE FINISHES OFF	If it is elaborate build up, close off the spaces, mark the players without the ball and press the one in possession. If it is immediate build up tell the defense to carry out the elastic correctly and the rest of the team to get back into position as soon as possible. For finishing touch techniques, see the relative paragraph.
DEFENSE SYSTEM	SEEING WHETHER THE DEFENSE SYSTEM USED BY THE OPPONENT (ZONAL, MAN OR MIXED) IS THE REALLY WHAT WE WERE EXPECTING	If our opponents are using a different defense system from the one we were expecting, give team the indications and advice connected with the behavior to use in order to get by - that which we have already seen in the related paragraph.
MOVEMENTS AND PARTICULAR PLAYING SCHEMES YOU WERE NOT EXPECTING	BOTH IN DEFENSE (e.g., OFFSIDE TACTICS) OR IN ATTACK (e.g., LONG PASSES)	Give specific indications to the team about how to oppose these playing schemes. See the paragraphs concerning how to oppose any defensive and offensive schemes that can be carried out by a team.
SITUATIONS AND ZONES OF THE FIELD IN WHICH THE OPPONENT IS HAVING TROUBLE	FOR EXAMPLE WITH VERTICAL PASSES, OR ON ONE OF THE FLANKS	Ask your team to insist with the right play to make the best of the opponent's difficulties and weaknesses (as we have already seen). Insist with the flank that is creating more problems for the adversaries.

INACTIVE BALLS	BEHAVIOR IN CONNECTION WITH ACTIVE AND PASSIVE INACTIVE BALLS	On passive inactive balls make sure you are in numerical superiority; otherwise ask one or two strikers to move back. Give your players indications on how to oppose themselves to the specific rival playing schemes. On active inactive balls, see if it is all right to bring a greater number of players into depth (depending on how dangerous the opponent's counter attacks really are.) or to change our specific playing schemes.
APPROACH AND STATE OF MIND DURING THE MATCH	DETERMINATION, CONVICTION, ANXIETY, TENSION, TRANQUILLITY, LACK OF EFFORT, ETC.	If the opponent's approach is positive, tell the team to keep up their concentration. If their approach is negative, ask the team to make the best use possible of this favorable situation for us by increasing our own determination, rhythm and intensity of play.
PLAYERS IN FORM AND IN DIFFICULTY	PLAYERS ON A GOOD DAY CREATING PROBLEMS FOR US AND PLAYERS WHO ARE IN PSYCHOLOGICAL DIFFICULTY	Attacking players in form: create specific doubling up on marking. Defense players in form: tell the strikers not to insist on keeping the ball and not to exaggerate with useless personal play. Attacking players in difficulty: tell our defenders to be more aggressive with them, carrying out invited pressing if possible. Defense players in difficulty: try even harder to play and bring the ball into their zone.
PLAYERS GOOD AT DRIBBLING	TAKEN BY SURPRISE BY PLAYERS UNKNOWN TO US WHO ARE GOOD AT GETTING PAST THE MAN	Create adequate doubling up on marking, telling the defenders to play for time until the team mate arrives to double up (or in any case if we are not covered).

SOURCE OF PLAY	WHICH PLAYER DO THE OPPONENTS DEPEND ON MOST IN THE ATTACKING PHASE?	Ask the team to put him constantly under pressure as soon as he gets the ball.
PLAYERS GOOD AT AERIAL PLAY	TAKEN BY SURPRISE BY PLAYERS WHO ARE GOOD WITH THEIR HEADS; OR IF YOU NOTICE THAT OUR PLAYERS ARE NOT UP TO HIM	Attacking players good with their heads: tell our defenders not to go and jump on long passes or when the opponents put the ball back into play, but to tighten up the marking on crosses. Defense players good with their heads: do not carry out long passes and cut down on crosses from the base line.
FAST AND ATHLETIC PLAYERS	TAKEN BY SURPRISE BY FAST PLAYERS WHO CAN PUT OUR DEFENDERS IN DIFFICULTY OR MAKE OUR STRIKERS LOSE EFFECTIVENESS	Fast attacking players: tell our defenders not to mark them too tightly, giving them a meter or two. Deeper diagonals. Carry out exchanges of position in defense, so that their fastest element meets our fastest defender. Fast defense players: place our best attacking player with his head in the zone of their fastest defender and move our fastest striker in the zone of their slowest defender.
GENERAL PHYSICAL AND ATHLETIC CONDITION	PHYSICAL STAMINA OF THE OPPOSING PLAYERS	If the opposing players are in good physical condition: keep control of our own energy without playing at a rhythm that is too high in order to be able to take the heat in the long run. If the opponents are in bad physical condition: press them with even more determination and keep the rhythm of play even higher.

In this table we have once again presented elements regarding the opposing team that we have already had a look at, omitting those that are not reasonably to be expected while the match is being played. As you can see, for every factor we have simply suggested the counter measures that we already spoke about before. For further details we refer you back to the longer paragraphs where each subject is given more in-depth treatment.

THE BEHAVIOR OF OUR OWN TEAM

It is of course important to analyze the possible variations of every kind present in the rival team in order to make whatever changes might be necessary - but evaluating the performance of our own players is even more important.

There is no point at all in following our rival team's attitude with care and attention, if our own team is playing in a negative way. Above all, then, the coach must make sure that his own team is playing as he wants and that the players are carrying out the countermeasures decided on during the week's preparation of the match.

As we will see, it is important to see to it that the team is playing both phases without meeting difficulty. As far as the attacking phase is concerned, the maneuvers must be fast, fluid, effective, varied (above all in connection with finishing touches) and unpredictable and build up must be going in the way we planned in training - that is, with the correct, continuous and coordinated use of collective movements without the ball. We must make sure the team is playing short and tight in the defense phase, that they are compact; that they are getting positive results from their pressing in various parts of the field (and that they are coming out on top in a great number of contrasts); and above all that they are not suffering under the pressure of the opponent's playing schemes and / or their personal plays. It is particularly important to look for any possible situations of numerical inferiority that we might be undergoing in important parts of the field.

To check on our correct implementation of the two principle phases of play (keeping an eye also on the transition phase), you must bear in mind the most important connected aims: to score as many goals as possible in the possession phase, or at least to create occasions for scoring; and, in the defense phase, to destroy the opponent's play, regaining possession, and trying in that way not to take goals.

Pinpointing the factors that do not permit the correct achievement of these aims is, of course, fundamental to resolving the problems.

Once again, what we are looking for, this time in connection with our own team, are the tactical, technical, athletic and psychological elements already seen above. These factors must also regard both the collective and the individual aspects of the team.

It is very important, therefore, to monitor things for the whole course of the match, and not only the tactical behavior of the team, but also the mental state of the players and their physical condition.

These are the aspects that very often convince a trainer to carry out variations, substituting the first choice players with reserves above all in the second half.

Aspects regarding the state of our own team are the principle cause of the changes made by a coach, rather than those connected with the opponents.

What the coach will be thinking of as he analyzes his team is their response to the work carried out until that moment, both in terms of the general organization of play and in those of our preparation of the match.

If the team is playing the match in the way the coach had hoped, then he will have no problems, but only a sense of satisfaction. If the team is behaving in a negative way, the coach's disappointment could be so great as to convince him to make some over-hasty or irrational move. In cases like this you must not lose your head, carrying out only those modifications or adjustments that are really considered necessary, keeping a check on your negative feeling about your players, who, already in psychological difficulty, would then have to face a very complicated situation.

In the following table, we will be looking at all the questions a coach should be asking himself related to the behavior of his team from different points of view. Every question can have various different replies, and we will be looking at the implications of these in terms of the possible moves the coach could make and the advice he could give.

QUESTIONS TO ASK YOURSELF	DESCRIPTION	POSSIBLE REACTIONS
HAS THE TEAM GONE ONTO THE FIELD WITH THE RIGHT MENTAL APPROACH?	EVALUATE THE PSYCHOLOGICAL STATE OF THE TEAM AS IT GOES ON THE FIELD: CONVICTION, CONCENTRATION, EFFORT, TRANQUILLITY, TENSION, FEAR	If their attitude is positive tell them to keep it up without changing their mental state. If it is negative, criticize the team (if they are not concentrating or not making much effort) or encourage them (if they are tense).
WHAT IS THE TEAM'S TYPICAL STATE OF MIND DURING THE MATCH?	EVALUATING THE PSY-CHOLOGICAL STATE OF THE TEAM IN THE VARIOUS MOMENTS OF THE MATCH. THIS WILL DEPEND ABOVE ALL ON THE ONGOING RESULT AND ON HOW WE ARE PLAYING	Those seen in the previous point. You must also pick out any single players creating possible negative attitudes in the team (tension, fear, depression, irritability, resignation, etc.), and consider substituting them with other fresher or mentally calmer players.
IS THE TEAM HAVING GENERAL PROBLEMS IN BUILDING UP PLAY?	SEE IF THEY ARE BUILDING UP IN THE WAY WE WISHED (SPEED, MAKING THE MOST OF WIDTH AND DEPTH, VARIATIONS, ETC.), AND IF THEY ARE GETTING PAST THE DEFENSIVE OPPOSITION	If there are any problems, indicate what mistakes are being made and what needs to be done. Reprimand those players that seem to be the cause of this lack of success, perhaps substituting them if we are already in the second half.

ARE WE MANAGING TO CONSOLIDATE THE SITUATION WHEN WE REGAIN POSSESSION, AND ARE WE IMMEDIATELY SETTING UP GOOD COUNTER ATTACKS FROM THE ZONE WHERE WE GET BACK THE BALL, OVERTURN-ING THE SITUATION?	EVALUATE THE EFFEC-TIVENESS OF OUR POST-CONQUEST PHASE, AND IN GENER-AL THE PHASE OF ACTIVE TRANSITION. THE TEAM MUST BE USING SHORT COUNTER ATTACKS WHEN REGAINING POSSESSION IN THE RIVAL'S HALF, AND MUST BE GOOD AT DECIDING WHETHER TO CARRY OUT IMME-DIATE OR ELABORATE COUNTER ATTACKS WHEN THEY REGAIN THE BALL IN THEIR OWN HALF	If there are any problems, remind the team how they are to behave in such situations, making sure that they are aware of the mistakes being made. .Tell the players to go and meet the player in pos-session rather than looking for the ball by going into depth. Consider whether or not to put on a striker who is good at keeping possession by himself and at bringing up the team
IS THE OPPONENT'S PRESSING CREATING PROBLEMS FOR US, ABOVE ALL WHEN WE ARE IN OUR OWN HALF?	HAVE A LOOK AT OUR ABILITY TO GET FREE OF THE OPPONENT'S PRESSING IN THE VAR-IOUS ZONES OF THE FIELD. ARE WE BEHAV-ING IN THE RIGHT WAY IN ORDER TO BE IN A POSITION TO BUILD UP OUR OWN PLAY	If we are in trouble, tell the team to make more frequent changes of play, so giving greater opportunities to the player in possession. When he is in trouble he should make more use of vertical passes to the strikers.
ARE WE HAVING MORE PROBLEMS WITH MANEUVERED ACTIONS OR AGAINST IMMEDIATE COUNTER ATTACKS?	SEE WHETHER THE OPPONENTS ARE PUTTING US IN GREATER DIFFICULTY BY CIRCULATING THE BALL HORIZONTALLY, SO INVOLVING A HIGH NUMBER OF PLAYERS, OR BY MAKING FAST AND PENETRATING VERTICAL PLAYS OVERTURNING THE ACTION	Give the team all the neces-sary recommendations and tactical advice relative to the opponent's way of building up play especially when that is creating the problem. For this, refer back to what was said in the specific paragraph of chapter 3.

IN THE TWO PHASES, IS THE TEAM MANAGING TO KEEP SHORT AND COMPACT SO THAT THE PLAYERS ARE ABLE TO HELP EACH OTHER AND TO CREATE NUMERICAL SUPERIORITY AGAINST THE OPPONENTS IN THE VARIOUS PARTS OF THE FIELD?	KEEP ON THE LOOK-OUT WHETHER THE PLAYERS ARE MAINTAINING THE DISTANCES FROM THEIR TEAM MATES WITH WHOM THEY SHOULD BE MOVING WITH THE RIGHT TIMING. IT IS ABOVE ALL DURING THE SECOND HALF THAT YOU WILL FIND THAT THE TEAM IS GETTING LONGER AND MORE DISUNITED, AND YOU MUST UNDERSTAND THE REASON WHY.	If the team tends to get disunited, keep telling them to coalesce. Tell them not to make the mistakes that tend to lengthen out the team, like using long passes for example, the fact that the strikers are not participating in the defense phase or the defenders in the attacking phase, the inability of the defense to keep their distance from the mid field by carrying out the elastic and offside tactics. If physical and / or mental problems are the cause of these difficulties, you should make substitutions.
ARE OUR DEFENSIVE PRESSING AND OFF-SIDE WORKING AS WELL AS THEY SHOULD BE? ARE WE DOUBLING UP ON MARKING? IS THERE THE RIGHT BALANCE BETWEEN OUR COVERAGE OF THE ZONES AND OUR MARKING OF THE MEN? ARE OUR SHIFTING MECHANISMS WORKING CORRECTLY (PARTICULARLY THOSE OF RECIPROCAL COVERING) AND ARE WE COMING OUT ON TOP IN OUR CONTRASTS?	SPECIFICS CONCERNING THE DEFENSE PHASE AND IN PARTICULAR IN DEPTH PRESSING AND OFFSIDE, WHICH SERIOUSLY COMPROMISE THE RESULT IF APPLIED BADLY. PROOF THAT WE ARE CARRYING OUT THE DEFENSE PHASE CORRECTLY IS IN THE NUMBER OF BALLS RECOVERED AND SO IN THE CONTRASTING PLAYS WON BY US (AS WELL AS IN THE NUMBER OF GOALS WE TAKE).	In cases where there are problems in our defense phase, try to resolve them by reminding the team and the single players how they should be moving in the various situations. When we have in depth pressing or offside being used badly, tell them to bring down the line where they go into pressing to the mid field and not to use offside. If we are at the end of a match and are having more problems than we should be because of these defensive errors, put on a more expert defender in the place of the one who is in difficulty (or a central mid fielder better at playing the defense phase in the place of one who is more undisciplined from this point of view).

GENERALLY SPEAKING, FROM THE COLLECTIVE POINT OF VIEW, IS PLAY BASED ON INCESSANT MOVEMENTS WITHOUT THE BALL OR IS THERE A TENDENCY TO RELY ON IMPROVISATIONS MADE BY THE PLAYER IN POSSESSION?	SEE IF THE TEAM IS BUILDING UP PLAY ON THE PRINCIPLE OF A PASS FOLLOWING ON A COLLECTIVE MOVEMENT TO FREE PLAYERS OF MARKING, OR IS THE PLAYER IN POSSESSION LOOKING FOR AN INDIVIDUAL SOLUTION WHILE THOSE WITHOUT THE BALL WAIT FOR THEIR TURN TO PUT THEMSELVES IN VIEW?	If things are going well, tell the team to keep it up. In cases where the team is not behaving as you wish, perhaps even from a particular moment of the match, tell them to get back in line, above all those players that are the principle cause, who should be substituted if they continue in this way.
IS THE TEAM RESPECTING THE GENERAL TACTICAL AND STRATEGIC OUTLINES THEY WERE GIVEN AND THE COUNTERMOVES THAT HAVE BEEN CHOSEN FOR THIS MATCH?	ASSESS WHETHER THE TEAM IS MOVING IN SUCH A WAY AS TO FOLLOW GENERAL STRATEGY AND TACTICS THAT SHOULD CHARACTERIZE PLAY. IS THE TEAM BEHAVING IN THE WAY ESTABLISHED BEFORE THE MATCH?	If the team is not behaving as it should, reprimand the players until they get back on tack. You can use the half time interval to convince them. If necessary, substitute the players who insist on not respecting your orders.
WHICH FINISHING TOUCH TECHNIQUES ARE GIVING US MOST SUCCESS AND WHICH THE LEAST?	IN ALL THE RANGE OF FINISHING TOUCH TECHNIQUES AT OUR DISPOSITION (CROSSES, CUTS, ETC.) WHICH ARE THOSE PUTTING OUR OPPONENT MOST IN DIFFICULTY AND WHICH ARE LESS EFFECTIVE	Ask the team to insist more with the most effective finishing touch plays, and make less use of those which are giving poorer results. Consider putting in players who are more skilled in finishing touches and shots that seem more effective (e.g., a player better at crossing and a striker better at aerial play if the opposing team are in trouble with crosses).

IF DURING THE LAST FEW WEEKS WE HAVE JUST INTRODUCED A NEW STRATEGY, NEW TACTICS OR A NEW SYSTEM (PERHAPS BECAUSE WE HAVE JUST TAKEN THE TEAM IN HAND), ARE THE PLAYERS APPLYING IT IN A SATISFACTORY WAY?	SEE WHETHER THE INNOVATIONS WE HAVE MADE HAVE BEEN ASSIMILATED IN A SATISFACTORY WAY OR IF THEIR APPLICATION IS CREATING DIFFICULTIES OR NEGATIVE EFFECTS ON THE TEAM'S PERFORMANCE, THUS HELPING THE OPPONENTS. TRY TO UNDERSTAND IF THE NEW SYSTEM IS MAKING US SUFFER TOO MUCH IN SOME ZONES OF THE FIELD.	If they seem to have assimilated sufficiently, just correct any mistakes made by the team in real time as they put the novelty into effect. If they have not assimilated things adequately, renew the team's old habits in part or completely. Even though they do not coincide with our own ideas, they will certainly guarantee a more reliable performance from the team. Above all in cases where the opponent is giving us a lot of trouble in important zones of the field it is important to restore the old system.
FROM AN INDIVIDUAL POINT OF VIEW, ARE THERE ANY PLAYERS WHO ARE NOT MOVING IN TIME WITH THEIR TEAM MATES?	EVALUATE THE PERFORMANCE OF SINGLE PLAYERS, ABOVE ALL IN RELATION TO THEIR INTEGRATION IN THE COLLECTIVE MOVEMENTS OF THE TEAM.	Reprimand the single players who are not behaving in the expected way. If they are creating too many difficulties for the performance of the team, they should be substituted, especially if we are in the second half.
ARE THERE ANY PLAYERS WHO ARE EXAGGERATING WITH THEIR INDIVIDUAL PLAY?	SEE WHETHER THE SINGLE PLAYERS ARE PERFORMING IN THE RIGHT COLLECTIVE WAY, OR IF THEY ARE INSISTING TOO MUCH WITH DRIBBLING OR OTHER INDIVIDUAL ACTIONS, ESPECIALLY IN PARTS OF THE FIELD WHERE SUCH PLAYS ARE NOT SUITABLE.	Go on reprimanding the selfish players until you get the desired results. This must be done by threatening to substitute them, and then by really doing so if they continue to behave in such a way - even during the first half.

ARE THERE ANY PLAYERS IN DIFFICULTY IN ONE OR BOTH PHASES?	TRY TO UNDERSTAND IF THERE ARE PLAYERS WHO ARE HAVING DIFFICULTY GETTING THE BETTER OF THEIR OPPONENTS WHEN CONTRASTING IN THE DEFENSE PHASE, IF THERE ARE ANY THAT ARE HAVING DIFFICULTY KEEPING THEIR POSITIONS, OR OTHERS WHO ARE HAVING A HARD TIME BECAUSE OF THE PRESENCE IN THEIR ZONE OF OPPONENTS WHO ARE FASTER OR MORE TECHNICALLY SKILLED THAN THEM. SEE IF THERE ARE ANY PLAYERS WHO ARE HAVING TROUBLE WITH THEIR INDIVID- UAL HANDLING OF THE BALL, PERHAPS MAKING BAD PASSES.	If these difficulties are the result of the fact that the play- ers are not trying to do their best or because they are not concentrating, you must repri- mand them. If the problems are due to other factors, encourage the players, trying to pick out the specific cause of the problem. If there are good opposing players in the zones where ours are in diffi- culty, invert their positions with others who are playing better. If the situation persists, substi- tute them with reserves.
ARE THEIR ANY PLAYERS WHO ARE TOO TENSE OR IRRITATED?	SEE WHETHER ANY OF OUR PLAYERS' PER- FORMANCES ARE BEING TOO NEGATIVE- LY CONDITIONED BY EXCESSIVE TENSION OR EXASPERATION, COMING ABOUT PER- HAPS ON ACCOUNT OF EPISODES THAT HAVE TAKEN PLACE ON THE FIELD (e.g., ARGUMENTS WITH OPPONENTS)	Either carry out a 'psychologi- cal intervention' on these play- ers, trying to calm them down or reprimand them if their behavior is having a bad effect on the team's performance. If you do not get good results, and above all in cases where the irritated player is running the risk of being sent off, it may be a good idea to substi- tute him.

WHAT IS THE PHYSI-CAL STATE OF THE TEAM AND THE SINGLE PLAYERS?	ABOVE ALL IN THE SECOND HALF AND AS THE MATCH IS DRAW-ING TO A CLOSE, KEEP AN EYE OF THE PHYSI-CAL AUTONOMY OF THE TEAMS IN TERMS OF STAMINA. LOOK OUT FOR PLAYERS WITH NO ENERGY LEFT	If the whole team is running on empty, ask them to lower the rhythm and intensity of play, even by bringing down the line from which they are going into pressing. If single players have run out of stamina, sub-stitute them.

The coach must be very clear about the questions to be asked - as shown in the table - and he must take his place on the bench expecting to get the replies. To make his job easier, he could rationalize it, drawing up a prospectus similar to the table above, writing down the results of the analysis he has made and the corrections and advice he wants to give the team during the interval, which, as we will see, is an important moment for rectifying negative situations.

At this point, having had a look at the aspects of the match connected to the performance of the two teams on the field, let us go into two other questions that are very important as regards the behavior of the coach on the bench: variations in the weather conditions and the importance of the match itself.

THE INFLUENCE OF THE WEATHER CONDITIONS

As we have already seen, the weather conditions are vital to establishing match tactics. The things that we have decided on the basis of our study of the opponent could be completely overturned by the presence of particular atmospheric conditions. Even the tactical set up of the team could undergo variations depending on the weather conditions rather than the characteristics of the opposing team. For example, a team that usually builds up elaborate play might hold to that plan against every team, but, in cases where the field is heavy as a result of rain, it would be foolish not to change playing style.

The weather conditions at kick off can sometimes change during the course of the match. To tell the truth a change in the weather is rarely so radical as to modify the conditions on the field and the temperature. In other sports, like Formula One motor racing, for example, this kind of change can effect the continuation of the competition, but this is not usually true of soccer.

However, in those cases in which the effects are extreme enough to alter the context in which we are playing the match, the two teams could begin to feel negative consequences.
Above all the coaches will be confused by this sudden change of context, but they must immediately come up with the indications to give the team so that their players will be facing the new situation better than the opponents.

You have to intervene on the tactical plane, changing the way of building up play, the level of aggression in the defense phase and, more in general, the rhythm and intensity of play.
The tactical behavior to be held by the team on the basis of the weather conditions is the same as that we saw in the table in chapter 7.

The important things, as you will see from the table, are that you must play soccer at a low rhythm with high temperatures, and, when the field is heavy, you must go for pressing and immediate build up.

The coach must be ready and able to perceive when it is necessary to intervene on the team in reaction to significant (or even trivial) changes in the weather, keeping in mind that it is always a great risk to the way a team plays.
Lastly, if you have to carry out tactical modifications during a match, there will not be time to train and instruct the team adequately on all the facets of the new playing system. The coach must be able to get across what he wants from his players in an immediate and easily comprehensible way, so that there are no misunderstandings and no confusion.

TACTICAL MOVES AND THE IMPORTANCE OF THE MATCH

Another important thing to keep in mind when speaking about the way the coach is to analyze the game is the importance of the match itself.

While the coach is observing what is happening on the field, he must concentrate more on certain elements, less on others, depending on their relevance to the match.

Then - and once again depending on the importance of the match - he should make a greater or a smaller number of tactical moves, even changing the whole set up.

If we are playing an important match, the coach will be making a detailed evaluation of his rival's set up, their behavior, their strong and their weak points. It is clear that you can risk more during an important match, trying to be more flexible even to the point where you are varying general elements in the set up which would normally be immovable. For example, if there are only a few minutes left and the team is losing, you could try putting on an extra striker as a desperate move, even though you would be changing the playing system that your men know well. In moments like that, however, any changes that you make must be more resolute. Another example would be abolishing offside tactics after a few minutes' play if you do not think it is giving positive results - and this would be done so as not to give the opponents a paradoxical advantage.

On the contrary, during an unimportant match like a friendly the coach should concentrate very little on the rival players, focusing his attention on even the smallest details in his own team's performance. Any modifications he makes in such circumstances must be very bland. There is no point in asking your team not to apply offside during a friendly match, or to bring back the initial point of pressing or to vary build up or finishing touch modes - not to mention the playing system itself.

Naturally, in cases where there has been a decided turn for the worse in the weather conditions, you will be obliged to give your team strong directives, because otherwise the match would mean nothing. The situation in which they find themselves will teach the players a lot, and they will have the opportunity of learning how to change play in such circumstances.

The deciding factor in the way the coach assesses the match and behaves as it is going on is the importance of the game itself. In any case, he must be coherent with his own ideas, at the same time acting in an intelligent way and keeping himself in line with what the circumstances require of him.

CHAPTER 10

MANAGING THE HALF TIME INTERVAL

As we have already said, the interval is an important part of the match, which can help to redirection things.

It often happens that a team which has played badly in the first half, comes out on the field completely transformed after the interval, overturning the ongoing situation and also the result. However you look at it, one of the moments when the team is concentrating hardest, is most determined and wants to do well is at the beginning of the second half.

This does not only happen as a logical consequence of the fact that during the quarter of an hour of relaxation the team recovers part of their energy, but also because of the psychological stimulus the coach can give the team and the possible modifications that he can easily bring to bear in the locker room.

We can say that the interval really is the moment during the match when the coach can be most important and decisive to his team. Consequently, he must prepare himself to carry out as well as he possibly can the work he has to do in the locker room.

Of course, whatever he says and does during this important period of time will be based upon his analysis of the first half of the match. It goes without saying, too, that the atmosphere of the interval will depend largely on the performance of his team. During these fifteen minutes, the coach has the chance to find a solution to the fact that the team is losing and / or playing badly, or, if the ongoing situation is a positive one, to make sure the second half will be on a level with the first.

As we have said above the interval can bring the following advantages:

❑ Physical and mental relaxation for the players

❑ The chance for the coach to manage his team from a psychological point of view, giving the players guidance for the second half.

☐ The chance for the coach to talk more calmly to the players, explaining the mistakes they have been making so as to try and correct them.

☐ The chance for the coach to carry out tactical modifications, in particular by substituting players and adjusting the system.

First of all, the coach must respect the fact that the players need some rest - from all points of view, also mentally.

You must not hassle the team in those fifteen minutes you have them to yourself, stifling them, in the mental sense. You have to communicate with them in such a way as to get their attention automatically, trying to speak in a 'relaxing' way, so as to inject a certain feeling of tranquillity into the locker room. You must not lose your temper, attacking the team verbally. The players must go back on the field with more determination, not even more afraid of making mistakes.

As far as the physical aspect is concerned, the classic 'tea' (or some other drink containing mineral salts) is always the best way of integrating part of the energy lost during the first forty five minutes. As well as that, some easy going stretching exercises are useful in order not to create too brusque an interruption to the work carried out by their muscles and so as to keep them warm and avoid sprains when they get back on the field.

As for the psychological management of the team, the coach must be working both on a collective and an individual level. On the collective level, you speak to the whole team in order to recharge them for their return onto the field, while from the point of view of the individual, you speak to those players who have not faced the first half with the right mentality, or who seem in the need of psychological intervention. In both cases, the guidelines we have put forward repeatedly in the book are still valid here: reprimand the players and tell them they must do their duty when they have put little effort into the first half; make sure they are aware of the potential and encourage the team (and the single players) if they have been playing with little conviction; tranquilize them if you have noticed a state of tension and anxiety; put their feet back on the ground if the team (and the single players) have been playing well but tend to be too full of themselves; give them praise if the team (and the single players) have played well but are becoming dispirited.

In order to correct the tactical or technical errors made by the team and the single players, you must point these out and give explanations. If the coach keeps shouting at the players during the match and getting at them about the errors they are making, this will tend to put the players in greater difficulty, and the interval is surely the best moment to try and correct mistakes and re-order the team from a tactical point of view. As well as that, you can show the team the analysis you have made during the first half, above all regarding the opponents. This will clarify your ideas concerning the corrections to be applied, making them understand how the match is going in order to get a better performance from them when they return to the field.

Lastly, the interval is the best moment for making tactical changes, because it is the one period during the match when you will be able to talk calmly to the team about any variations to be made in their behavior on the field. During the interval you can give them satisfactory explanations about what you want them to do when the match starts over.

Coaches very often carry out substitutions during the interval. There are good reasons for this: first of all, in order to send an overhauled team back on the field, which will be enabled to turn the screws on the situation that existed before going down to the locker room; in the second place, it may be taken as a humiliation for a player to be substituted for technical reasons in the first half, and so the interval is the right moment to change one or more men without them feeling it too much on the psychological plane (you should also console them and explain why you have made this decision).

In reference to the substitutions to be carried out during the interval there is another point to be made: if the whole team has been playing badly, you should not change any players. You ought really to change the whole team, but as that is not possible, substituting some of the players would be like giving negative signals to the entire group, giving them the impression that some have passed the exam and some have failed (the substituted players). Instead, it is better to give them your confidence for the moment, and then carry out any substitutions during the second half.

The coach has to manage the interval in such a way as to make the best use possible of the time at his disposal. Explanations about their mistakes, your analysis of the first half, your definition of the tactical moves and the corrections to be carried out, your psychological management of the group and each single player - you must find time for all these operations during the fifteen minutes at your disposal.

Clearly, the coach must be good at organizing and carrying all this out before the teams have to return on the field, focusing on one or another aspect depending on what seems necessary as a result of how things were going in the first half. For example, if you have to make particular tactical variations, it is better if you take more time to explain them, shortening up on your report about how things were going. In other cases, the most important aspect is undoubtedly the psychological management of the team followed by any explanations concerning their mistakes.

Remember that the principle aim on which you should be basing your management of the interval is to send back onto the field a team that has been transformed from the mental point of view if the first half has not been positive, or to assure yourself of the same approach when the match starts over if things have been going well in this sense during the first half.

To sum up, you can think of the interval as a strategic instrument to be exploited as well as possible to guarantee a positive performance when the match gets going again. The aspect of the coach's job belongs to the submerged part of the figurative iceberg we have already spoken of. It only goes to show that the coach's most important tasks are the invisible ones that the general public never notices.

Let us now go on to assess what happens after the interval: the second half.

CHAPTER 11

THE SECOND HALF

The first thing to do is to make a quick comparison between the characteristics of the two halves from the coach's point of view. The coach must be much more careful and patient when making any possible modifications during the first half, especially as far as substitutions - and there usually are not any - are concerned. A coach should not make substitutions during the first half, first of all because that could turn out to be an over-hasty move, and secondly because you would be giving the player in question a psychological blow. Any changes that take place during the first half should come about as a result of injury or in cases where a player is performing in a truly disastrous way, in which case he might even be content to be changed.

In the second half on the other hand, you can be freer with your substitutions because the nearer you are getting to the end of the match, the more you can gamble on making changes: As well as that, the players will be more mentally prepared to leave the field, and when they are called in, they will not find it so hard to take from a psychological point of view.

Even tactical modifications are encouraged as we approach the final whistle. Changing the tactical set up of the team might be a risk in the first half, whereas in the second part of the match they could even turn out to be indispensable.

In addition, the players are often both physically and mentally exhausted in the second half. We have to consider telling the team to take up a more provident attitude (bring down the line where they go into pressing, the speed with which the ball circulates, the vehemence of their movements, and the general rhythm and intensity of their play). During the second half you must continue to incite the team so that they do not let up from the mental point of view, but you must not put them under excessive stress, showing comprehension towards the players if they are finding it difficult to carry out what you are asking of them. You must always remember that physical fatigue brings a loss in mental lucidity.

Lastly, the team will tend to lengthen itself out in the second half, and the players may even cease to respect the orders of the coach, which rarely takes place in the first half.

All this is connected with the fact we mentioned above - little by little as we get near the end of a match, the players tend to lose their mental concentration and their athletic crispness. The coach must recommend that the group does all it can to keep hold of its tactical diligence. The team that stays solid and compact is the one that often has the edge, and the coach must do all he can to make sure that this takes place.

You often see end of matches where the two teams have lengthened out and are no longer doing anything about it: the mid fielders and the strikers are not moving back to defend, the defenders do not shorten up on the rival's half, all attacking play relies only on the long pass in building up, so causing the opposing team to disunite as well in a viscous circle without end. The coach must do all he can to force his players not to make these mistakes, lengthening themselves out in such a way, even telling them to maneuver themselves horizontally and to cut down on the rhythm of play so as not to waste their energy, dedicating all there is left to keeping compact.

As for the coach's behavior during of the second half, initially he must evaluate the first minutes immediately after play has resumed.

First of all, he must be watching his players' approach to the second half. As for the very beginning of the match, it is important to be sure that the team has come on the field with the right positive attitude that we have already listed more than once. On this basis, he will decide what he now must say to the team (inciting the players to keep it up or reprimanding them).

It goes without saying that if the team has got off on the wrong foot at the beginning of the second half, the situation could turn out badly. The coach will no longer have the time to intervene psychologically with calm, and will have to limit himself to calling the team to order as it comes.

The coach must evaluate the effects of what he has done during the interval. Above all, from an entirely personal point of view, this will enable him to judge his own behavior, but it will also give him a greater insight into the mental characteristics of the group and their sensitivity to his calls to order. All this will help him to improve his ability to manage the interval, so that he will be able to organize things better on another occasion.

The coach should also try and sum up all the changes that have taken place in the rival team during the interval, evaluating the work carried out by his opposite number. He, too, will have made substitutions, small changes to the tactical set up and the necessary mental transformation of his team for when play gets off to a new start. As a result, we will have to make a careful new analysis of the opposing team, keeping in mind all the elements we have already set forth in chapter 9, regarding the set up and the performance of the opposition.

Generally speaking, then, the coach will have to renew his analysis of the two teams already carried out in the first half. He will have to identify all the changes that have followed on the way his rival colleague has managed his session in the locker room. He will have to resolve all the new tactical situations that are putting his team in any difficulty, at the same time trying to turn the others to his own advantage.

As the second half proceeds, the coach must keep his own team's mental and tactical attitude constant, making sure that his players are 'alive' until the end of the match.

As we have already said, the coach will have greater reason in the second half to carry out new tactical moves, changes to the set up of his team and above all substitutions.

As the match draws to a close, the coach will be letting go of his 'behavioral brakes', changing things that he would never have modified earlier. For example, if there are only a few minutes left and the team is under too much pressure, you can ask them not to carry out offside tactics any longer, but only the simple defense elastic. This will make sure that we are not running any useless risks, especially if our team is not particularly good at these tactics.

In any case, we will be dealing with such critical situations and how to react to them in chapter 13.

You must be more decisive in carrying out substitutions as time goes by, above all to put in new energy. You should not, however, make the three substitutions permitted (unless, that is, you are playing a friendly match in which you can make as many as you wish) until at least the eightieth minute, because otherwise, in cases where there is an injury in the last minutes of the match and you have already used all your changes, you may be left in numerical inferiority. Clearly, however, if the match is important and / or you have to resolve a situation, you can use up all three substitutions early on.

On the other hand, there is no point making the last substitution when the match is just about to finish - for they would then be completely useless.

Another thing you should not do is make strategic substitutions as soon as you are one goal up or down. If the tactical situation were to change again, your replacement of players would be wasted.

When carrying out a substitution, remember first of all to psyche up the new players (also getting them to warm up a minute or two before they go on), explaining which position they are to take up and giving them the relative tactical point of reference. You will then need to console the player coming off the field, making him understand that the move has not been carried out because he has failed in any way, praising him if his performance has been good. It sometimes happens, unfortunately, that a substituted player does not accept the coach's decisions, even without being able to give a logical reason. As he leaves the field he can behave badly towards the coach or even towards his team mates, thereby creating problems for the group's serenity. A coach must be good at dealing with such situations without losing his temper. For the moment he should try and close an eye, especially if he thinks the player is just using his anger to hide his disappointment. When the match is over, he should immediately have a talk with this 'rebel' player, asking him to explain his attitude, and, above all, to apologize to his team mates and to the coach. In cases where the man in question keeps behaving in this intemperate way, the coach must take strict measures, putting him off the team and even asking the club to send him away. The following is some advice about how to manage the psychological state of players.

When we are sure that the match is going to end in a positive way we can substitute those players who have performed particularly well so as to allow them to receive a 'standing ovation' from the public - which will be more or less noisy depending on the category in which we are playing and the number of spectators watching the match. The player in question will react to this situation positively from a psychological point of view, and indeed it will be like a sort of seal, a collective approval of his performance.

On the contrary, if the game is at an end and is irreversibly compromised, there is no point in substituting players that have played particularly badly, because the only effect of such a move would be further to depress the players coming off, who would have to undergo the public's disapproval.

Lastly, remember that in the second half, you should try and correct the errors made by the team in real time. This will also make the players feel the coach's presence and keep them concentrating.

When the match is over, the coach has not finished his own work completely because he must carefully manage the moment when he comes face to face with his players once again. He should avoid making technical or tactical comments as soon as he gets into the locker room, putting them off until he sees the players again during the training sessions of the following day. At this point the match is over and beyond all thought of the result, the players only want to wind down. Talking to them immediately about the match would be no good - that is, it might even be counter productive. On the other hand, the coach must immediately try to manage the psychological emotions deriving from the match, striking while the iron is hot. If the team has played well, the entire group and the particularly effective single players will receive your compliments. This will help to build up the confidence of the players in themselves and in their coach, who will show that he is not simply rigid and demanding but is also able to give merit its due. Of course, in the following days the coach will invite the team not to become over-optimistic if they tend to be doing so.

When the team have performed badly the coach must reprimand the players only in cases where he thinks their failure is the result of a lack of effort on their part. Otherwise, the best thing to do is to console the group, particularly those players that have been playing worse than the others. You must make sure that the team does not get too depressed and to do that you give them a list of all the good things they have done so as to bring up their morale.

After this quick but important intervention on the emotions immediately after a match, the coach must allow the team to relax so that they can get rid of the tension and stress they have accumulated during the game and recharge 'their mental batteries'. In any case, the coach will now have put down the foundations for his work of the next few days, having concluded those of the game he has just concluded.

CHAPTER 12

HOW TO MAKE A DIFFERENCE TACTICALLY

Unfortunately, particular critical situations can come up during a match, giving the team tactical and psychological difficulties in one or both phases of play. It does not matter how well the team has been prepared during the course of the week and how good the organization may be - these negative situations can make their appearance in any case, generated by bad luck or by the fact that the team is having an off day.

The coach needs to be specifically able to manage such situations as well as he can, making due tactical corrections where these may be necessary. There is no doubt about it, a complete coach must be in possession of such abilities. A coach who is particularly skilled at giving a top class general organization to his team and to prepare the match in detail, but who is unable to read and find a solution to the various situations of the game which are giving trouble to his team, may be an excellent coach but cannot be said to have reached the apex of his professional maturity. The fact is that the match itself is the key to soccer, and being able to manage the match is certainly not a thing to be neglected. That remains true, though, of course, we have said again and again in the course of the book that the coach's main work takes place during the daily training sessions.

We often see matches during which a team betrays serious difficulty for a certain period of time, and the first thing both the more or less neutral spectators and observers will be expecting is to see the coach carrying out various tactical modifications, starting out with substituting first choice players with reserves. If after making such operations, the coach manages to get results, then he will be praised to the sky, whereas if the situation does not vary he will be accused of being unable to read the match. This last judgement will seem even more factual in cases where, facing a critical situation, the coach does nothing - or the public believes he has done nothing - to correct the situation.

The first thing we must say is that it is not right to judge a coach only on account of this responsibility because we must also consider all the others which are certainly more relevant. A coach who is able to give play and a precise mentality to the team but who is not able to resolve the critical situations in the match is to be preferred to one who carries out one substitution after another (meeting the approval of the public) but who just does not seem able to send a team on the field which is presentable, from an aesthetic point of view or in terms of tactical organization. We could go so far as to say that it is the continuous emergence of these tactically critical situations (like for example the inability of the team to become dangerous in attack) which is a sign of the coach's weak ability at organizing his team from all its points of view. The more frequently such situations are making their appearance, the more the coach in question should tell himself that he must try to improve his team's competitiveness, quite apart from any minute by minute decisions he might make to resolve them as they come up. You must also keep in mind, as we have already said, that critical situations may come up even for teams that are generally well-organized.

We must also point out that a coach with personality and with his own ideas about soccer must not allow himself to be influenced by the public. It often happens that a coach carries out substitutions and tactical changes only to keep the critics happy, foreseeing their behavior when his team as been defeated. In this way he ties to reduce his own responsibility in the failure, fully aware of the charges the critics will be making about him.

In any case the coach must not allow himself to be maneuvered by people that probably know little or nothing about his work. He must go his own way, aware that he is the real and only judge of the work that he is doing. And he must read the match as well as he can, carrying out only those changes that he really feels to be useful and necessary to straighten out the moment of difficulty. When he does not succeed in resolving them and he knows that he is responsible for this negative outcome, he must try and understand why it has happened so that he can gain experience from this point of view, affronting the next match in a better way. In order to improve in this sense, the coach must watch his team's match as many times as necessary after it is over, making a detached analysis of the critical situations they have met with and evaluating not only the effectiveness of the moves he made but also those that he should have carried out.

THE VARIOUS MEANS AT THE COACH'S DISPOSAL TO RECTIFY CRITICAL SITUATIONS

Before we make a list and explain the moves at the coach's disposal to rectify critical situations, we must first consider exactly how much should be changed and in what way.

First of all, you must remember that there are some elements in the organization of a team which should never normally be changed: their mentality, their attitude in terms of offensiveness, the playing system, the defense system and the general set up during the attacking phase, especially in terms of the ways of building up. You must never expect a coach to change the system or the team's attitude as if there was nothing more to it than that, especially when the situation is not really desperate.

Changing the team's tactical physiognomy will only put the players in even more difficulty and confusion, creating a negative effect that will be worse than the critical situation that we are trying to resolve.

In the second place, there are ethical and sportsmanlike considerations that should prevent coaches from expecting negative attitudes from their players just because critical situations have emerged.

You must always remember that an important aim of a soccer team, and also of its coach, is to offer a pleasing spectacle to those who are watching the match, above all the neutral observers. If teams were constantly to play badly, the grandstands would be empty in a month or two and soccer would lose its importance and its following. This duty not to make conjectures about results, adopting submissive measures detestable to those who want to see soccer being played (and not only to watch a war of positions), is further underlined by the positive idea that the result should go to those that really deserve it.

Every team should do all they can to gain the victory, which must be a consequence of the performance on the field and not a mere number independent of the rest. If we win playing badly for a part of the game (and a defensive team, as such, does not play well in a global sense, even though some people maintain that it is to be appreciated because it is good at destroying its rival's play), or because we makes calculations about the result after having scored a goal, we should not say that we are good, but only lucky. We also give the impression of being guilty of not respecting our part of the unwritten 'contract' expected by the spectators, who have bought a ticket valid for the whole of the ninety minutes and not just a part of them. You must play in an active way for the whole match, accepting the final result even when it is negative.

You often see teams that attack, even in a spectacular way, until they go a goal up, when they close themselves on purpose and give up playing. In this way, such teams disclose their real pragmatic identity, according to which 'attacking' and 'defending' are equally valid strategies leading to the result itself, which is their only real target. What can we say? Of course you must try and resolve any critical situations even by making tactical moves so as to reach one of your aims, which is victory; but such moves must never conceal the other objective, your 'duty', which we have spoken of above. As a consequence, tactical moves like closing yourself in defense after having gone one goal up, or bringing the opponents into depth with the only aim of counter attacking are not the right things to carry out in the face of your double objective. It could be added that your simple aim of bringing home the result may not be aided by behavior like this: the best way of succeeding is to continue to attack even if you are winning, in the spirit 'the best form of defense is attack'.

As we begin to speak about these moves at the coach's disposal, we must say at once that they are not all of a tactical nature, but also psychological and having to do with communication.

In fact, the coach does not only have 'tactical instruments' at hand - like for example substitutions or the inverted placement of the players on the field - in order to resolve critical situations. He can also give advice and make recommendations, and he can encourage his players and use other psychological methods that we have already seen in the course of the preceding chapters.

Let us now have a look at all these moves, underlining how and in what contexts they are to be used. So as not to become too repetitive, we will not be going into details here about the single situations in which it is useful to use them, because we will be studying that in a later section. As we are looking at each critical situation we will point out the most appropriate move to resolve it.

SUBSTITUTING FIRST CHOICE PLAYERS WITH RESERVES

This is certainly the most widely used move to straighten out critical situations. Spectators at a soccer match will always be expecting the coach to play the card of substitutions during the second half. Everyone will suddenly hold the coach in greater consideration if the match really is resolved as a result of the substitutions he has carried out. However, when the players he has put on reveal themselves to be decisive, the coach can also be heavily criticized because he kept them on the bench at the start. In any case, the coach must not give any weight to such things, but go on his own way, acting on the ideas coming to him as he watches the match.

The situations in which it can be useful to carry out substitutions are more or less the following:

☐ He chooses to put in new energy.
☐ He needs to take off players in difficulty or injured
☐ He needs to get a substantially balanced situation into his own favor near the end of the match.
☐ The team are having problems carrying out a phase of play and this must be resolved as soon as possible.
☐ He chooses to change the playing system by making a substitution.

For every substitution that he makes, the coach must keep in mind that he has one less at his disposal, and that, in cases where the situation that he wants to straighten out changes face once again, he will not be able to go back on his tracks. For example, it can happen that a coach decides to put on mid fielders who are better in the defense phase because his team is one goal up but is destined to suffer in that the players are no longer able to press and keep possession. Then, a few minutes after the substitution, the opponents score a goal to draw, and he finds himself with the wrong players, who are no good to him in attacking the opponent's goal. The thing is that before carrying out substitutions the coach must be very sure they are necessary at the moment, keeping in mind above all the difficulty the team could have if the situation suddenly changes again.

Remember that you have to give psychological assistance to the players going on and coming off the field. As far as that is concerned, we refer back to the chapter about the second half, in which we explained how a coach should behave in these situations.

CHANGING THE PLAYING SYSTEM

When the coach starts to think about changing his system, he must weigh up the advantages this will bring and the disadvantages of taking away their points of reference from the players. If he thinks the advantages prevail, he must not hesitate to change the system.
There are two ways of doing this:

☐ Adapt the players already on the field to the new system, moving some of them around and inverting their positions.
☐ Substituting first choice players with reserves.
☐ Clearly, these two methods can often be carried out together.

You can change the system in the following general contexts:

☐ You can try and improve the execution of one of the two phases of play when the match is coming to an end and you no longer feel there is any advantage in leaving the system unchanged.
☐ You have just begun to introduce a new system, perhaps because you have just begun to coach the team, which is not applying your new system well enough, perhaps because the opponents are creating problems in various parts of the field.
☐ We are in numerical inferiority as the result of a player having been sent off, and we need to invent a new tactical set up.

When you change system you must explain to the team how they are to place themselves as a result of the choice you have made. You must very quickly give your indications to the players on the team who are to make up the new sections, and in what way and how they are now to move on the basis of their different positions.

When the change of system is brought about by the insertion of a player who was on the bench, it can be a good idea to give him detailed explanations not only about where he is to place himself and how he is to move in the two phases, but also how the whole team is to line up in the new system. The player going on will then be able to explain things to his team mates, which will make it easier for the coach to communicate his directives concerning the new system.

AN EXCHANGE OF POSITION BETWEEN PLAYERS ON THE FIELD

Deciding to invert the position of some of the players can be a very useful way of improving the performance of the coach's team.

Sometimes the team is not able to express itself to the top in one or both the phases because of the simple fact that some of the players are working in zones that are either not congenial to them or occupied by opponents with characteristics that are putting them in serious difficulty. For example, a mid fielder who usually plays on the flank might not be able to find his feet in the central position assigned to him for this particular match. Or a defender whose speed is not his strong point is facing a very quick striker with or without the ball in his zone of competence. Or again, our aerial striker has the tallest of all the opponents in front of him, while our fastest and most technically skilled striker is playing in the zone of the quickest and athletically most agile rival defender. In order to put our players in a position to express themselves to the best of their ability, improving the performance of the whole group, we must always be ready to make a resolute exchange of positions.

Before carrying out this exchange of positions, we must remember to consider carefully whether the results will really be positive. If you invert the positions of two players in order to improve their performance in the defense phase, but then, when the team is attacking, both of them are still having difficulty participating in the play in their new positions - then the final results of the move are not to be considered very good.

However, changes of position are moves to be carried out freely because, if they do not bring the desired results, you can easily re-establish the preceding set up.

It is useful to change positions when:

☐ Single players are in difficulty during the defense phase against rival players superior to them.
☐ Single players are facing opponents that can inhibit their technical skills in the attacking phase.
☐ Single players are acting in parts of the field that are not congenial to them.

This move can be considered the best one to make if you consider the proportion between risk and advantages. It is easy to carry out changes of position (even from the point of view of communicating them to the team); they can often turn out to be very effective in resolving situations that seemed complicated; and, in cases where the result is negative, it is very simple to correct them, on condition that the coach is keeping a careful check on the results of his moves and is ready to go back on his tracks. However, if the critical situation does not improve after the change of positions, you must think about what other moves to make.

CHANGING THE EXECUTION OF ONE OR BOTH THE PHASES (VARIATIONS IN STRATEGY)

Changing the team's way of attacking and defending is the most frequently used way of straightening out critical situations, especially when it is not yet necessary to make 'all-out changes'. It is relatively easy to make little modifications to the way in which the team is carrying out one or both the phases of play, and, at the same time, they can be changed again at any moment. You can ask your team to make better use of the depth of the field by using vertical passes, and then rectify that again barely a minute later.

For the same reasons, you can make changes in the execution of the phases of play even in the first half.

One thing should be said, however: these modifications should only involve particular details, without calling into question the general way in which they are carried out. For example, it is complicated to ask a team to go from a zonal defense system to one marking the man (or to a mixed system), just as it is not easy to change from elaborate build up of play to immediate construction based on long passes.

Variations can concern: the application of pressing (in terms of the zones in which to carry it out and not to carry it out) and offside, the shifting movements, single movements and playing schemes to be carried out in the attacking phase and whether to make more or less use of the depth of the field rather than the width and vice versa. We can carry out these changes in cases where our opponent's counter moves, which we have been studying during the week, should turn out to be ineffective, or if we need to make new ones perhaps on account of a different tactical set up assumed by the other team.

You can ask your team to modify the way in which they carry out the playing phases in the following contexts:

- ☐ Difficulty becoming really dangerous in the attacking phase.
- ☐ Difficulty regaining possession in the defense phase, where we are also giving the opponents too many goal scoring opportunities.
- ☐ The need to give extra strength to the effectiveness of one of the two phases: the attacking phase if we have to score one or more goals, the defense phase if we are winning but suffering too much.

Once again, in cases where you decide to modify the execution of one or both phases, you have to explain things to the players as clearly as possible so that there will be no misunderstandings.

ADVICE AND RECOMMENDATIONS

Something you must never neglect when thinking about how to resolve difficult situations is to give advice and recommendations to your team and to the single players about how to behave in the two phases. As we have already seen, you often need to take resolute actions in order to safeguard against difficult situations. There are many situations, however, where it can be an equally intelligent and effective move and quite enough in the circumstances simply to say a couple of words to your players. This is particularly true during the first half, when the decision to carry out tactical variations could turn out to be decidedly hazardous and premature.

Advice and recommendations are particularly useful on account of the fact that teams often have difficulty in the execution of one or both of the phases of play not because what they have decided to carry out against a particular opponent turns out to be ineffective, but for the simple reason that the players are not doing what the coach has asked them to, both as far as the counter moves chosen for the match are concerned and in terms of the level of tactical organization in general. At this point the coach must recommend that they carry out the things they have been instructed to do during the training sessions of the week before, reminding them of the moves they are to make.

As well as this, when the team is having difficulty making determined movements in both phases of play, or when a particular player has problems in the defense phase facing up to the rival who is operating in his zone of competence, or, in the attacking phase, carrying out that which is expected of him - then it is important for the coach to give suitable tactical advice. This advice will not lead to a change in the execution of a phase of play, but only to our improving it, eliminating the difficulty in which the players are finding themselves.

The circumstances in which it can be useful to give the team advice and recommendations are the following:

☐ The team is having difficulty carrying out one or both phases of play deriving from the fact that the players are not carrying out that which is expected of them.

❑ The players are having trouble facing the opponents in an effective way, especially on an individual level.

In conclusion, the coach must decide whether the critical situations are a result of inadequate tactical behavior on the team's part, which will require more resolute interventions, or on the players' insufficient tactical discipline, in which case the coach must intercede verbally. In any case, it is always better for the coach to try and resolve a critical situation by giving advice. You can always use the other tactical moves later if the situation does not improve.

PSYCHOLOGICAL INTERVENTIONS

Connected with advice and recommendations, there is another move at the coach's disposal in order to resolve critical situations - a move that must never be underestimated: the psychological intervention.

It can often happen, in fact, that these negative situations come about as a result of the fact that the players are psychologically 'blocked', or influenced by other mental conditions that we have seen in the preceding pages (they are not making enough effort, presumption, etc.)

It is above all in the first half that a team will run into critical situations generated not by tactical factors but by negative psychological states.

The coach must be able to pick out such grounds and reasons, and then intervene on them at once.

A psychological problem can have a collective or an individual nature. Sometimes the whole team can undergo such a predicament and at others only certain players, thus compromising the group's performance.

This type of situation can often have both a tactical (i.e., it is connected with the opponent's behavior) and a psychological nature. In such cases, the coach must apply different kinds of moves: psychological interventions, advice, substitutions, changing the way one or both phases of play are carried out, etc.

To sum up, you can carry out psychological interventions in the following circumstances:

- ☐ The entire team is have psychological difficulties (of all types) in carrying out one or both the phases of play.
- ☐ Some of the single players are having psychological difficulty in the various situations of play.

It will be clear, lastly, that such interventions must come about verbally. As concerns managing negative psychological states, we refer you to the relative parts of the book.

CHAPTER 13

RESOLVING CRITICAL SITUATIONS WITH TACTICAL CHANGES

In order to resolve the various critical situations you can run into during a match, you must first of all be able to see and pick them out. A coach must make sure that his ability to read the match is as well developed as possible if he wants to notice everything that takes place on the field of play. In order to observe the match in the correct way, and so also to read it, we refer you back to what we said in chapter 9.

In every situation of play, the coach must be asking himself the following questions: how is the team behaving in general? How did it behave in the play that has just finished? How should it have been behaving? What should it be doing in order to improve its performance?

However, the real key to reading a match is this question: in what kinds of situations are we in difficulty?

By asking these mainly tactical questions we learn more about the critical situation itself, but there are many factors that can create such problems for us. The ongoing result in particular can very often create a moment of difficulty for the team: if we are winning we may start suffering because the opponent is trying to force the situation so as to get even; if we are losing we may be having problems in making ourselves dangerous and overturning the situation; if we are drawing we might be too subdued in front of the adversary's play, and risk going under.

Another very important factor that can influence the creation of critical situations is whether we are playing at home or away. We might not have trouble against our rivals in the first case, but there is a high risk of us running into critical situations when playing an away match. For example, when playing away our team will very often tend to yield to the opponent's attacking play, and will have more trouble making itself dangerous that when playing at home.

However, when dealing with the various critical situations we will not be keeping tags on whether the match is at home or away. The situations to resolve are not always so desperate. For example, if there is tactical balance between the two teams, or if we have almost complete control of the territory but we just can not make ourselves dangerous, then we find ourselves in a difficult situation, but not so critical as to compromise the match if we can not resolve it. We are risking too much , for example, if we cannot resolve the situation when our team is continuously recoiling under the rival's attacking play.

As well as that, you must always remember that the correct reading of the match requires that the coach observes and evaluates the two teams on the field from all the different points of view. In this connection, we refer you back to the tables underlining the factors to be taken into consideration and analyzed about the rival team, and the questions to be asked in order to verify the performance of our own.

Lastly, when he has identified a critical situation, the coach must understand the nature of the factors that are causing difficulties to the team.

The following can give rise to problems:

- ☐ **Tactics**: (difficulties in carrying out the specific movements in both phases).
- ☐ **Technique**: (difficulties on the part of single players in facing up to opponents who have superior skills to them).
- ☐ **Athletic**: (difficulty on the part of the team to sustain the rhythm exacted by the opponent - and which, clearly, we are not able to impose).
- ☐ **Psychological**: (mental difficulties on the team's part in affronting the match).

It is by analyzing these four aspects that the coach will choose the modifications he must make. As we will see, if the critical situation is of a tactical nature, we will have above all to modify the way we are carrying out the two phases. If the negative situation is of a physical kind, we must make substitutions, but also tactical moves like bring back the line from which we start pressing and lower the general rhythm of play. If the critical situation has to do with psychology, then we must make a mental intervention on the group. And, lastly, if we are having technical problems, we can make substitutions between first choice players and reserves but also interchange positions between players already on the field. In all four cases, it is always useful to give advice and make recommendations before making any more resolute move.

The coach must then evaluate the results obtained after carrying out these moves: if he has managed to resolve a situation, he must make sure at all times that it has not reappeared; if he has not managed to resolve it he must not get discouraged but choose something different and some other kind of modification to bring to the team.

Before having a look at all the possible critical situations with the relative moves to resolve them, we must make one other consideration: difficult moments can come up in almost every moment of the match, and the coach must not wait too long before intervening even if we are still playing the first half - hoping that everything will work out by itself. You must make quick moves to resolve these situations, especially in situations where the team is having problems from the point of view of the defense and running the risk of taking a goal, which would create a new complicated predicament: having to revive and rally round and get on top again. If there is still a lot of time to go, you could decide not to make decisions that are too drastic, like carrying out substitutions, but softer solutions - perhaps asking the team to vary the details of their ways of attacking or defending.

We will now, at last, have a look at these critical situations.

UNBLOCKING A BALANCED SITUATION IN YOUR FAVOR

DESCRIPTION: This is not really a critical situation in that the team is not about to take a goal or compromise the result. The match is still wide open and anything could happen, but the team which manages to break this balance and take control of the match has a good chance of winning it. The coach must not simply stand about waiting, but must make sure that the balanced situation resolves itself in favor of his team, so preventing the opponents from becoming dangerous and getting the better of the situation. These circumstances come about above all in the first half when the teams are still not able to impose their own play with courage and determination, perhaps on account of the tension that will slowly dissolve with the passing of time. When one of the two teams manages to move the balanced tactical situation into its favor, it will be difficult for the other to recover. You can also find balanced situations throughout the match, during any of its periods of stagnation, perhaps even towards the end when the two teams are running short of energy.

From a tactical point of view, these situations are characterized by the fact that play is slumping in the mid field, where the two teams are crowding in and neither is able to get control of the action. When one manages to gain a few meters, the other beats back immediately without closing itself up, regaining possession and then giving way to a new turn of front. These rotations of front are typical of this tactical situation.

From this point of view things can become really critical when your team is obliged to win. The tactical balance will lead naturally to a draw, and in that case it becomes urgent to resolve the situation.

MOVES TO RESOLVE THE SITUATION: The first thing the coach must do in this type of situation is make sure that his moves will not prejudice the team's performance in the phase that is not under correction. For example, if you modify the attacking phase, the defense phase must not suffer, otherwise, far from being improved, the situation runs the risk of becoming seriously compromised.

To resolve situations of balance, the coach must intervene on both a tactical and a psychological level. From the tactical point of view, it is a good thing to modify both the attacking and the defense phase - the first by changing the specific playing schemes in build up, inversion of players' positions, increasing play on the flanks or into depth; the second by giving new indications about how to carry out pressing, shifting movements and the doubling up of marking, by asking the strikers to participate more in the defense phase, by getting the team to keep compact and by making any necessary changes in position between players. From a psychological point of view, you must eliminate the tension in the team, which leads them to assume attitudes that are not particularly aggressive or resourceful. You will need to make suitable interventions from that point of view.

However, if the match it only at the start, you should wait a minute or two before make any real tactical decisions, limiting yourself to simply giving some advice. If the balanced situation should come about towards the end of the match on the other hand, you should be making some resolute moves: carry out substitutions to improve the possession phase, but also, if we are really running out of time, a change of system by putting on more offensive players.

GETTING OVER THE DIFFICULTY OF CONQUERING THE OPPONENT'S HALF: WE ARE TAKING THE BRUNT OF THINGS

DESCRIPTION: Although the coach was expecting to see his own team in control of play, the very opposite can come about: the opponents are commanding the territory and forcing us to suffer dangerously. This type of situation can take place at any moment of the match. If it is still only the beginning of the first half, it may well be caused by our bad approach to the game - or at least an inferior approach to that of our opponents. If this type of situation comes up towards the end of the match, it is very probably caused by physical fatigue.

If it is happening during the course of the match it may be caused by a drop in concentration. Another thing you must keep in mind is the ongoing score: if we are winning, you must expect the opponent's forcing to grow progressively stronger, which will give our team the consequent difficulty in continuing to play in their attacking half keeping ball possession all the time. If we are drawing but our team is taking all the pressure, we run the serious risk of going a goal down, which would complicate the situation and make it difficult for us to win the match. It goes without saying that the situation will be even more desperate if we are losing and are still getting the worst of play.

However, we will be having a more detailed look at critical situations connected with the result later in the chapter.

From a tactical point of view, our team is crushed back into their own half (low point of balance), we just cannot manage to regain possession with in depth pressing (which, in fact, our players are not even carrying out) and we never manage to become at all dangerous in attack, where, in any case, our players only appear sporadically.

This critical situation requires rapid resolution, not only because we want to apply our own play, but also to prevent the opponent from scoring, which would make the situation even more complicated.

MOVES TO RESOLVE THE SITUATION: Once again, the moves to make here are both tactical and psychological. Tactically speaking, what you need to do is try to improve the effectiveness of the defense phase. To do that, you need to:

- ☐ Get the team to bring up the initial line of pressing, which will make them move towards the rival half.
- ☐ Tighten the marking on the 'hinges players' of their opponent's actions.
- ☐ Ask the strikers to become more involved in the non-possession phase.
- ☐ Tell the players to keep more compact and to give each other a hand, above all trying harder to double up on marking.
- ☐ Put on a mid fielder with defensive tendencies if the match is drawing to a close and we are continuing to suffer - in that way we will find it easier to regain possession.

The attacking phase has to be consolidated as well. Our team might be finding it difficult to raise their point of balance because the opponents are very good at pressing. We must, therefore, ask the team to be faster and more careful during the post-conquest sub-phase. You can advise the players to pass immediately forwards the moment they gain possession and are undergoing immediate pressing. This will give the team the chance and the time to move into depth and press where the ball lands, so entering the opponent's half. It might also be an intelligent move to put on a striker good at defending the ball, which will give his team mates the time to move up behind.

From a psychological point of view, a team very often has trouble because of the fear and tension that prevent the players from carrying out in depth pressing and from imposing the maneuvers through reasoned ball possession. The fact that you are not able at the beginning of a match to play the soccer that you have been studying in training can make the players feel frustrated. It is a good thing for the coach to make careful and well-aimed interventions directed at the whole collective in order to unblock the situation.

THE RESULT IS POSITIVE BUT WE ARE CONTINUING TO HAVE PROBLEMS

DESCRIPTION: This critical situation is connected to the one that we have just seen. There are, however, a number of differences principally in reference to the psychological attitude of the team. As we have already seen, the fact that we are undergoing repeated attacks from the opponent can have different meanings depending on the result. When we are winning but our opponent's play is creating problems for us, we must first of all analyze to what extent the situation is due to the rival's offensive plays and to what extent to the more or less voluntary attitude of submission that our players are putting on.

Of course, as the opponents are one goal down, they will be trying to attack with more determination and continuity, attempting to crush us into our own half. Their forcing will become more and more intense as we get nearer and nearer to the end of the match. And in fact it is in the last part of the match that the situation becomes more delicate and, as we will see later, the coach will have to make a couple of more resolute, not to say, drastic solutions.

It very often happens that players in advantage get resigned to seeing their opponents come forward looking for the drawing goal: it is almost as if they accept it, considering it a normal, and at bottom even the right thing that their role is now to defend themselves, putting all their cards on counter attacking.

In cases where the critical situation is due to the fact that the opponents are attacking with such a rhythm as to prevent our players from getting control of play even though they are trying as hard as they can without losing heart - then the coach will also have to manage their state of psychological frustration.

In cases where the critical situation depends on both the opponent's forcing and our own player's resignation (they have simply accepted the necessity of defending in their own half), we must get at them psychologically by giving them a vigorous mental shakedown.

There can also be cases connected to those above where the rival team is not carrying out particularly incisive or intense offensive play, but are being favored by the mistaken behavior of our players, who allow them to move into depth on purpose. Once again, here, the coach must make a verbal communication on the team, reprimanding them severely for this completely avoidable tactical, behavioral error.

These two cases, in which the team itself is strictly responsible, are all the more dangerous the further away the end of the result is, and they must not be tolerated even for a moment by the coach. When the end of the match is nearer, they become more acceptable.

In all three cases, however, you must work on mental, and not only tactical, factors relating to the team so as to make sure things will improve.

Having problems with the opponent's attacking play when we are winning is different from the previous situation that we analyzed, because its psychological aspect is more important.

On a tactical level everything is more or less similar. The opposing team is dominating the field and attacking with determination and intensity, forcing us to stay far back and making it impossible for us to get control of the situation on account of the pressing that our rivals are using in every zone. The tactical difference from the situation above may be that the opponent is attacking more actively with more men than usual, and is applying more constant in-depth pressing than usual.

MOVES TO RESOLVE THE SITUATION: The same moves that we have already seen regarding the general situation can also be applied here. For the defense phase, you need to: bring up the initial line of pressing; get the strikers to collaborate more; make sure the team is more compact; make sure the team tries to double up on marking more; insert a center mid fielder able to rob the ball so that you will have more chance of getting back possession. For the attacking phase you need: more concentration and diligence in the post-conquest sub-phase so as to improve our consolidation once we have got possession, making sure we can get past the opponent's pressing; to fall back on an initial long pass if the rival team's pressing is so asphyxiating as to make it difficult for us to carry out maneuvered counterattacks; to put on an attacking player able to defend the ball, who will permit the team to move into depth behind him.

From a psychological point of view, you have to be able to manage the mental state of the team in order to resolve the critical situation. The tactical moves might turn out to be less penetrating if you do not also eliminate the negative psychological states which, as we have seen, are to be considered an important cause of the critical situation in question.

If our team is closing itself in on purpose, or if they are simply accepting the opponent's play in a passive way, we must call the players' attention to the mistake that they are making. Remind them that this inactive behavior is not part of the project and of all the hard work they have carried out in training - that everything will have been in vain if the result is now compromised. You can add that the best way of getting a positive result is certainly not to leave the ball to your opponents, letting them come towards our goal, but if anything the very opposite. It would be foolish ruin both the performance you are offering to the public and the result of the match because of an error of this type.

If our team wants to get out of this situation but just cannot succeed you must do something about the consequent psychological frustration. You have to keep the players calm, telling them to think carefully about what they have to do on a tactical level to resolve this difficult situation, without getting angry or giving way to resignation. Tell them that they will get hold of play with patience and tactical diligence, calling on the conviction they should have in their own ability. You can win them over by telling them that carrying out pressing is a great way of letting off steam and tension, which tends otherwise to grow without giving way to the necessary aggressiveness.

As we have already said, the further away from the end of the match we are, the more intransigent the coach should be about not accepting such situations.

We must, however, give separate treatment to cases where, at a few minutes from the end of the match, the opponents really bring us to our limits in order to get back on top. If you think that there is no hope of our players to reacting actively to this situation, gaining the rival's half with their pressing and ball possession, we will have to resign ourselves to the situation and take specific measures. The first thing is to ask the defense line to

limit their application of offside, so as not to be running into useless risks. Then, once we have got back into possession, we
must not accelerate the rhythm of play, but rather, take advantage of the situation by making sure the opponents cannot do so.
If you have any substitutions left to make, this could be a useful
moment to carry them out in order to keep down the rhythm of
play being imposed by the opponents, and, at the same time, to
give your players a chance to take a breath. Apart from their
other reasons for being, which we have already discussed, these
substitutions are made in order to interrupt the rival's forcing for a
minute or two. Some coaches even try to calibrate the marking
on the attacking players in these moments, and more in general
on any of the opponent's more dangerous players so as to be
able to control them with fewer risks. To do that, we have to modify the set up so that we will be in numerical superiority over the
opposing strikers. You can, for example, very often see teams
which, in the final minutes of the match, having by now 'lost half
the field', pass from a 4-4-2 to a 5-3-2 in order to have personal
marking on the rival strikers.

However, in cases like these you must ask your team to make a
last physical and mental effort in order to bring home the match,
convincing them on the basis of the fact that the game is all but
over and we have the means to carry it off. If we make it in the
end, we must, in any case, do a lot of work during the week to be
sure that we do not find ourselves in the same situation during
the next match.

THE RESULT IS NEGATIVE AND WE CONTINUE TO GO UNDER

DESCRIPTION: This is a complementary situation to the last. In
this case the team is not only losing, but is continuing to suc-
cumb to the rival team, who, having the game in control, wishes
to consolidate their favorable result. When we are winning and
having trouble it is a difficult situation to resolve but is not to be
considered disastrous, because, if we take a goal, we will have to
roll up our sleeves and start over, though the match has not been
compromised. The situation is really serious when we are losing,
but we still are not able to attack: not only are we in no position
to overcome the opponents and managing to draw the match, but

we are also running the risk of taking another goal, so further compromising the game.

This situation is principally due to our opponent's extraordinary determination in continuing to attack even though they are in advantage, demonstrating their positive and commendable winning mentality. But their incessant offensive onslaught might easily be helped along by the psychological backlash that our own players are undergoing in this situation. The fact that we are one goal down and there seems to be nothing we can do about it but just continue to give way, demoralizes our players from a mental point of view because they now have two problems to resolve (draw the match and take control of play).

This psychological difficulty becomes a tactical problem, and our players cannot find the clearness of mind necessary to resolve the critical situation by carrying out what they should do correctly. Such a state of things can come about immediately after having taken a goal (the most frequent case), or in the subsequent period of the match (perhaps because resignation takes hold of them). If we take a goal towards the end of a match, it can be very difficult to find the psychological and physical force necessary to get back on top of the situation.

You must not neglect the fact that the team might not be able to react because they are at the end of their tether as far as physical energy is concerned.

Once again, the tactical situation here is characterized by the presence of the opposing team in our own half. Our side is decidedly unable to carry out the defense movements correctly (above all, those connected with pressing), or those connected to the post-conquest sub-phase.

However, if we react well, above all mentally, the opposing team will not be able to keep up such attacking incursions for a long period of time and will slowly let go of the reins of play. In the last minutes of the match we will in all likelihood be able to gain our opponent's half, on condition that we still have the energy to do so.

One last consideration about this situation. which can come about on account of the evident superiority on the part of the rival team from almost all the points of view. For the moment there is very little we can do to straighten out the match in course, but in the future we must work hard in order to bridge the gap between us and any team superior to us.

MOVES TO RESOLVE THE SITUATION: From a tactical point of view the same moves we have already seen in relation to the other two connected situations will also be useful here. There is no point repeating ourselves, but remember that you must strengthen up both phases of play: the defense phase in order to improve our ability in regaining possession; and our attacking phase so as to improve positive transition and consolidate as well as possible the fact that we have regained possession, and then to move up towards the rival team's half.

One thing must be said - because this situation is more critical than the preceding two, we will need to be more resolute in carrying out substitutions even when the end of the match is not really near.

Again, we will also have our work cut out from a psychological point of view to resolve this delicate situation.

The first thing to do is to urge the team not to let go, not to resign themselves to the negative result, insisting that they recover their positions and must remain convinced of their ability by which they will be able to get back into the opponent's half. We must convince our players that if they oppose themselves with more determination to the opponent's offensive attitude, their rivals will get discouraged after a little while, and will resign themselves to waiting in their own half.

Nevertheless, it is not easy to manage this situation in a psychological way, above all if the end of the match is near. In such moments it is difficult to convince the team that they must keep their heads and assume a determined and aggressive attitude. It might be a good idea to put on a number of players from the bench who have not gone through this mentally frustrating situation, and who could therefore give their team mates a positive shake-up, acting as an example and an incitement to them in order to try and get back into the opponent's half.

If we can in no way resolve the situation, then the coach must make an in-depth study of the causes of this psychological (but also tactical) problem during the following week. All our work during training sessions is being thrown away because once the match begins we are not able to express any attacking play of quality.

Lastly, if the situation is due to a lack of physical energy, and the end of the match is still far off, we must try to 'lengthen out the game'. You tell your players not to apply in-depth pressing, to keep the rhythm and intensity of down so that the opponents are dominating play, but we in turn are controlling them. When there are only a few minutes left, the time has come to ask our players to give all they have got and organize themselves for the final assault. All this will be done reluctantly if the coach has more active and resourceful ideas about soccer. But this type of behavior is without doubt more intelligent in these particular circumstances, and must therefore be adopted without too much remorse. We can do the same thing even in cases where our team is too technically or tactically inferior and the match seems to be too long - we can insist on the defense phase (even making a change of system) although we are losing. This will help us give as much as we can in the last ten minutes when the opponents might have physical or psychological problems handling a sudden change in the tactical situation.

THE RESULT IS NEGATIVE AND THERE ARE ONLY A FEW MINUTES LEFT

DESCRIPTION: In this situation our team is losing (or we are drawing but this is not a satisfactory result for us because of the classification tables or an aggregate score in a return cup match), and there are only a few minutes to go to the end of the match. We must do all we can to resolve this type of critical situation and the coach must be resolute with the team, using so-called 'desperate' tactical moves.

This is true, however, only when the team is down by one or at the most two goals. Things will be somewhat different if we are undergoing a crushing defeat. Later, we will be having a look at the type of critical situation that sees our team down by a number of goals.

When we are under by a goal, we can still make that up even if there are few minutes left to play, though of course you are going to have to organize a real assault on you opponent's goal. Two things can happen in these circumstances, depending on your opponent's behavior. If they take up a nonresistant attitude we do not have to face the problem of getting past their pressing in order to gain their half, but we will have difficulty breaking through the barrier that they have erected around their area. If the opponent assumes a more active attitude by pressing in depth and trying to gain possession far away from their goal, then we will have the opposite problem. In fact, our aim is them to keep possession near the opposing goal so as to be able to create goal scoring opportunities.

In order to resolve such situations a team must be well lined up from every point of view. Tactically speaking you need to have good discipline in the attacking movements, which must be clear and suitable for the job of opening out the rival defense system, especially if it is closed; from the physical point of view, you must have enough energy left over to carry out the final forcing, and, as concerns psychology, you need to have the force, the will and the mental determination to try and create and finalize goal scoring opportunities without giving up right until the referee blows the final whistle. You very often see teams that attack the opponent with great verve in the final moments of a match, frequently getting positive results and managing to resolve a critical situation. At the same time teams regularly have great difficulty in becoming dangerous at this point, letting their opponents control play even when they are losing a match.

From the tactical point of view, then, the critical situation may see our team play all the time in their opponent's half without managing to become dangerous or finalize the goal scoring opportunities that are being created, but we could also be having difficulty keeping possession and getting near the rival goal. This last case could be due to an active attitude on our opponent's part and / or a tactical, physical or psychological flaw in our own team. In any case, this situation is connected to another that we will be having a look at later - a team that is finding it difficult to become dangerous in the offense phase and to finalize play.

MOVES TO RESOLVE THE SITUATION: As we have seen in our description, you have to work on three fronts in order to resolve this critical situation: the tactical, physical and psychological front. Tactics first of all: you have to start making 'desperate' moves which will completely overturn the normal set up of the team. The first thing is you have to put on a greater number of attacking players, so changing the playing system. This will give you more players who can finalize the maneuvers, intensifying the action taking place in the last twenty meters. Then you must insist on actions along the flanks, so as to get to finishing touch-es by crossing. Crosses are a very important type of finishing touch play when you want to create problems for a defense lined up around their area. When using crosses, in fact, it is not impor-tant to create situations of numerical superiority, but it is enough that the attacking player gets to the ball first (either because he jumps high or because he has jumped at the right moment). The most unusual, or last ditch moves are the following. You can decide to bring up one or two defenders good at aerial play into the position of real strikers so as to be able to make the most of crosses. Depending on just how urgent it is to straighten out the result you can also ask your goalkeeper to come into attack with all the other players when there are corners to be taken or free kicks in the cross zone - keeping one man at most in relative pre-ventive coverage. It goes without saying that this is a move to use when there is nothing left to lose, and, as there are only a couple of minutes left to play, taking another goal will not make any great change. Still talking about the attacking phase, and apart from counting on crosses even from behind and on shots on goal from far out, to accelerate play without losing any time you can ask the players and above all the defenders to make great use of long passes to the attacking players. These long passes, which in any case must not be carried out any old how, can create difficulties for the already very tense opposing defense line, above all if we have a great number of players posi-tioned far into depth who can manage to cover the areas where the ball will fall.

All this will depend on the fact that the opposing team is at the end of its tether with our pressing and our forcing. If they are managing to keep possession far away from their goal, the situa-tion is more complicated and our players will have to press in a constant and well-organized way, looking for finishing touches with cuts and central combinations following on vertically oriented build up rather than by using crosses after horizontal actions. For the defense, apart from going for suffocating pressing on the whole field, you will have to ask the back line to intensify the almost exasperating tactical application of offside. That is very important in order to regain possession at once, making sure that the opponents cannot keep possession without our decided opposition.

From a physical point of view, you must make sure that the team has the necessary energy to bear up against the final forcing. If the match is to be won at any cost, you have to ask your players to make a final effort, unless this might damage their health. In situations like this, you must not hesitate in carrying out substitutions among players if there are any still at your disposal, so that you can put on fresh energy that will be able to give extra life to those who are already over tired.

Form a psychological point of view, lastly, it is important to keep inciting the team in the last few minutes. You must ask your players to give all they have got, not to capitulate and not to leave anything untried, so that, even if they have not been able to resolve the situation, they will have done their duty at least. Psychologically speaking, you have to ask your team to 'hurl their hearts beyond the obstacle'.

WE ARE LOSING EVEN THOUGH WE ARE PLAYING WELL

DESCRIPTION: This situation comes up when our team takes a goal, or even worse more than one, when in fact they are playing well and deserve to score themselves. The same thing can happen during their best part of the match, even if they have not been expressing themselves very well up to that moment.

This is a situation of an entirely psychological nature. It is never a particularly happy moment when a team takes a goal and goes one down. But if this happens when our team is dominating the match both in terms of possession and of opportunities created, or, in any case, if we do not deserve to be at a disadvantage - then the psychological backlash can be very strong.

The fact of having played well without getting positive results, but actually being defeated is a paradox that can make the players lose their conviction in their own means and deprive them of the force to go on playing as they were before. Even though we have tried to convince the players over and over again that the important thing is the way in which they play (and that the result should be a consequence of that), in situations like these they can totally lose confidence in such concepts and feel lost and victims of injustice. In some cases, the players could lose their faith in the philosophy and the tactical set up proposed by their coach, to the point of being tempted to copy that of their opponents from whom they have received a 'lesson'.

Another thing is that in this situation the rival who does not deserve to be winning gets a psychological kick from the circumstances and can start to play better immediately after the goal on the wings of this new enthusiasm.

A situation like this cuts our players down to size, having such an influence on their minds as to impede them from running and moving around as they were doing until just a moment before. From a tactical point of view, our team has been in full control of play and master of the field, the number one in the number of goal scoring opportunities created. It can then happen following on the fact that they have gone one down, that they are suddenly incapable of attacking with ant continuity and they are allowing the opponents to come dangerously forward and attack as if there is nothing they can do about it.

The first thing to say is that there must be some tactical flaw at the basis of this situation. If the team fails to be concrete in terms of goal scoring opportunities created by all this play, then they are not very effective or are not using their chances in a cynical enough way.

As well as that, the situation will get even more complicated if the players do not have much energy left, which will make it difficult for them to find greater drive in order to rectify the result.

If there is still a long time to go before the end of the match, the coach has the advantage of being able to get his team back into line psychologically; while if we are near the final whistle, it will be more difficult to get them to react.

Lastly, this is a similar situation to the one where our team was in advantage and playing well, only to take a goal from the opponents with the risk of going down. You can refer back to what was said there for this context as well.

MOVES TO RESOLVE THE SITUATION: To resolve this situation you need to act above all on a psychological level. You must make sure that the players do not give up in the face of an unfair predicament, giving them the force and above all the motivation to continue playing as before. The greatest problem is to make sure that the players do not lose confidence in the mentality and the tactical method created by the coach, maybe even blaming the negative result on these very things. We must convince the players straight away that, despite the disadvantage, the proce-

dure must remain what it always was - the highway to be followed in order to get the result in this and in future matches.
The players must be animated by a positive desire to get back what has been lost and not by a negative sense of resignation and by the loss of conviction in their means.

The coach must do a good job of straightening out this situation whenever it comes up, though of course the more time there is still to go in the match, the greater his responsibility will be because there will be more time to put things in their place. If there is little time left to play it will be much more difficult for the coach to set things on the right track, and he will be less to blame in such situations.

Apart from these continuous and selective psychological interventions in the direction of the team and the single players, the coach will also have to decide whether or not to carry out small tactical changes to make things easier for the team in difficulty. You must be careful, however, not to send negative messages to the team: applying tactical modifications to the playing system might give the players the impression that the negative result is due to the inadequacy of the system itself.

In the attacking phase, you could now ask the team to apply certain playing schemes more frequently than others, and to develop play more in depth than in width. This can be useful in the final minutes of the match when the need to make up on the result calls for a more incisive and immediate attitude in building up play.

In the defense phase, you can give new instructions on the shifting mechanisms and on the application of pressing and offside, so as to increase the team's aggressiveness and their ability to regain possession.

You also need to pick out any players that because they are particularly de-motivated, might be having a negative influence on their team mates. Such players must be substituted at once, as well as those who are not physically or tactically suitable for carrying out the assault against the rival defense.

After the match, you must discover the tactical reason for this situation, working hard to make the team more effective and prolific in the attacking phase. Above all, you must talk to the players, convincing them that they are to go on in this way, even if in this case we have lost without deserving to. They must be told that by playing well they will get the better of things in the long run, even against more cynical opponents.

GETTING OVER THE INABILITY TO BE DANGEROUS IN THE OFFENSE PHASE

DESCRIPTION: Even though we are keeping possession and have control of the field, it can often happen that we are just not able to become dangerous in the attacking phase creating goal-scoring opportunities with a certain continuity.

This situation can come up in any moment of the match, but it will become more and more critical the nearer we get to the 90th minute. At the beginning the team will take this inability to unlock the match with a certain calm, but the nearer we get to the end of the match, the more nervy and frenetic the players will become if they are not able to score. Single players might even start thinking that their own attacking organization of play is inferior to the opponent's ability to defend. The players could get into a psychological condition of frustration and lack of confidence in their means. The consequence will be that, playing without any tranquillity or rationality in possession, we will become even more ineffective in attack, so favoring the rival's defensive play. So it is that this situation creates big problems of a psychological nature. The inability to set up goal-scoring opportunities is a critical situation, especially if we are drawing or losing. If we are winning, the fact that we cannot reinforce the result even though we are still attacking is not to be considered a true negative situation: we must only be careful that the situation does not change, continuing to keep hold of play and waiting with patience to score other goals.

A situation in which we are having trouble capitalizing on attacking play is often caused by a rival team's surrendering and stand-by behavior, moving back in mass around their penalty area. From a tactical point of view, our team will keep possession, crushing the opponent into their half, but ball circulation will be slow and predictable just as the maneuver will be distinguished by insufficient collective movement to free players of marking with inadequate use of the flanks. Even in cases where the maneuvers are well built up, we will be having great difficulties during finishing touch play: we get to the opponent's area easily enough, but then we have no clear ideas about what to do.

So, apart from the opponent's ability at placing themselves correctly in defense of their goal, this critical situation is above all created by our team's inadequate execution of the attacking phase.

MOVES TO RESOLVE THE SITUATION: In order to resolve this situation, you must keep in mind not only the tactical difficulties of the team in the attacking phase, but also those psychological repercussions that form themselves little by little as time passes and we still have not scored. From the tactical point of view, we must first of all invite the team to move about and circulate the ball in the way studied during training. The most important thing to ask them is to move around incessantly without the ball, speeding up and varying play to the limits and heightening the rhythm. Another thing is to insist that they carry out intense pressing to as to make sure that the rival defenders are dealing with as many psychological problems as we can give them and trying to get past them with sharp, short breaks.

As well as that, we must do something about improving the effectiveness of our attacking play. If the end of the match is still a long way off, we can ask the team to build up by giving preference to playing schemes that have not been very much applied until that moment instead of others that have not been creating great problems for the opponent. Without doubt, you will have to encourage the team to go for their assaults along the flanks to arrive at crosses and not to come forward in the center where it is to be supposed the rival defense will be more tightly closed. You will also have to ask the defenders to participate more assiduously in the maneuvers, so as to be in numerical superiority against the rival defense and to have more attacking solutions at our disposal. In making this choice, we must make sure that the risk of finding ourselves in numerical inferiority in defense are not too high in case we undergo a counterattack - above all if the result is still unsure.

Another useful thing in order to unblock the situation is to carry out exchanges of position between players so that strikers and mid fielders with marked offensive characteristics can play in zones that are right for them and against opponents that do not inhibit their particular strengths.

When the match is drawing to a close we must make more drastic decisions, i.e., change the system by putting on more strikers
ready to make the best of crosses into the area (remember that
the opponents must be 'bombarded' with high balls coming in,
counting on the fact that sooner or later one of their members will
make a decisive mistake).

From a psychological point of view, it is very important to make
sure that the team does not become prey to panic and get nervy,
so becoming more sterile and predictable in their play. You must
keep the players calm, telling them to play without anxiety with
the conviction that sooner or later the situation will unblock itself if
they make use of reasoned, rational build up - and reminding
them that there is still enough time to create goal-scoring opportunities. especially in the final part of the game, you must ask the
team to do its duty in the defense phase, convincing them that
their play is superior to the opponent's ability to destroy it, and
that if we are not scoring that is because the soccer we are
expressing is influenced by anxiety and exasperation. It is all
important to keep the players' tranquillity and reasonableness in
order to unblock the situation.

UNBLOCKING ANY DIFFICULTY IN FINALIZING THE MANEUVERS

DESCRIPTION: This is not really definable as a critical situation.
It would be better to call it an unlucky or an 'odd' situation. Our
team is playing effective, convincing soccer and is respecting the
tactical and behavioral orders given by the coach and studied in
training sessions. The problem is that the many goal-scoring
opportunities created are not being finalized by the players, in
particular by the strikers. As a result, the team is not very effective in the shooting sub-phase.

Logically, this is generally due to the technical inability at shooting on the part of those players who are kicking at goal. Yet, it
can often happen that the difficulty the attacking players are having in finalizing their opportunities is not due to technical flaws,
but rather to psychological difficulties. You can quite commonly
find attacking players with good technical skills which they show
to the full in training, but which they seem to lose during matches, failing the easiest of opportunities. This is due to their lack of

clear-headedness and to the tension of the moment, which does not give them the chance to think and to choose where, how and when to shoot at goal.

It is clear as well that this critical situation can be caused in part by bad luck which conditions the episodes in a negative way.

In this sense, the trainer's job is not only to resolve the problem of not being able to finalize the goal-scoring opportunities created, but he must also prevent another: the loss of conviction and continuity on the part of the players, who might therefore end up by being no longer dangerous in the attacking phase. We could even say that the coach should worry most about making sure there is no change in a situation that sees our team so effective in creating opportunities in the attacking phase.

If the match is about to finish, we will easily be able to go on creating opportunities, above all if the result is not in our favor. If there is still a long time to go, it is not easy to keep attacking in a satisfying way until the end.

To conclude, the situation will be more or less urgent depending on the result we have reached: if we are winning, the coach will not have to worry too much; if we have to score a goal in order to make up for a negative result, he must do everything he can to ensure that the critical situation finds a solution.

MOVES TO RESOLVE THE SITUATION: To resolve this situation, the most intelligent thing to do is to put on strikers who are more capable and 'cold-blooded' in shooting at goal and who are not, above all, as overcome by frustration as the first choice players will be on a negative day like this. Before carrying out these substitutions, we have to make sure that the effectiveness of the offense phase will not be undermined, which would, of course make the move devoid of meaning. If we put on a striker who is technically skilled at shooting at goal, but who is not sufficiently part of the team's playing schemes (and this would damage the choral movement of the build up), the situation will not have been improved, but might even become really critical. As well as this, we must keep in mind that if the match is about to finish, we can carry out more than one substitutions aiming to improve the technical ability of the team to conclude the actions that it produces. If you judge that the situation will now remain stable until the end of the match because the opponent is relinquishing its play, you can make a change of system so as to put new strikers on the field keeping the ones that are already there.

If the final whistle is still far off you must make the changes in a rational way. The first thing to keep in mind is that the tactical situation might change again, and new moves will be required which we must be in a position to carry out. As well as that, you must remember not to make all three substitutions before a certain part of the match, because otherwise, if one of our players should get an injury, we will be playing for too long in numerical inferiority.

Speaking generally, however, it is a good thing to put on at least one player good at scoring in the second half. That is fundamental in the moment that we are creating opportunities with ease, keeping in mind that, unfortunately, situations like that might not last too long.

From a psychological point of view, you must tell the strikers to play with calm, keeping their heads clear in the moment when they have to shoot at goal.

In order to manage the most important aspect of this situation, that is, to make sure we keep on creating goal-scoring opportunities, get the team to persevere with what they are doing.

You must encourage the players who fail their chances, so as to make sure they are not losing heart. And you must give the group the conviction that if they continue to attack as they are doing, the goal will arrive sooner or later.

As soon as you see that the team is becoming resigned to their inability to score, you must take them up on this, making them aware of the fact that by behaving in this way they are taking a step in the wrong direction, and that resignation will bring no advantage at all.

WE ARE LOSING BY A LARGE MARGIN: LIMITING THE DAMAGE

DESCRIPTION: It can unfortunately come about for various reasons (a terrible performance in terms of play, a much better opponent from all points of view, bad luck, etc.) that our team is losing - down by a considerable number of goals. This situation could be the consequence of the one above, where our team was at a disadvantage and unable to become dangerous, but it is now

definitively compromised and will be almost impossible to overturn. The overall shape of the situation will change depending on
the moment of the match when the result becomes impossible to
reverse. If there is little time left to the final whistle there is nothing to be done to straighten out the match. If we have time on
hand the situation could be fixed up, or at least we can try.
We must keep in mind that the team's performance heavily conditions its psychological state (which in its turn is a very important
thing at such moments), and consequently the possibility of getting back on top. If the team deserves the bad result because
they are playing badly, this will not give problems from the mental
point of view because the players are aware that they have not
done their duty in one way or another. However, if our side have
been playing a good match and do not deserve this negative
result, the players will logically feel annulled from a psychological
point of view, without there being anything we can do to resolve
this - and they will finish up by compromising their own performance in terms of the quality of play. In both cases, it can easily
happen that the team gets depressed and gives up, at which
point the final result will be more or less deceptive with regard to
the real difference in value between the two teams. This often
happens because of a perverse mechanism which detonates in
the mind of a player in great difficulty. Lowering your guard, playing with little or no drive and without even really trying - this is
typical of a player who, seeing that the situation is compromised,
prefers to lose badly rather that fighting on until the end. On the
psychological plane, in fact, a defeat following on a performance
which is below your real standard is more acceptable that one
that comes about when the players are putting everything they
have into the match. You must also consider the fact that in critical situations the player with little personality prefers to haul in his
oars and hide himself in the middle of the team, from where he
can always lay the blame on the whole group. Critics will often
give negative judgments on a team that has lost by a large margin of goals, full of surprise when in they next match the same
players come out on top, perhaps even against a stronger team
than the one from whom they took such a hiding. These 'experts'
do not keep in mind the psychological aspect that leads a team
to surrender when they think there is no longer anything they can
do about the result - they stop playing, in fact, and run the risk of

taking more and more goals from their opponents who become ever more stimulated by the ease of their success.

At this point our opponents will have brought our team to the end of their tether from the tactical point of view. They will be able to press in depth and keep easy and effective possession in our half of the field. As a result, our group will not be able to press with any constancy or effectiveness and they will not be able to keep possession, which is the only thing that would give them the chance of becoming dangerous in the offense phase.

MOVES TO RESOLVE THE SITUATION: You must keep in mind that there is not much that can be done to resolve this type of situation. If we cannot find a solution, that does not mean that we are not capable enough to do so, but, if anything, that we were not able to prevent this particular difficulty from coming out. As this situation can be compared to the one that saw our team down by a goal but unable to react, the coach has the responsibility, in such cases, of not having found a solution right from the beginning.

However, though there may not be any real chance of overturning the situation, there can be no doubt that the coach must leave no stone unturned in carrying out his duty and making sure that the same thing goes for his team. There is not much to say from the tactical point of view except to incite the group to go on behaving as has been established: pressing, ball possession in the attacking zone, speed of maneuvers, etc.

But it is above all on the psychological plane that you must act. As we have already said, in cases like these the team can get almost irreversibly depressed and finish up by giving up completely with the consequent risk of taking even more goals. To avoid this mental collapse, you must incite your team not to let go, to put everything they have got into it so as to be in a position to say at the end of the match that they have done all they could until the end. It is not so easy to carry this off, but if you can work on the team you may be able to manage. You could try and convince them not to take an interest in the result, almost as if we were drawing, concentrating in a free way on the spectacle they are offering to the public, having a careful look at the result obtained in this way only when the match is over. All this will vary, however, on the amount of time still to play. The longer the time remaining, the more the coach has to insist on his players trying to overturn the situation; the nearer we are to the end of the match, the more the coach must see to it that his team can save face, trying hard to limit the damage. If the critical situation is created by the clear superiority of the opponents, we must ask our players to do their best in any case, trying to make sure there is no increase in the disadvantage.

Clearly, when we manage to score a goal that shortens the distance, the coach must immediately make a psychological intervention to incite and encourage his players. In the end, we can decide to change the most resigned players, putting on others that are more motivated from a mental point of view and who, because they do not play very often, will want to put their qualities on show.

The degree of physical preparation is not often a predominating factor in these critical situations. The only thing you will have to look into is whether such a highly negative result is to be connected with a serious physical low in the group. If that seems to be the case, we must ask the team not to behave in a wasteful way from a tactical point of view and the most fatigued players should be substituted immediately.

At the end of the match, whether or not we have been able to straighten out the situation, we must make a detailed in-depth analysis of all the tactical, technical, psychological and physical factors that are at the base of the critical situation we have had to affront so as to make sure it does not come up again in the future. Of course, if the team has managed to recuperate the negative situation in question we will also have to praise them for the character they have shown.

CONTAINING THE OPPONENTS IN THEIR ATTEMPT TO OVERTURN THE SITUATION

DESCRIPTION: This is the opposite of the preceding situation. In this case, in fact, our team is initially at an advantage by more than a single goal, but the problem is that the opponents are closing in on us little by little again. It goes without saying that the last situation was more serious. This is not only because in this case we are at an advantage, but also and above all because this type of situation can be resolved, while, on the contrary, the last was almost irreversible. Naturally, the players must make sure they can contain their opponents who are fighting back, but it not difficult to make sure that actually happens.

This situation is very probably due to two things: the rival's attacking drive and our players' loss of concentration. The first factor comes down to the positive way in which the opponents are playing, showing character and the ability not to give up. It is the second facet that is of greater interest to us, testifying to the fact that the team is behaving badly, deciding not to play, that is, believing that they are already sure of the result and showing that they do not have a winning mentality. The situation is similar to another we have already had a look at, where we were winning but submitting too much to the opponent's attacking play. As well as that, as the distance between the two teams in terms of the result is gradually reduced, precise and decisive psychological states will make their appearance on both sides, and these will progressively increase the chances of the rival team to overturn the score. In fact, the opponents will believe in themselves more and more, increasing their determination and conviction and giv-ing all they have got to overturn the result. On the contrary, our team will be more and more shocked and afraid by the attacks it is receiving and might even begin to panic feeling impotent in front of it rival's offensive drive.

The situation is characterized by two psychological states in our players: the initial de-concentration which made it easy for our rivals to fight back; followed on by fear and a feeling of impo-tence, which make it more and more possible for the opponents to get back on top.

Mentally speaking, the more time is left to the end of the match, the more complicated the situation will be. If there is little time remaining the players will be less 'desperate' because the oppo-nents have less chance of making it: they know the critical situa-tion will soon be at an end and they have almost won the match. This will give them the necessary force to react to the rivals attempt to get back on top. On the contrary, if there is a long time to go before the end of the match the players will be panicking more knowing that the opponents have a good chance of draw-ing. In this case, the group's feeling of being at a loss runs the risk of lasting longer or of not even coming to an end.

There is little to say from the physical point of view about this situation. It is very rarely caused by sudden and terrible athletic collapse, and it will seldom happen that the team cannot react for this reason.

From the tactical point of view, lastly, our team is crushed in their half and is having difficulty carrying out the defense movements with order and effectiveness, which would allow them to face their opponent's decided forcing play. When we do manage to get possession, we just cannot get past our opponent's pressing and enter their half, and there is no question of us ever becoming dangerous in attack.

MOVES TO RESOLVE THE SITUATION: As we saw in the descriptive section, in order to resolve this situation you really have to intervene on a psychological level. It is important to act at once, the moment you see the first signs of the problem and not only when it has already become critical. At the first goal that we take, therefore, and no matter how great the difference in the scores still might be, we must start to communicate with the team, making them as aware as possible of the risking we are beginning to run, waking them up as it were. You must tell the players to keep their concentration, insisting that they apply the attacking and the defense plays with continuity, and reprimanding the players even when their mistakes regard tiny errors in what they have to do. You must make them concentrate as hard as they can, without worrying that you might be stressing them.

In cases where the situation is already critical because the opposing team has already made up ground, you must take up a decisive and very strict attitude in order to make your players react, though you must also understand the difficulties they have in front of them. When a tam realizes too late just how dangerous this situation really is, they will normally do all they can to react without needing to be asked, but it is clear that they will not always be able to do so in a clear-headed way because the are blocked by their fear. The coach's intervention must help them and not make them even more strained and tense. The coach must be good at calming the players, telling them to go on playing and to ignore the result, pretending even that it is unfavorable to us. You must prevent them from making the bad decision to defend the advantage they have in a passive way, placing themselves in their own half and allowing the opponents to come dangerously forward. This can happen above all during the final minutes of the match, when all our players minds are possessed by the opponent's onslaught.

In itself, pressing can be an important outlet for this tension. When there is still a long way to go before the end of the match and the situation is even more critical, you have to convince the players that they, too, have the advantage of more time at their disposal in order to close the game definitively, rolling up their sleeves to attack and score more goals.

To make all this easier, the coach can make other changes, especially on the tactical plane. First of all, he can substitute the most shaken players, the ones who are in the greatest difficulty from the psychological and physical point of view. He can also improve the defense phase by putting on a mid fielder who is better able to regain possession, asking the strikers to work harder by moving back in assistance and the whole team to keep compact. Telling the defense not to apply offside in an active way is another move to consider, keeping in mind that the back line can easily make mistakes in this situation of tension and worry. In attack, it can be very useful to put on a striker who is more capable of bringing the team up, and you must tell him to manage the ball with calm and order, without being in too much of a hurry to carry out an immediate but confused change of front.

In any case it is important that in the week to come the coach should try and resolve this disturbing loss of concentration which has led to this worrying critical situation. He must speak about it with the players to make sure that it does not take place again.

THE MATCH HAS ONLY JUST BEGUN AND WE ARE ALREADY ONE GOAL DOWN

DESCRIPTION: The critical problem here is that the match has only just begun and our team is already down by one or more goals. The game has suddenly and dramatically become an upward slog for us because we are at once obliged to make up for a negative score and all our plans have been upturned. Psychologically speaking, it is as if we have been hit on the head by a cudgel - finding ourselves in deep water in a match for which we have made detailed preparation and which we have been looking forward to for days - and which has now begun in the worst of all possible ways. The players may get a growing sense that they are no good, and they may begin to think that the reason why they are undergoing such a beating is the ineptitude of the playing schemes created by their coach, even those relative to the countermoves they have studied during the week in preparation for this match. In cases where the group has not yet assimilated the playing system required by the coach, it can easily happen that the players lose confidence when they see things going so badly. It follows that the coach may have trouble convincing the players to make the required movements with determination - even if, form the tactical point of view, they are exactly what is needed to get back in control.

This situation can be due to factors of different characters, but which can be verified in connection to each other. Perhaps the opposing team has started the match with unequaled attacking drive; maybe our team's approach has been completely inadequate; our players ma be having great difficulty in applying a newly introduced playing system or new tactics; we might have undergone a series of unlucky episodes during the first minutes of the match even though there is a substantial situation of balance; or could it be that the opposing team is to generally superior to our own?

If the coach is not quick to put his team back on the right track, the situation could become even more complicated. On the contrary, if we manage to get over the few minutes following on the goal (or goals) that we have taken, then we can still consider the match to be completely open. You often see teams that go one or more goals down in the first minutes of the match, passing through another difficult moment immediately afterwards and running the risk of taking other goals, but who then get on top of the situation and overturn the result without too many problems. Obviously, if the other team has scored only once, the situation is less desperate than those cases where we are down by a number of goals. It is up to the coach to make sure the situation does not degenerate.

When we have gone down during the first minutes of the match, our team will usually be confused and disordered also from the tactical point of view, finding itself crushed in its own half and unable to get anywhere near the opponent's goal. We will be at our opponent's mercy, and they will be attacking and pressing with incredible force - though this will become less and less as time goes by, especially if we are good at reacting.

MOVES TO RESOLVE THE SITUATION: To resolve this situation you need to act carefully from a psychological point of view. The first thing is to make sure that the players react to this moment of havoc. You must convince the team not to give in, which can easily happen especially when the disadvantage is due to bad luck, underlining the fact that they have more than enough time to get back on top. You must make them aware that everything is still possible and that their chances depend above all on them. To get them to keep their heads regarding their opponents incredible and apparently incessant attacking drive following on their psychological feeling of being on top, tell them that this aggressive attacking play will not last too long, and if they can get over this moment with determination their opponents will not be able to increase their lead.

It is very important that the players do not lose their confidence in the organization of play created by the coach and in the specific tactical moves he has got them to adopt for the match itself.

For this reason you must insist with the players concerning the tactical errors they are making, so as to convince them that if we are losing that is not to be accounted to the unsuitability of the playing system but to the fact that it is being applied in a mistaken way.

You incite the team so that they do not get the impression that they are alone in this moment of crisis, and in general you must never aim to depress the players whatever you say to them, making sure that they do not lose confidence in their means.

If the situation is due to a lack of concentration, the coach must reprimand the players, and then go to work during the week to improve the team's approach to the match.

When we have got over the moment of difficulty during which the opponent was on the point of scoring other goals, we have resolved only half the problem. At this point we must make sure the team makes up the negative score, which still persists. You must encourage the players, telling them that the difficult moment has passed and that we now have all the time we need at our disposal to overturn the result, which we will be able to do if we constantly apply the tactical instructions given by the coach. If these do not work out in a positive way, we can begin to adopt the tactical moves that we were looking at in the critical situation that saw us having difficulty becoming dangerous during the attacking phase.

In cases where the initial situation is not managed correctly and we have taken other goals, the coach will need to give a bigger psychological turn of the screw. He must be severe and at the same time near the team, participating in the shock they have received.

However, no real tactical move should be made immediately after being put in disadvantage. You could invert the positions of any players under particular psychological duress and who are also facing a difficult opponent, above all as concerns the non-possession phase. It is much too early at this point to carry out substitutions.

If this critical situation has been created by the fact that there is too big a difference between the two teams from every point of view, we must ask our players not to give up in any case, inciting them to do what they can during the rest of the match

THE TEAM HAS NOT ASSIMILATED THE COACH'S TACTICAL INSTRUCTIONS

DESCRIPTION: The team might be showing that it has clear limits in both phases, giving the coach to understand that the players have not assimilated his tactical instructions. When the team does not carry out a part of what has been asked of them, this can take place either on the level of the general tactical organization or on that of the countermoves for this particular match that we have established during the week.

As regards the general tactical organization, despite all the work that has been done during training, it can happen that the team is just not managing to carry out what they have been practicing. This can be due to the fact that there was no time to get to the end of the short training course that we set up for them, or that they are not yet sufficiently able to apply what they have learned in a natural way because of the tension that is always present during the match. When a team has still not fully assimilated the movements to be carried out in both phases, these difficulties are made even greater by the emotional state against which the players are struggling and also, of course, by the force of the adversary. However, it is evident that situations like these will come about when a new coach had just taken on the team. If that is not the case, then it is obvious that the players are so mentally conditioned (perhaps because they are not trying, or concentrating, hard enough) that they are just not able to carry out what they really know how to do.

A third possible factor that might inhibit the team's play could derive from the still precarious level of physical preparation they have reached.

Going into the tactical particulars of this situation, the team is not moving with the ball following the right timing; they are making banal mistakes in passing; are having difficulty building up and at the same time keeping possession; they are making space / time errors in applying pressing and carrying out shifting moves, which therefore end up by becoming useless or even dangerous; and the defense line are making continuous mistakes with offside, moving at the wrong moments and / or in the wrong ways.

As for the countermoves, it may be that the team has not assimilated them correctly, and now, either they are not doing what was asked of them during the week, or they are applying them in the wrong way. This is less critical than the other, relative to flaws in their general movements. While errors in connection with the tactical organization of the team give us great problems in building up your own play, or opposing yourself to you rival's actions, the unsatisfactory implementation of the specific countermoves for the match, will only make it happen that you cannot exploit the rival team's weaknesses or annul its strengths. In such cases, however, the match will not be completely compromised.

From a tactical point of view, therefore, our team will be having more or less evident difficulty in building up play or destroying the rival's actions. The opponents will be playing at their ease, magnifying our limits and annulling our strong points.

MOVES TO RESOLVE THE SITUATION: The first thing is to understand whether our team's problems in applying what the have been asked from a tactical point of view stems from the fact that they have not learned these things very well or from any particular mental states.

In the first case, it is clear that we cannot leave the team's tactical set up as it is in the empty hope that the players will start to carry out the movements correctly any moment now. You have to judge which movements in both phases the team is not able to implement very well. The tactical element that you must not hesitate to change if it is not being carried out correctly is the use of offside. Offside tactics are very advantageous if they are implemented in the right way, but if not they can become a danger. Obviously, you will need to tell the team to use only the defense elastic. Another tactic to change, if the team demonstrates that it is having difficulty applying it, is offensive pressing, because otherwise our half will be easy prey for the opponents as it would be dangerously open to them. In this sense, you will without doubt need to tell the team to bring back the initial pressing line so as to make the situation in which we are having trouble less dangerous than before. Then you must ask your players to build up play in a simple way; they are not to worry about applying complicated playing schemes which require more that one player to get free of marking in synchrony, but must move in an easy, linear way. Lastly, you have to ask yourself whether the new system that we are getting the team to apply is creating problems for them, especially concerning those cognitive points of reference that every player needs to have on the field. If you think that is the case, then you must ask the team to go back to the system they were using before your arrival. Where a new defense system has been introduced, and in circumstances where the players are having such great problems executing the new one that it could even compromise the match, you must return to the old one even if you do not like it.

In the face of all these tactical elements, you could decide to wait before making any strenuous moves, just reminding the team for a minute or so of how they should be behaving in both phases. As far as countermoves are concerned, you must first of all insist that they are applied correctly, reminding the team of what they have studied during the week. If the team continues to behave negatively from this point of view, you must try and supply them with new, simpler countermoves to carry out, aiming as always to put their strengths on show and weaken those of the opponent, keeping our own defects hidden and underlining theirs.

In cases where the bad execution of the tactical instructions has to do with questions of a psychological nature, the coach must do what he can to resolve them. He must try to calm the team, giving them back confidence in their ability. You must tell the players that by carrying out that which we have learned during the training sessions we can be superior to the opponents, and that otherwise we will be getting nowhere. If the team goes on full of tension and just cannot reason in a tactical way, you must lighten their workload in the ways we have seen above.

THE TEAM IS PHYSICALLY TIRED AND IS SUFFERING

DESCRIPTION: This situation is characterized by the bad physical condition of the team in terms of stamina, which comes out in a certain moment of the match. Even though the players have had good athletic preparation, they can sometimes have a fall from this point of view during a match for a number of reasons. Perhaps their preparation was not as good as we thought, and so the physically testing strategy that we have chosen for the match turns out to be inadequate, or the weather conditions (high temperature) are forcing the team to use up too much energy. It could also happen that the players have not been able to dose out their energy, running around too much and for too long during the match, perhaps to keep behind the high rhythm that the opponent seems to be able to take.
The situation will be more or less critical depending on the moment when the players seem to have run out of fuel. Clearly, if the match is just about to finish, there is nothing serious about the fact the team is physically tired - it is quite normal, in fact. The situation is worrying for the coach when there is still a long way to go. However, it is usually during the second half that the team starts to fall short of physical energy, even if it has had good athletic preparation.
Another thing is that when a team has run out of energy, there is also a mental reaction. Exhaustion provokes a fall in the players' ability to think clearly, and that in turn will create problems from the tactical and technical point of view. The team will lengthen out, it will insist on long passes in the attacking phase and will be more likely to make fouls in defense because the players no longer have the force to contrast their opponents. To add to that, the single players will begin to make mistakes with the simplest of techniques, like their passes or their stops.

All this will help the rival team, which, if there is enough time left and providing they are not in a precarious physical state themselves, will have a very good chance of winning the match.

That is another thing: the score reached at the moment of our physical collapse will contribute to our definition of just how critical the situation really is. If our team is winning, the situation is less acute. If we are drawing the match, or, worse still losing it, only a very well-chosen intervention by the coach will be able to save the situation.

Tactically, our team will be shut into their half, with the opposing team easily managing to carry out dangerous plays for our defense system in difficulty. In cases where the opponents are not in good physical condition either, the match will be fairly grey, played predominantly in the mid field, without the players being able to propose continuous or effective moves. The situation will be characterized by the teams being lengthened out with wide open spaces between the players.

MOVES TO RESOLVE THE SITUATION: Naturally, the coach should first of all be good enough to realize that the team is running out of energy before that actually happens - and then he will easily be able to resolve the situation. There is a good chance of continuing the match in the right way if we make the right moves at the right time, because otherwise it might be just too late.

To resolve this situation you need to modify the tactical attitude of the team. You must ask the players to apply less physically tiring tactics and ways of playing in order to help them save up the small amount of energy left in their 'tanks'. Tell them to bring back the initial line of pressing, at least to the mid-field. Even the use of offside tactics can be cut down on, until they are only using the defense elastic, so that the players in the back line are running less. For the attacking phase, tell the players to move less without the ball, trying pass it round principally in horizontal lines so as to slow down the rhythm and intensity of play. The defenders must go less into attack, above all to save themselves those long gallops to get back into position when the opponents are counter attacking.

The plays must develop slowly, moving the ball up with short passes, and then crossing from the base line or trying to carry out a final acceleration. You must tell the players not to make long passes forwards because this tactic, far from helping a team that is short of stamina, will put it in even greater difficulty, at the same time causing the players to lengthen out. As far as possible, you have to try and adopt an attacking attitude in any case, or at least one that is not excessively yielding, trying always to keep possession. By keeping our own rhythm low, we can try and force the opponents not to accelerate in their turn.

To help the players get a clear mental vision of each ongoing situation, and because they will not be thinking very clearly as we have seen, you must tell them not to be in a hurry to get rid of the ball after a few touches - the very opposite of what you have asked them to do during training. In this way, also the players without the ball have more time to get free of marking.

In cases where, unlike us, our opponents are in good physical shape and are attacking and forcing us to stay in our half of the field, we should try and 'lengthen out the match' as we have already seen.

You also need to give psychological support to your players, keeping in mind that their physical suffering creates mental distress, and that the more time there is still to go, the worse this will actually be.

Clearly as well, you need to make a couple of substitutions, taking the more exhausted players off the field without actually using up too much time to ponder things over. You must ask the new players to give all they have got in order to make up for the fatigue of their team mates, but also to align themselves to the new tactical attitude of the team. For example, if you are putting on a new center mid fielder, he must not go to attack parts of the field where we have decided not to apply pressing, just as he must not speed up the attacking play increasing the rhythm in a way that the other players will not be able to bear.

When the results of these moves are still negative, you must decide whether the team has the energy to take on a more aggressive and offensive attitude in the last few minutes. If you think the answer is yes, ask your team to make one last all-out effort. Otherwise, you must resign yourself, remembering that you should by no means compromise your players' health.

SHORING UP A SITUATION OF NUMERICAL INFERIORITY AGAINST THE OPPONENTS

DESCRIPTION: In this situation we are in general numerical inferiority against our opponents, and this can be due to two factors: the first and most frequent is that one of our players has been sent off; the second, which can come about during the last minutes of the match, is that one of our players has been injured and we cannot substitute him. It goes without saying that in this second case, the player's injury must be serious enough not to enable him to continue with the match. In the first case, the player who has been sent off is to blame for this numerical inferiority that we are undergoing, but the coach himself might be responsible for the second case, if he has been in too much of a hurry to carry out the three substitutions allowed to him. Obviously, if the injury takes place after the eightieth minute, we cannot call the coach to account.

This is without doubt a critical situation, which could even seriously compromise our match. Apart from the initial psychological backlash coming from this situation of numerical inferiority, our whole tactical set up will be displaced as well. The necessity to play with one fewer men can move the existing balance of the match into the opponent's favor. If our opponent already had control of the play and /or the result, it will now be even more difficult for us to straighten out the situation. The situation will of course be less critical if we were on top, although we will now have to expect even more drive from our opponents, who will feel even stronger because they now outnumber our own men.

There is another important factor in working out just how serious the situation is - how long we have on hand before the end of the match. If the final whistle is near, it will be enough to resist for a minute or two in numerical inferiority and this situation should not compromise the positive ongoing situation; if anything, it will be difficult to overturn the result in the last few minutes if this is a negative one. If there is still a long time to go before the end of the match, the situation is more complicated and the coach will need to make a well-aimed intervention to convince his players not just to wait for the 90th minute.

To return to the mental aspect: paradoxically, once the players have got over their initial shock at having lost a team mate, the players generally have a positive reaction to this situation. When they are in numerical inferiority against their opponents, they will often find it easier (under the coach's encouragement as well), to double the concentration in order to make up for the absence of their team mate, with the result that the team's general level of attention and determination is even higher than it was before. As well as this, the opponents will probably decrease their own level of concentration, believing mistakenly that everything will be easier at this point. Psychologically speaking, the weight of responsibility which until this moment was balanced out equally between the two teams will now tend to lean more on the one playing with eleven men who will feel that it is their duty to win the match. Many experts believe that this situation of numerical inferiority has a good general effect on a team, or that the side is not really damaged by it in an excessive way.

This is also true because from the tactical point of view it is not too difficult to place the ten remaining players on the field. Perhaps we will no longer be able to apply in depth pressing so as to have greater compactness in the team, but for the rest there are no real handicaps. We are not running the risk of being at a serious numerical disadvantage in any particular part of the field, and you can often see a team attacking with a certain effectiveness and continuity even though they are playing with ten men.

Of course, if we are missing more than one man, the situation will become more complicated from the tactical point of view (it becomes more difficult to set up the team so that it does not have problems in any part of the field), from the psychological angle (the players are now discouraged and convinced that the match is compromised, and they will end up by giving in) and in connection with their physical state (the team has to run much more to make up for the lack of some of its members, and they will not be able to put up with that for long). As well as this, the opponents will now be much more determined, and will no longer show any of the tension that they may have been suffering from earlier.

MOVES TO RESOLVE THE SITUATION: The best way to manage this situation is to act on the tactical and the psychological plane. On the tactical plane, you must give the team a new and precise set up on the field. We are talking about inventing a new system on the basis of which to line up the players. There are two ways in which the coach can go about this. The first, the easiest and the most widely used is to decide on the new 9 moving player system on the basis of the circumstances in which we find ourselves in this moment of the match. You keep in mind the result, how many minutes there are still to go, the general condition of the opponents and their system and so of the places on the team where they could outnumber our own men if we make any changes. After that, the classical move in these kinds of situation is to substitute a striker with a defender or a mid fielder depending whether we need to strengthen the second or the third line. When we are in numerical inferiority, the coach will usually try to set up his team in a defensive way, thinking that offensive play should now limit itself to counterattacking. At this point, you try to reinforce the defense or the mid field, leaving a single player in a forward position.

However, you must not overturn the tactical arrangement of the team and take away the players' points of reference.

The second thing that can be attempted will require some organization during training. You have to study and create a playing system with 9 moving players to be put into effect in these situations, and which does not depend on the situation in the team will find itself during the course of the match (result, performance and set up of the opposing team, time to go until the end of the match, etc.), but which has another important characteristic. That is that the 'special' system will not invalidate the typical set up of the team, and therefore also the application of the tactics and the specific playing schemes that we want to see. For example, if a team using the 4-4-2 loses a defender, the typical move is to put on a player in the same role in place of a striker, transforming the system into a 4-4-1. In that way, it will not be possible to apply in depth pressing (there is only one player positioned in such a way as to be easily able to press the rival defenders), and in the attacking phase we will no longer be able to base ourselves on the perfectly synchronous movements of the two strikers, on which the movements of the other players were earlier depending. The coach may also have created and taught in training a system of 9 moving players which will permit the team to continue with their pressing and to carry out the usual attacking plays: such a system could be the 4-3-2, some of its particulars maybe even adapted to the tactical needs of the moment.

In any case, it is up to each single coach to decide which of these two ways is the most intelligent and in line with his own way of thinking. When we are in numerical inferiority by more than one player, we must in any case adjust ourselves to the situation, doing what we can and trying to limit the damage.

On a tactical level, such changes of system are often carried out by making substitutions, but in cases where the numerical inferiority is created by an injured player who we can no longer replace, we will have to make interchanges of position between the players on the field in order to adjust the team.

On the psychological plane instead, we have to make the best use possible of the surprising potentiality of this critical situation. You must order the team to double their concentration, telling them that a part of the responsibilities of their team mate who has left the field is now on their own shoulders, and that each individual player can no longer limit himself to carrying out his own particular duties. You must convince the group that they are not to give up hope by simply waiting for their rivals in their own half. If they do the very opposite, the opponents, who are already running the risk of losing concentration, could be surprised by our drive and at a disadvantage. If you think that the team is assuming a passive attitude, you must dress them down, or, in any case, keep encouraging them until the end of the match.

To finish off, even the opposite case could be a critical situation from a mental point of view - when we are the ones to find ourselves in numerical superiority. In cases like that, you must make sure the team does not lose concentration believing that the rest of the match will be downhill. The very opposite: you must put them on the alert to the fact that the opponents will now multiply their attention and determination, and that we must do the same. In this situation as well, we must modify the details of our two phases in order to make the most of any possible situations where we will be in numerical superiority in different parts of the field and the tactical hindrances that our opponents will now be coming up against.

RESOLVING PROBLEMS CONNECTED WITH PLAYING EXTRA TIME AND THE PENALTY SHOOT OUT

DESCRIPTION: You will not often find yourself in this critical situation. Playing extra time and then perhaps even penalty shoot outs can only happen in those matches that do not foresee a draw and the end of regular time, i.e., in tournaments where there is direct elimination. Extra time and penalty shoot outs are a protraction of the ninety minutes of the match, and this subject could perhaps have been included in the preceding chapters treating the match and its various stages. Yet, because this extended time is a difficult moment to affront for the players and therefore also for the coach, it is more correct to treat it as a real critical situation. In fact, when, after having reached a draw (during the course of the match or as result of the calculation of the goals scored during the double face off), we are forced to play extra time, the players of both teams will have great athletic, psychological and therefore also tactical difficulties to face. You can say that both teams will share the problems of this situation, and so the coach who manages things in the better way will be giving his men the greater chance of coming out on top.

From the athletic point of view and after ninety minutes of playing time, it is clear that the team have little energy left, especially if they are using an exhausting system, and they run the risk of not being able to keep on their feet until the end of the extra time. It is very likely that the players will start getting cramps during this part of the match, and that they will have to come off the field, unable to go back on. In any case, we will not easily be able to carry out the required movements and tactical behavior, because the players will no longer be up to running so much. On the psychological plane, the players' moral will be hit hard, with the idea that, despite their mental and physical exhaustion, they are going to have to play for another half hour, continuing to run and keep their concentration. As a result of their physical and mental fatigue, and from a tactical point of view, we can no longer ask them to carry out tiring playing schemes. Unfortunately, you can forget pressing, speed of maneuvers, rhythm and intensity during extra time. The two teams will now appear very blocked up, lengthened out and slack, slow in passing the ball and ineffective in the attacking phase - in other words, they will carry out simple and essential movements in both phases of play. Both teams could even end up by taking on a stand-by attitude, above all because if one scores a goal it will be very difficult to draw back even, or the whole match could even be over if the rule of the 'golden goal' is in use.

In these cases then, the teams will be full of fear and tension and they will be more, worried more about not taking a goal than about trying to score one. Unfortunately, extra time will rarely be spectacular, and in these situations the coach will not be in a position to ask too much of his players.

Also from the tactical point of view, the players will tend to make individual mistakes, even when doing simple things. The players will not be clear headed enough and their legs will be shaking.

As for the penalty shoot out, here the psychological and in part the physical aspect will be more important than the individual's technical ability. You often see players who are very gifted in the basics of the penalty and who surprisingly mistake their kick, while others, who are technically speaking weaker, convert without problems. It is even more significant that in friendly matches you rarely see mistakes in the final shoot out which usual continues well beyond the first five players. In official matches the shoot out usually finishes before the first five kicks have been taken, and there are usually a high percentage of mistakes.

When you are kicking from the penalty disc you need great cold blood and there must not be too much tension or the fear of making mistakes. Also from the physical point of view, if you are too tired you will find it more difficult to make decisions about how to kick and your precision will be reduced. As far as the goalkeepers are concerned, they will be under less pressure and responsibility. If they do not save they are not generally blamed, while when they carry out decisive interventions, they are considered heroes.

MOVES TO RESOLVE THE SITUATION: As we have already said, it is important for the coach to manage this situation as well as he can, because his rival will have to try and do the same, and beating him in these circumstances will give the team a good chance of coming out on top. The coach will have to act on the three fronts that we have seen in the descriptive part: the psychological, athletic and tactical planes. These three factors determine the peculiarity and the extreme difficulty of the situation.

From the mental point of view, you will have to encourage the players to go through another thirty minutes of the match. You must tell them to start playing again with drive and determination, making the most of the fact that their opponents are 'in the same boat', and if they can resist they will make the best of the situation. It is important to make the best use of those few minutes of rest between the end of regular and the beginning of extra time. You must group the players around you and tell them that at this point they must go over the top.

When play is going on, you must make the players feel your presence, inciting them whenever you feel they are losing concentration.

On the physical plane, hopefully you will still have some substitutions to make. If you have, there may be the problem of deciding who to take off the field if all the players are in more or less the same athletic condition. Each single coach will have to make his own choices, on the basis of each player's integration in his playing schemes and all the other criteria that we have been looking at previously. If we think that our team will not be able to dispute the extra time in an offensive way because the players are physically at the end of their tether, we could put on a mid fielder who would carry out decisive tasks in both phases, or a defender who would guarantee more stability to the back section, which will be under pressure by the rival - rather than a striker who would run the risk of being cut out of play. But you could also decide to count on fresh forces in attack, so as to have more chance to shoot during the rare goal scoring opportunities that we will be creating.

Lastly, from the tactical point of view, we will need to modify our application of the two phases of play, so as to lighten and simplify the players' tasks, but especially in order to make them less tiring. You have to keep in mind that the players do not have much energy left in their legs and they will not be able to carry out plays which depend on good running ability. You have to bring back the initial line of pressing to the point where you think it is viable for the players. You must also cut the attacking movements down to the bare necessity, asking the players for essential action, moderate rhythm in the circulation of the ball and less continuous and less frenetic movements with and without the ball, which should however be just as effective. The maneuver must not build up too much in a vertical sense, even when their is the temptation to do so. The team must not lengthen itself out too much, keeping in mind that this can often happen during extra time because of the players' mental and physical exhaustion. In any case, you cannot expect the team to be playing brilliant and spectacular soccer, and so you must be indulgent towards the players.

If the team seems to be too contracted, scared and tactically blocked up on account of the fear of taking a goal, especially if there is the 'golden goal', you must encourage them to play with moderate calm, trying above all to score that first crucial goal. You must convince the players that by anxiously waiting for the opponents in their half of the field, they are running the great risk of undergoing the opposite result -taking the goal themselves. If they can keep the ball in their opponent's half, they will have much more chance of making a go of things, especially because it is not easy to counterattack in these circumstances of physical exhaustion.

If we take a goal it is not easy to raise the players' spirits, but you must do your duty to the end, trying as hard as you can to make the players react.

As far as the penalty shoot out is concerned, the first thing to say is that the coach should make out the list of the players who are to take them, without thinking too much about the specific technical ability of the single men, but keeping in mind their emotional level rather, their cold-bloodedness, and also their physical condition. As we have seen in the descriptive section there is a high emotional content in such moments. You must give psychological support to the five you have chosen and to the goalkeeper. Especially those who will be taking the penalties need calm and serenity, and you must tell them not to feel excessively responsible about the way they shoot, and that however things may go, the force of their performance has been put on show during the one hundred and twenty minutes of real play. You could tell the players to concentrate only on the physical act to be carried out, without thinking of the rest and about what will happen if they fail. As far as the goalkeeper is concerned, you must build him up and make him feel important and in advantage over the rival shooters because he has nothing to lose. You must praise his ability to save penalties even if these are not so evident.

If the penalty shoot out goes on beyond the first five, you choose the others and give them your moral support in the same way that we have explained above.

However the penalty shoot out ends, you must compliment the players on their admirable physical and mental stamina, without blaming them in any particular way if they have been defeated.

AN ANOMALOUS SITUATION

Having now concluded our treatment of the important critical situations a coach can run up against during a match, we must mention another particular circumstance, which not everybody will consider really critical. Or rather, though this situation may not be critical for our team, it will certainly be so for the public. We are talking about a situation when our team is and deserves to be solidly in the lead, but, at a certain point of the match begins to feel that it has done enough and stops producing spectacular play, taking up a passive attitude in order simply to wait for the referee's final whistle. As we have already implied, this kind of behavior shows no respect for the spectators, who - apart from those supporters who care only about the results, will surely not be very happy to see the show ending too early. When the team stops playing just a few minutes before the end of the match we can close an eye to it, even if the public has paid for a ticket valid for ninety minutes. But when there is still a lot of time to go, it is just not right for our players to bring the 'final curtain' down. If it is only the opposing team to take up a passive, non-spectacular attitude after which the match will be unwatchable, our own conscience will be at rest. But if we are the ones with the negative attitude, the coach should certainly intervene immediately, and this will also turn out to our own advantage. In fact the players should never get into the habit of making dangerous calculations about the result, playing well only now and then depending on the particular moment. Even during the course of a match in which the team think they have played sufficiently well and feel the result is now safely in their hands, it can happen that the opponents continue to attack and begin to gain ground, so putting our players into crisis because they were not expecting this. You must also remember that in order to give a positive winning mentality to the team, you must insist that they always play to the hilt, for the public's benefit and their own. Even if there are those coaches who are not at all interested in the real show their team is putting on, there are also those for whom it is a question of personal satisfaction and realization to see their team expressing quality soccer for the whole course of the match.

Having said that, we can have a look at how to intervene.

The first thing that you will need to find out is whether the team is taking on this passive attitude because of its negative mentality or because the players have run out of physical energy. If the second is the case, you should not intervene with the players, understanding and justifying the difficulty they are having in pro-posing active and aggressive soccer. If, on the other hand, the physical problems are not so serious as to justify the team's atti-tude, you can make some substitutions, asking the new players to try and attack without however keeping the rhythm too high. In the defense phase, they should not exaggerate with pressing.

In the first case, you must intervene with the players at once. The players should be called on to do their duty, making it clear that if they continue in this way, we will judge their performance in a negative light, even if they win the match. You must get this con-cept across to the players: that they must never feel satisfied with the result they have reached until that moment, but, on the con-trary, must play until the end, and only then can we make any judgments about their performance.

It is almost impossible that there are any tactical problems at the basis of this critical situation. If the opponent's attacking force is so strong that the players are no longer in a position to come out of their own half and gain that of the opponents, we will have to make some tactical modifications, the same that we have already seen for those situations when our team is having trouble getting into the opponent's half and cannot make themselves dangerous in attack. If the team reacts positively to our reprimands from the bench, at the end of the match we can just give them a dressing down. If not, you will have assume a severe attitude for the whole of the following week, speaking to the team in such a way as to make them change their mentality so that this kind of situation does not crop up again in the future.

This and many other things will be done during the post-match phase, part of the coach's job that will be having a good look at in the conclusion of the book.

CHAPTER 14

MANAGING THE POST-MATCH PHASE

During the course of this book, we treated first of all the problems
connected with, and the way of preparing a match. Then we had
a look at all that concerns the match as it is being played and
how to manage that. Lastly, we analyzed the various critical situations that can come about during the game itself, supplying
instruments and ways of resolving them as they come up. To
conclude, we must say something about the time after the match,
which we could consider the last of the coach's tasks in this cycle
connected with the single match, and which we defined as 'micro-
programming' in chapter one. You must always remember that
the coach's tasks in relation to the single match do that end when
it is over, which may, instead, be the case as far as the players
are concerned.
For a coach, the post-match phase begins as soon as the referee
has blown the final three whistles, and we could say, practically,
that it goes on until the kick off of the subsequent match. As we
will see, the coach will be working for the whole of the following
week with the last match played as his point of reference and the
base on which he will prepare the upcoming game.
If a coach were to neglect the post-match phase, if he were to
reduce it to the day immediately after the match itself, or even
worse, to the few minutes that follow the final whistle, then he
would not be carrying out his duties to the full, and would not be
making the best use of the potential inherent in his work. Quite
the opposite, if the coach is to get his team continuously to
evolve from every point of view, and especially as far as the winning mentality is concerned, he must give great consideration to
the post-match phase. This period of time will allow all of us to
improve in every sense on the basis of the mistakes made by the
team and by the single players, and it will also give us the
chance to acquire greater conviction in our means in relation to
all those things that have been carried out correctly.
It must be underlined at once that the coach should do this part
of his work carefully whatever the result obtained by the team in
their last match. The coach must never 'file' a match just because

the result was positive. Even in cases where the team has won by a large margin, without, let us absurdly imagine, committing the tiniest of mistakes, the coach must base a part of the training sessions of the following week on the match that has just been played, above all in order to extend in his players that conviction in their fundamental potential so necessary to building up and evolve their winning mentality. However, you must always remember that absolute perfection is not of this world, and the coach should always think that he could have done better in the last match, being the first one not to feel entirely satisfied. The coach's principle aim during the various training sessions should be to arrive at the highest possible level of perfection, and the last match played is the point of reference and the base from which to begin. Of course, the week's training sessions must not be based only on the preceding match. You must keep in mind any part of the teaching schedule still incomplete, the various technical or tactical amendments to give the team and above the strict preparation of the next match, which requires accurate study of the opponent to be met.

Having made these introductory remarks, which were necessary in order to understand the importance of this long post-match phase, we can now take a look at how to organize it.

The first thing to say is that it is divided into three large sub-phases: the immediate post-match phase, the analysis of the game that has just been played and any action that the coach should take during the following weeks in the light of their last performance.

The immediate post-match phase, that is the minutes running on the end of the match in question, are important because they lay the foundations for the work to be carried out during the following week. As well as this, the psychological impact on the players can have a vital effect on your men in that moment. Remember that when you come face to face with the players in the locker room, you should make no tactical reference to the match that has just finished, just as it is inadvisable to reprimand the players about any errors that they have made, unless they have clearly not been trying hard enough. On the contrary, you must make the best of such moments in order to leave a mark on their minds. If the match has been a success you will immediately intervene to compliment the players, praising their performance and speaking only about the good things they have done. This will not only increase their confidence in themselves but also in their coach because his congratulations represent a sort of momentary recognition of their performance. In that way, the players see their coach not only as a distant figure always expecting more and more of them and merely capable of dealing out criticism, but as a person close to them and able to see merit where it is deserved.

In any case, the interventions carried out by the coach immediately after the match must never harass the players who are exhausted by ninety minutes of concentration and tension, but should be relaxing and not require real attention on their part. They must not go on for too long either. After having given the players their 'freedom' as regards the match that has just been played, the post-match period will begin again at the first training session in the following week.

However, the coach's job extends beyond the training sessions, and here we enter the second phase of the post-match period. In order to decide how best to face the players and to organize the training sessions during the course of the next week , the coach must make a detailed study of the last match to have been played. It is a little like what happens for the preparation of the match, as we have seen in chapter 2. Just as the coach must study his next opponent in order to prepare the match against them, so, in the post-match period he must dedicate a good deal of his time to the match that has just been played. And as we have seen regarding the study of the up and coming opponent, so our analysis of the match that we have just played must be done in the presence of the team.

For all notions concerning methods to be used in studying and analyzing a match, we refer you back to what we have already said in chapter 1.

In looking back over the match the coach must make a careful study of its crucial moments, even going over them again and again because the post-match period will hinge on this particular investigation. In order to make a correct analysis, he should refer more or less to the table in chapter 9 relative to the questions to ask yourself about the performance of any other team. There are a great number of benefits to be derived from looking back at the match. In fact, in viewing the last match to be played over again, the coach will be able to:

- ❑ Carry out a new more composed analysis of the match.
- ❑ Compare the analysis carried out while the match was in course with that which can be surmised in the light of this second viewing.
- ❑ See new aspects and tactical elements that were missed in the heat of the moment during the match
- ❑ Become aware of mistakes of all kinds (tactical, technical, behavioral) made by the whole team or the single players, and also of any negative psychological conditions (fear, tension, lack of determination) that they might have shown.
- ❑ Pick out all the things that the players have applied correctly from all points of view.
- ❑ Prepare the 'lesson' that he is to give the players on the match they have just played.
- ❑ Evaluate how good their preparation was for the match in question.
- ❑ Evaluate his own behavior during the match, trying to see whether he was making the right adjustments to face the various critical situations as they came up.

Let us have a closer look at some of these points.

As we have already said, our analysis of the match carried out in real time will certainly be imprecise and incomplete, however attentive the coach may have been. Looking at the match again means trying to catch hold of tactical details that we missed out on during the game, and at the same time confirming all the things that we managed to note. It should be said at once that the feelings you get in real time are always important. You will not have those same sensations when you watch the match again, but you must keep them in mind, remembering, however, that a calm analysis is more reliable. You will surely be able to pick out every mistake made by the single players and by the team as a whole: mistaken individual and collective tactical behavior and individual technical errors, but above all any general behavior that does not come up to the required mentality. It is very important to understand, in cases where there have been mistakes, whether the players have tried to carry out what the coach is asking of them, or if they have made no attempt at all. On the basis of this, the coach will be more or less severe with the team during the next training sessions. Our analysis of the critical situations that have come up during the match is important as well in order to understand the team's limits and to try and resolve them.

You must not forget to take note of all those things that the players have done and applied correctly from all points of view. Show them these, not only to build up their confidence, but also to give them confirmation that they have been behaving correctly. It can happen, in fact, that the players have got some tactical movements right, but are still not sure that it is so. And the coach must be the one to confirm their precision in the execution of these movements. All this will be useful to us in order to see up to what point we have been able to get the right things over to the group. You must try and realize what psychological states have characterized the team during the course of the match, above all as far as their approach was concerned. You must keep in mind both the positive and the negative states: the first must be confirmed in training sessions, the second eliminated. It is very important to have a close and detailed look at the psycho-tactical behavior of the team with all its strengths and flaws.

With a view to the 'lesson' that he will be giving the team, the coach must make detailed preparations for all he has to say to the players, and especially about how to organize the week's training sessions. First of all, he must establish how he is to behave himself in relation to the team, but he must also make a plan for the technical and tactical exercises he is going to propose to them.

When in the company of the players the coach runs through the film of the match that has just been disputed, he must be clear in his own mind about what to point out to them, what to insist on and above all at which moments of the game there are episodes that are significant to his purposes. For this reason, he will have made out a prospectus in which he has listed all the mistakes made by the single players and by the whole team, as well as all the things that have been applied correctly. If he thinks that there is not enough time for the players to have a look at the whole match, beside each item on this list he can make a note of the moments (or even the precise instant of the match) which show most clearly the errors made by the team, and also the things that they have carried out particularly well.

It is useful and reasonable for the coach to discuss the match with his players, listening to their opinions. You must remember that they have had the chance of experiencing in first person the events that the coach has only been able to see from the bench and on film. Their feelings can be important for the coach, who will now have the chance to perfect his own analysis, improving his own vision of those aspects that only the players will be able to understand fully. It is important to remember, however, that the coach's word is final and absolute, or almost.

Lastly, the coach has the chance and the duty to evaluate his own performance as he makes an analysis of the match. First of all, he will be able to establish whether the preparation he has made in the preceding week was valid or not. Also, he must tray and see whether the countermoves he worked out were really effective. If they were not, he can then decide what tactical and behavioral modifications he should have imposed upon the team. He must establish whether he behaved correctly during the match making the right decisions. Especially during whatever critical situations came up, did he manage to affront them in the best way possible? Once again, if the answer is no, what would have been the best way to resolve them? On the basis of the comparison between what he did in the heat of the moment and what he considers would have been right when he looks back over the play, the coach must sound out his own ability to read and analyze a match. If there is a large difference between these two readings, you must look into the reasons why that is so, in order to improve this aspect.

Another thing to keep in mind is that by making an analysis of the team's performance you can measure out how far they have been able to assimilate your instructions, especially regarding the all-important tactical organization. After that, you can evaluate your teaching methods.

In any case, the match is not only a way of evaluating his performance for the coach as well the players - it is also and above all a formative instrument that allows him to improve his own ability.

We will now take a look at the third stage of the post-match phase, concerning how effectively to manage the training sessions of the week after the game we have just played.
The first thing to do when we are face to face with the players once again, is to adopt a stance that is different from the one we have seen immediately after the end of the match. In that moment we praised the players, congratulating them on all the positive things that they had done without mentioning the negative aspects of their performance - but now we must change our conduct. The players must be brought back down to earth, and in general we will be mainly stressing the negative or unsatisfactory aspects of their play - things to be straightened out as soon as possible. Especially if the players are already too full of themselves, you must by no means further build them up when reporting on their performance. Of course, what we have just said will have only marginal worth in cases where out team tends towards depression. In such circumstances, you need to build up the players on the basis of what they have carried out correctly and so as to increase their conviction in their means.
The coach must then give the team his global report on the last match. His evaluation on the players' performance must come out during the report, which should in any case be sincere and honest. After this the coach must tell the team clearly what he is expecting from them in the coming matches. It is important to make the team participate in our programs and they must also be aware of the methods that will be used to improve their performance and eliminate or reduce mistakes.
At this point we come to the part of the post-match phase that regards putting our ideas for training into action on the playing field - ideas, of course, which we have arrived at on the basis of the last match played.
In order to eliminate the mistakes made by the team, we must propose an adequate series of technical and tactical theme exercises. These exercises correspond to those that we have seen in chapter 8, which are, however, merely some examples, founda-

tions upon which to create other more personal drills responding to these specific needs. These exercises must keep in mind the limits and all types of mistakes shown up by the team in the last match, as well as any critical situations we have bumped into - and they will last for the whole week. One thing must be considered closely. When you have to prepare the training sessions for a whole week, you must not consider only the last match that has been played. You must always keep in mind the performance of your team in all the preceding matches as well as the various different analysis that have been made. You must never cancel out your team's recent past, and the errors the team have made, as well as all the good things they did in the last match must be compared with the mistakes and the positive points that have characterized their play in all recent games. In this way, we can get a view of the steps they are making in the right direction, the things to be confirmed and the things that are getting worse. The steps forward and the elements to be confirmed are an achievement for the coach, who must try and make sure that they remain and that there are no reverse moves. It is a good idea to revise things at times in order to strengthen that which the team is carrying out correctly. Any deterioration or negative confirmations must be made up for by an intensified recuperation program, to be carried out again by using the same technical, tactical exercises. The coach must compare the degree of didactic progress now arrived at by the team with what came out from his studies of the last match. He must then decide whether it might be a good idea to modify the didactic program, going back over things again. In cases where the team has already worked their way through the program, it is always a good idea to see if they need tactical 'refresher' lessons or if it might even be the best thing to begin the course over from a certain point.

It is always necessary to get the team to revise the various tactical elements in the general organization, dedicating a couple of exercises to these during the week's training.

You must also keep account of any limits in individual technique, to be made good with good exercises coinciding if possible with more tactical ones. Along with this tactical and technical program, the coach must look after the psychological aspect of his team as well as possible during the week.

This psychological approach aims to give the team the necessary winning mentality. This must come about in the light of the psychological and behavioral state made evident by the team in their last match, once again keeping in mind the comparison to be made with the other recently disputed games. Clearly, we have to try and eliminate any negative psychological states that have come up in the last match, and to maintain the positive ones. This can be done by using appropriate exercises coinciding with the tactical drills. For example, for a team that has been low on concentration, we can propose tactical exercises and, generally speaking, whole training sessions where the rhythm and intensity are to be kept at the highest levels, forcing the team to be always on the alert. If the team has shown excessive tension during the match, which has led the players to make mistakes in the easiest of technical actions, it might be a good idea to propose exercises in individual technique in moments when they are tired or psychologically tense, (and so in difficulty), so as to create situations that are similar to those of the match.

Generally speaking, on the basis of errors of various nature made by the team, the amount of drive that they have shown and the difficulties they have met, the coach must decide whether his behavior towards his players should tend towards intransigence or sympathy.

In any case, all the general aspects relative to the psychological management of the group have already been treated in chapter 8, to which we refer the reader.

Apart from the psychological aspect, you must not neglect the physical athletic condition of the players either. Depending on the physical state of the team as shown in the match, you must decide whether to confirm or modify the program of athletic preparation.

Having now set out this phase of work relative to the post-match period in general, there is one other thing to be said about the week's work to be carried out by the coach. The coach must not only study the match that has just been played and decide the week's training program basing himself on that. As we have already seen, he must also prepare the next match, making studies of the up and coming opponent in the ways that we have detailed in the chapters two to six.

Following on this double task of the week - studying the last match and preparing the next - the coach must divide his time between the analysis of his own team's last match and that of his next opponent. On this basis, he will plan out the timing and the content of the various training sessions. Generally speaking, it is advisable to dedicate more space to the post-match phase during the first days of the week, while the second part will give more care to the preparation of the following match. General exercises and the various psychological interventions should be blended in with both these needs.

It is a good idea in any case for the coach to prepare for the next match with great care because our attention should be turned mostly to the future. The most important thing of all is to do all we can to make sure that our future performances and up and coming results are always of a high level.

You must remember, in fact, that the soccer match is the primary aspect of this sport - that which really interests and attracts a great number of people. Studying the most recent matches is important above all from a formative point of view because it gives us a chance to improve, but paying all the attention we can to the next match to be played is a form of respect and a duty towards all those people who are in love with soccer and its central event. As well as this, it will allow our team to express itself better increasing its chances of coming out on top against its next opponent.

To conclude, it is important that the coach puts all his efforts into all those primary aspects regarding the match that everybody is looking forward to seeing - but that he always keeps in mind that soccer is a sport, and that there is nothing in it that we can think of as absolute or mathematical.

Then, let the match begin, and may the best team win!